"Few facts are more important to the future of our country and our understanding of the nature of our species than the identities and motives of the persons responsible for the assassinations of Martin Luther King, Jr, President John F. Kennedy, Robert F. Kennedy and Malcolm X. These deaths have affected more than mere events. They have torn our people between belief and disbelief. Conscious, persistent pursuit of the truth of these assassinations is essential to our character and faith.

"No one has done more than Dr William F. Pepper to keep alive the quest for the truth concerning the violent death of Martin Luther King who in courageous and important words once said 'The greatest purveyor of violence on earth is my own government.' In *An Act of State*, Bill Pepper argues that very government violence was turned on America's greatest prophet of non-violent change."

Ramsey Clark, 1 November 2002 (Ramsey Clark was appointed Assistant Attorney General by John F. Kennedy in 1961 and was Attorney General under Lyndon Johnson from 1967 to 1969, during which King was assassinated)

"Dr Pepper, a trusted associate of my father in the anti-war movement and a dedicated follower of his teaching, has conducted exhaustive research and shed new light on all of the critical questions including the extent of the involvement of government intelligence agencies, military units and organized crime in the assassination, the motives behind it, and the individuals who ordered and participated in it."

Dexter King

"William Pepper's book is by far the most thorough critique of the official story of the King assassination. The result of Pepper's decades of determined investigative efforts, it should be carefully read by every serious student of King's life and his tragic death."

Professor Clayborne Carson, Director, Martin Luther King, Jr., Papers Project

"One juror, David Morphy, said after the trial, 'We all thought it was a cut and dried case with the evidence that Mr Pepper brought to us . . . everyone from the CIA, military involvement, and Jowers was involved."

New York Times

AN ACT OF STATE

AN ACT OF STATE

The Execution of
Martin Luther King

WILLIAM F. PEPPER

V

VERSO

London • New York

First published by Verso 2003
© William F. Pepper 2003
All rights reserved

1 3 5 7 9 10 8 6 4 2

Verso
UK: 6 Meard Street, London W1F 0EG
USA: 180 Varick Street, New York, NY 10014–4606
www.versobooks.com

Verso is the imprint of New Left Books

ISBN 1–85984–695–5

British Library Cataloguing in Publication Data
A catalogue record for this book is available from the British Library

Library of Congress Cataloging-in-Publication Data
A catalog record for this book is available from the Library of Congress

Typeset in 10/13pt Janson Text by SetSystems Ltd, Saffron Walden, Essex
Printed by R. R. Donnelley & Sons, USA

CONTENTS

PART ONE

PART TWO

PART ONE

1

THE BEGINNING

In spring 1966, US carpet-bombing had systematically devastated ancient village-based rural culture in South Vietnam as napalm rained from the sky, slaughtering helpless peasants. As a freelance journalist, I had witnessed and chronicled these atrocities and in early 1967 opened my files to Dr Martin Luther King Jr, who had been awarded the Nobel Peace Prize two years earlier.

At this time when I discussed the effects of the war on the civilian population and the ancient village road culture of the Vietnamese people with Dr King, he was already inclined to formally announce his position on the war. He had previously voiced his growing concern about his country's ever greater role in what appeared to be an internal struggle for control of the nation by a nationalist movement seeking to overcome an oligarchical regime in the south, which was previously beholden to western economic interests.

It occurs to me that he would likely react in much the same way today, opposing American, unilateral opposition to nationalist revolutionary movements around the world, which ostensibly is being mounted against terrorist organizations.

In the Museum of History in Hanoi is a plaque with the following words: "All men are created equal. They are endowed by their creator with certain inalienable rights; among these are life, liberty and the pursuit of happiness." It was with these words and pro-American spirit, which Ho-Chi Minh said he took from the Declaration of Independence of the United States of America, that he proclaimed the Democratic Republic of Vietnam on 2 September 1945.

It was not lost on Martin that Ho-Chi Minh's reverence for Jefferson, Lincoln, and American democracy, as he idealized it, made him the legitimate father of a unified Vietnam. So, on April 4 1967, Martin declared his formal opposition to the increasing barbarities in Vietnam. By July 1967, against the disastrous backdrop of the Vietnam War, America began to burn not only through enemy attack but from racial tensions and riots sparked by mounting anger over living conditions at home.

At the Spring Mobilization anti-war demonstration in New York on April 15, before 250,000 cheering and chanting citizens, after I had advanced his name as an alternative presidential candidate to Lyndon Johnson, Dr King called on the government to "stop the bombing."

He was emerging as a key figurehead in a powerful coalition of the growing peace and civil rights movements, which were to form the basis of the "new politics." The National Conference for New Politics (NCNP) was established to catalyze people nationwide. I was asked to be its executive director. From this platform, Dr King planned to move into mainstream politics as a potential candidate on a presidential ticket with Dr Benjamin Spock in order to highlight the anti-poverty, anti-war agenda. He called for conscientious objection, political activity, and a revolution in values to shift American society from materialism to humanism. As a result, he came under increasing attack.

During the Second World War, Ho-Chi Minh parachuted, as part of an American OSS team, behind Japanese lines to supply his nationalist Vietminh forces. Only when America turned its back on his nationalist-anti-colonialist movement against the French, did he seek help elsewhere. Eventually, of course, the Americans, whom Ho-Chi Minh saw as being an anti-colonialist republic and very different from the Europeans, replaced the French, and mounted their own effort to control and rule Vietnam.

During the years of that futile and wasted effort which resulted in a humiliating defeat for the United States, it dispatched its greatest ever land army to Vietnam, dropped the greatest tonnage of bombs in the history of warfare, forced millions of people to leave their villages and homes and by accrual bombardment used chemical agents in a way which devastated and altered the exposed environmental and genetic structures, virtually petrifying some of the most beautiful and lush lands in the world. In excess of 1,300,000 people were killed (I estimated over a million by 1967) and many others were maimed for life; of these 58,022 were American.

By 1970, Vietnamese babies were being born without eyes, with deformed hearts and stumps instead of legs. Six pounds of toxic chemicals per head of population were dumped on the people of Vietnam. President Reagan referred to this as a "noble cause."

Therefore, when in 1967 I confronted King with the devastating effects of napalm and white phosphorus bombing which had been unleashed on the young and the old of that ancient land, his prodigious conscience compelled him not only to formally announce his opposition to that war but to actively work and organize against it in every corner of America he visited.

There was great concern in the halls of power in America that this most honored of black Americans had decided to use the full force of his integrity, moral authority, and international prestige to challenge the might and moral bankruptcy of the American state, which he freely characterized as the "greatest purveyor of violence on earth."

His formal announcement of opposition and condemnation of his government generated serious apprehension in the boardrooms of the select list of large American corporations which were receiving enormous profits from the conflict. These, of course, included the range of armament, aircraft, and chemical manufacturers as well as favored construction companies (like Texas and Lyndon Johnson's own Brown and Root) which had multi-billion-dollar contracts, and the oil companies, again including those owned by Texans Johnson and Edgar Hoover's friends, H. L. Hunt and Clint Murchison.[1] It is hard to imagine oilmen becoming more upset about this threat to public policy which had benefited them since John Kennedy's commitment to end the 27.5 percent oil depletion allowance. This list, of course, should not omit the powerful multinational banks, who are the bankers to these corporations and which arrange financing so that they themselves greatly profit from the loan syndications and leasing contracts. And there are the large law firms who advise and provide legal services on every aspect of every deal, contract, lease, and sale.

When one assesses this awesome array of private established, non-governmental, institutional power, it is eminently reasonable to consider those in government decision-making positions as being compelled to listen to, protect and serve the unified interests of this corporate establishment. When business speaks with one voice, as it did in respect of the war or the purported extreme threat of war at the time when Martin King set himself up in opposition, the relevant government agencies and their officials become mere footsoldiers for the mighty economic interests. Out in front in time of war are the armed forces, the intelligence and law enforcement communities. Not far behind are the executive, the legislative and the judicial legitimizers, who sanction the necessary actions, and the media conglomerates who, as the publicists of government policy, posing as independent voices of the people, vigorously support and defend the official policy in serious national security instances of significant concern to the corporate establishment.

Virtually unanimously, and with one voice, the mass media condemned Dr King's opposition to the war. In the shadows were the forces they serve.

When one understands this context and those times, more than three decades ago, it is understandable that when Martin King began to crusade against the war, he would cast a long shadow over the economic forces of America. Little wonder that they shuddered at the possibility that his efforts might result in the tap of the free-flowing profits being turned off. Should the American people come to demand an end to the war and should the war end, the losses were not something they could accept.

Perhaps it was for this reason alone that King had to be stopped.

If this was not reason enough Dr King gave these awesomely powerful forces another inducement to eliminate him. He had been wrestling with the problem of economic injustice for some time. It was, he said, one thing to gain the civil right to eat at a formerly segregated lunchroom counter but quite another to be able to pay the bill. This was the next and, in a capitalist society, an essential component of freedom and equality, and one which was the essence of the movement for social justice. The war had made things worse. Not only were a disproportionate number of blacks being sent 10,000 miles from home to serve as cannon fodder, but the cost of the war increasingly required that essential social services and programs in their communities be curtailed. The poor knew better than anyone that President Johnson's commitment to "guns and butter" could not be fulfilled. In effect there was an undeclared cease in the "war on poverty."

So, for Martin King, opposition to the war against the people of a poor, non-white ancient culture was in harmony with, and a natural extension of, the civil rights struggle against oppression and the denial of basic freedoms and essential services at home.

By mid-1967, he began to formulate a strategy to address the widening gap between the rich and the poor. The project gradually took the form not of a march by itself but the extensive Poor People's Campaign and mobilization culminating in an encampment in the shadow of the Washington Memorial. The projection was for the establishment of a tent city of some 500,000 of the nation's poorest and most alienated citizens, who would regularly lobby their elective officials for a range of socio-economic legislation. They would remain as long as it took to get action from the Congress.

If the wealthy, powerful interests across the nation would find Dr King's escalating activity against the war intolerable, his planned mobilization of half a million poor people with the intention of laying siege to Congress could only engender outrage – and fear.

They knew that it was not going to be possible for the Congress to satisfy the demands of the multitude of poor, alienated Americans led by Dr King, and they believed that the growing frustration could well lead to violence. In such a situation with the unavailability of sufficient troops to control that mass of people, the capital could be overrun. Nothing less than a revolution might result. This possibility simply could not be allowed to materialize, and neither could Martin King's crusade against the war be permitted to continue.

When the NCNP convention was held on Labor Day weekend, many of us believed that nothing less than the nation's rebirth was on the agenda. But a small, aggressive group had urged each arriving black delegate to join an obviously planned Black Caucus which at one point threatened to take Dr King hostage. He made a spirited speech, calling for unity and action, after which I had to arrange for him to leave the stage quickly under guard for his own safety. Black Caucus delegates voted en bloc. There were walkouts, hostilities, and splits. Though we didn't admit it at the time, the NCNP died as a political force that weekend. We had not realized the power of the forces ranged against us to divide the emerging coalition and to infiltrate and manipulate movement organizations.

Dr King stepped up his anti-war efforts and threw himself into developing the Poor People's Campaign which was scheduled to bring hundreds of thousands of the nation's poor blacks, Hispanics, whites, and intellectuals to Washington in the spring of 1968. He would, of course, not live to see it.

Since their plight was the very epitome of the condition of the wretched of America, Dr King lent his support to the Memphis sanitation workers' strike by predominantly black non-union workers. On March 18 1968 he addressed a meeting at the Mason Temple and called for a general work stoppage in Memphis. He agreed to return to lead a march and did so on March 28. Chaos descended, and the march was disrupted. Because he was determined to lead a peaceful march, it was rescheduled for April 5. He returned to Memphis on April 3, checking into room 306 at the Lorraine Motel. At 6:01 PM the next evening, he was shot dead on the motel balcony.

The FBI hunt led to fingerprints on a map of Atlanta found in a room in the city hired by a man calling himself Eric S. Galt. They matched those of a fugitive from a Missouri penitentiary – James Earl Ray. He fled to England, but eventually, on Saturday June 10, he was arrested at Heathrow Airport and extradited to the United States.

The case never came to trial because James Earl Ray entered a plea of guilty on Monday March 10 1969. He was subsequently sentenced to 99 years in the state penitentiary. Within three days of arriving there, Ray had written to the court requesting that his guilty plea be set aside and that he be given a trial.

Any reservations I had about another lone-assassin explanation for the removal of a progressive leader were sublimated by the combined feelings of grief, sadness and disgust with all politics.

During the next nine years, I had virtually nothing to do with the civil rights and anti-war movements. I had no hope the nation could be reconstructed without Martin King's singular leadership. Then, in late 1977, Ralph Abernathy, who had succeeded Dr King as the President of Southern Christian Leadership Conference (SCLC) but had been replaced in 1976 by the Reverend Joseph Lowery, and who had been a close friend of Dr King, told me that he had never been completely satisfied with the official explanation of King's murder. He wanted a face-to-face meeting with the alleged assassin. Although I was surprised by his interest I told him that I had assumed that the right man was in prison and that I knew very little about the case. If I was to help him, I would need time to catch up on the facts.

In the absence of a trial, the prosecution's scenario had been put out to the world as the final word, bolstered by books written by publicists of the official story and media coverage. To the general public, Ray was a loner, motivated by race hate, who sought to make his mark in history.

The state claimed Ray began stalking Dr King on the weekend of March 17 in Los Angeles, arriving in Memphis on April 3 with the murder weapon and booking into a seedy rooming house above Jim's Grill. It had a bathroom overlooking the Lorraine Motel balcony, where Dr King was standing when he was killed. Ray, according to the state, locked himself in and fired the fatal shot.

Then, in haste, he neglected to eject the spent cartridge. Straight afterwards, he gathered up a few belongings from his room and ran down the front stairs, allegedly seen by rooming house tenant Charles Stephens who became the state's chief prosecution witness. Supposedly seeing a police car parked near the sidewalk of the fire station, Ray allegedly dropped the bundle in the recessed doorway of the Canipe Amusement Company on South Main before jumping into his white Mustang and heading for Atlanta, where he ditched the car. He then made his way to Canada. His prints were found on the gun, scope, binoculars, beer can, and copy of the Memphis *Commercial Appeal* dropped in the bundle.

During this period, the House Select Committee on Assassinations (HSCA) had been set up to investigate the murders of President Kennedy and Dr King. Following Ralph's request, I began to read everything I could about the killing. Meanwhile in early June 1977 after a failed escape attempt, James Earl Ray was returned to his cell at Brushy Mountain Penitentiary.

Finally, on October 17 1978, with Ralph Abernathy and a body language specialist in attendance, I met Ray. He told us he had been set up, his actions leading up to the assassination coordinated through a shadowy figure called Raul. He had met this man in the Neptune bar in Montreal in August 1967 while on the run, looking for a way to leave North America.

At the end of the interview, Abernathy and I agreed. Ray was not the shooter. As we left the prison, Ralph Abernathy told waiting journalists that Ray's answers to questions convinced him more than ever a conspiracy had led to Martin Luther King's death and Ray should get a trial. I was troubled by the discrepancy between the public image of James Earl Ray and the person we interviewed, as well as by the unanswered questions of which I became aware. The more I thought about the issues, the more concerned I became. I decided to quietly probe the official story. It was the beginning of a quest that was to last more than a quarter of a century and which would ultimately expose the dark underbelly of American government and the covert activities of its military and intelligence organizations and their fealty to corporate interests and organized crime.

The House Select Committee on Assassinations report

In January 1979, the House Select Committee published its final report on the assassinations of John F. Kennedy and Martin King. It found no evidence or complicity on the part of the CIA, the FBI, or any other government agency in the assassination of Martin King. Ray, it concluded, was a lone gunman. Raul did not exist, so Ray couldn't have been a fall guy manipulated by others (even though racism was not the motive). The report itself was widely publicized, but the accompanying thirteen volumes had a very limited distribution. Only the interested few would learn that information buried in these documents frequently conflicts with conclusions in the report itself.

The volumes provide a detailed account of the FBI's wide-ranging legal and illegal communist infiltration organization (COMINFIL) and counterintelligence programs and activities (COINTELPRO) conducted both before and after the assassination. They were designed to tie Dr King and the SCLC to the influence of the Communist Party and to discredit Dr King.

Way back in 1957, when the SCLC was founded, FBI supervisor J. K. Kelly stated in a memo that the group was "a likely target for infiltration." As the SCLC mounted an increasingly high-profile challenge to segregation and the denial of voting rights to blacks across the South, the Bureau began actively infiltrating meetings and conferences.

On October 23 1962, Hoover sent a memo authorizing the Atlanta and New York field offices to conduct a general COMINFIL investigation of the SCLC and asked the New Orleans office to explore COMINFIL possibilities. COINTELPRO activities specifically targeted against Dr King began in late October 1962. The Bureau's campaign embodied a number of felonies according to a Justice Department report in 1977. This was noted in the HSCA report.

In December 1963, less than a month after the assassination of President John F. Kennedy, Bureau officials met in Washington to explore ways of "neutralizing King as an effective Negro leader." The conference focused on how to "produce the best results without embarrassment to the Bureau." Officials agreed that hidden microphones be placed in Dr King's hotel rooms as he traveled in an effort to pick up evidence of extramarital sexual activity which could be used to tarnish his reputation or even to blackmail him. Numerous hotels nationwide were bugged from late 1963 to the end of 1965.

Documents reveal wiretaps on the SCLC's Atlanta office ran from October 1963 to June 21 1966. Dr King's home was tapped from November 8 1963 to April 1965 when he moved. In 1966, FBI director Hoover, fearful of a congressional inquiry into electronic surveillance, ordered that the monitoring of Dr King be discontinued. When Dr King and the SCLC turned their attention to Vietnam and the Poor People's Campaign, a request to Attorney General Ramsey Clark to approve renewed telephone surveillance was refused. We would learn that surveillance never ceased.

The Bureau also engaged in surreptitious activities and burglaries against Dr King and the SCLC. The HSCA estimated 20 such events took place between 1959 and 1964. The Bureau would maintain that Dr

King was not officially a COINTELPRO target until late 1967 or early 1968. In fact, a massive campaign was under way from 1964 aimed at destroying him through dirty tricks and media manipulation.

The HSCA revealed FBI infiltration of the SCLC through a "black probe" operation. Former agent Arthur Murtagh, assigned to the Atlanta field office between 1967 and 1968, testified that the office's primary informant was a member of the SCLC's executive controlled by agent Al Sentinella. The informant was, said Murtagh, also embezzling organization funds. He informed on the SCLC right up to the assassination, providing details of Dr King's itinerary and travel plans.

The HSCA firmly rejected the FBI's contention that Ray was a racist and that was why he shot Dr King. But it advanced a convoluted scenario that he carried out the killing to collect a bounty from two St Louis racists, both dead by the time the committee reported.

The report accepted the fingerprint evidence of the dropped bundle but also noted that there were many unidentified prints in the rooming house and on Ray's white Mustang.

The Memphis City Engineers analysis of the fatal bullet's trajectory could not conclude whether it came from the bathroom window of the rooming house attached to Jim's Grill or the brush area behind the building. But the HSCA dismissed the possibility that the shot had been fired from the brush area. It concluded that the bullet had been fired from the bathroom, ignoring the statement from witnesses including Solomon Jones, Dr King's Memphis driver, that it came from the brush area, where he saw someone right after the shooting. Any person seen in the brush, the HSCA concluded, must have been a quick-responding Memphis Police Department (MPD) policeman already on the scene. It also concluded no cutting back of the brush had taken place after the killing – and did not interview Reverend James Orange who said he saw smoke "rise from bushes right by the fire station" seconds after the shot.

MPD undercover agent Marrell McCollough said he was the mysterious figure kneeling over Dr King after he was shot on the balcony. He had infiltrated the Invaders, a black group trying to address local needs in the city, supplying Lieutenant Eli Arkin, his MPD intelligence division control officer, with regular reports. He subsequently acted as an agent provocateur in activities as a result of which members of the Invaders were convicted and sentenced. He has never admitted that he was recalled to military service on June 11 1967 and assigned to the MPD from the 111th Military Intelligence Group, as I learned years later.

Several conspiracy theories, some implicating the Mafia, were covered and dismissed in the HSCA report. It strengthened my growing conviction that Dr King's murder had not been solved. It also provided me with leads.

In early 1979, I traveled to Memphis to follow up some issues touched on by the HSCA. John McFerren, a civil rights leader in 1968, eventually told me how he had heard Frank Liberto, president of the Liberto, Liberto and Latch Produce Company in Memphis, shouting down the phone on the afternoon Dr King was killed. McFerren, who was at the back of the store, heard Liberto say "I told you not to call me here. Shoot the son of a bitch when he comes on the balcony." Liberto told the caller he should collect his money – $5,000 was mentioned – from Liberto's brother in New Orleans. McFerren had heard Liberto had underworld connections – and was astonished when, an hour later, he learned of Martin Luther King's assassination.

McFerren told Baxton Bryant, Executive Director of the Tennessee Council on Human Rights, who insisted that he tell the FBI. McFerren was reluctant until Bryant promised his name would be kept secret or he and his family would receive protection. In the early hours of April 8, he told his story to Frank Holloman, Director of the Memphis Police and Fire Departments, MPD homicide chief N. E. Zachary and FBI agent O. B. Johnson at the Peabody Hotel. They taped McFerren's account, got him to sketch the scene, and promised to check it out thoroughly. Three days later, Bryant was told that the FBI believed that if McFerren had heard the call at all, it was not related to the killing. McFerren was left feeling like a criminal.

The HSCA had similarly dismissed allegations from Louisville police officer Clifton Baird that there was an attempt to assassinate Dr King in 1965, emanating from named Louisville police officers collaborating with FBI agents. The claim, backed up with a tape recording he took, mentioned a $500,000 contract to kill Dr King. It was another glaring instance of the HSCA's failure to follow leads and solve the crime. Since Martin's brother A. D. lived in Louisville, Martin visited that city from time to time. In a lengthy meeting in a darkened bar Baird shared his evidence with me. He impressed me as an honest, courageous policeman.

Relocation and more investigations

I moved to England in 1981 and engaged in the practice of international law. Though I did some work in my practice during this time, it was primarily concerned with attempting to understand what role, if any, James Earl Ray had played. I was driven to uncover the truth behind King's murder. James Earl Ray was desperate to get a trial. He had been denied an evidentiary hearing by the Memphis federal district court magistrate, but was convinced he'd have a chance with the Sixth Circuit Court of Appeals. Hugh Stanton, co-defense counsel in Ray's court case, was appointed to represent Charlie Stephens, the prosecution's chief witness, when the state sought a protective custody order against him. Stephens had also applied for the publicly offered reward for identifying James. Thus we had a defense co-counsel who had, in the same case within the same six months, represented the primary prosecution witness against the defendant. Vigorous cross-examination of Stephens would obviously be required to mount an effective defense. This meant the case couldn't go to trial. Stanton would be precluded from examining Stephens because he had no waiver from him. James would thus be unable to confront the man the prosecution was putting forward to accuse him. This appeared to be a blatant violation of James's Sixth Amendment rights to independent counsel and his right to confront an accuser. James's lawyer in 1988 decided he didn't want to handle the appeal. Having become convinced of his actual innocence, I reluctantly agreed to take it on myself. I thus voluntarily placed myself in a bizarre situation, for I would be defending the man who was officially legally guilty of killing my friend and colleague. In October 1988, I formally filed Ray's appeal and continued investigating.

I tracked down former taxi driver James McCraw who had refused to transport a drunken Charlie Stephens sometime before the assassination. He told how, when he arrived to pick up Stephens sometime before 6:00

PM, he'd noticed a delivery van and two white Mustangs parked within a 50 yards of each other, one in front of Jim's Grill, the other just south of the Canipe Amusement Company.

On entering Stephens's room, he saw his fare slumped on the bed. The hall bathroom door was open, and the bathroom apparently empty, both as he approached and as he left the drunken man's room. As he drove away, it was not very long after he heard instructions over the radio to avoid the downtown area because of the shooting.

This was an exciting discovery. If true, the MPD, FBI, and HSCA conclusion that the shot came from the bathroom made no sense at all. Confirmation that Stephens was drunk shortly before the shooting and that the bathroom was empty supported Ray's contentions that he wasn't there and contradicted the official scenario.

In a meeting in Columbus, Ohio, Myron Billet, occasional driver for mob leader Sam Giancana in the 1960s, gave me a chilling description of the working relationship between the mob and the federal government. In January 1968, his boss and fellow mobsters Carlo Gambino and John Roselli met with three federal agents in Apalachin, New York. One of the "feds" announced there was a $1 million contract on Dr King's life. Giancana immediately said "no way," making it clear he wanted nothing to do with that job. Billet's story was also dismissed by the HSCA. I came to believe that his description of how the mob works with the federal government was disturbingly accurate.

The MPD investigation concluded there was only one white Mustang in the area near the shooting as, by implication, did the HSCA. I gained first-hand evidence that this conclusion was wrong. Charles Hurley told me how he arrived to pick up his wife from a company directly opposite the rooming house at around 4:45 PM on April 4. He remembered pulling up just behind a white Mustang with Arkansas plates parked in front of the rooming house but south of Canipe's amusement store. Hurley said that a young dark-haired man was sitting inside the Mustang just in front of him. Ray's Mustang, of course, had Alabama plates, and he was dressed in a dark suit, white shirt, and dark tie that afternoon. Ray had always maintained that he didn't move the white Mustang he parked outside Jim's Grill (north of Canipe's) until he finally left the area.

I learned that the paid informer on the SCLC's executive staff was

James Harrison, who joined the staff in 1964. Harrison reported to agent Al Sentinella, Atlantic field office from Autumn 1965, and was still doing so on the day Dr King was shot. On that day he was in Memphis, checking in with the Memphis FBI Special Agent in charge, Jensen, when he arrived.

A BBC documentary on the assassination researched in 1989 included an interview with Earl Caldwell, then a young reporter covering Dr King for the *New York Times* in 1968. He was staying at the Lorraine Motel on April 4 and said he saw the figure of a white man crouching in the bushes behind Jim's Grill and the rooming house. No one from the FBI, MPD, or HSCA had ever tried to talk to Caldwell. His observations also directly contradicted the official position that the shot came from the bathroom window.

Program researchers unearthed another key lead. Taxi driver James McCraw casually mentioned a gun being in Jim's Grill around the time of the murder. McCraw later told me that late in the morning after the shooting, Loyd Jowers, the grill's owner, showed him a rifle in a box on a shelf under the counter. Jowers told him he found it "out back" after the killing. He said he was going to turn it over to the police. I found this disclosure startling. Was the second gun in fact the murder weapon? If Jowers was telling the truth to McCraw it was becoming increasingly clear the shot came from the brush area, not from the rooming house inside. Police swamped the murder area within minutes – why had they not found the gun? I had met Jowers numerous times before, and he had not mentioned the gun. And why was there no mention of it in the HSCA report? I set out to try and get answers.

Meanwhile, the Sixth Circuit Court of Appeals denied the appeal I had filed on James Earl Ray's behalf. As a last resort, on June 19 1989, I filed a petition for a review by the US Supreme Court. This was denied. The trial James Earl Ray had so long been denied seemed as far away as ever.

2

THE TELEVISION TRIAL OF
JAMES EARL RAY

I had to find another way to get the case heard and began fleshing out the bones of an unscripted TV trial, featuring real evidence, witnesses, judge, and counsel before an independent jury. It would be conducted strictly according to Tennessee law and criminal procedure. James liked the proposal from the outset, believing if he could tell his story to an independent jury, he had a good chance of winning, though material evidence in the files of the federal government was sealed and unavailable to the defense.

In 1992, I signed a contract with Thames Television in London. Former US Attorney Hickman Ewing agreed to be the prosecutor; Marvin E. Frankel, a former federal district court judge, now practicing law in New York, the judge. I would lead the case for the defense. The jury was selected from a pool of US citizens initially secured by a consultant research group. Hickman and I agreed on twelve jurors and two alternates. In putting forward our case, we intended to go well beyond the actual murder and demonstrate the existence and extent of a cover-up.

The evidence we unearthed strengthened and tied together earlier findings. There could no longer be any doubt the prosecution chief witness was drunk, and that Dr King's room at the Lorraine Motel was switched from one on a secluded ground-floor courtyard to a highly exposed one with a balcony.

Eyewitnesses Solomon Jones, Dr King's driver in Memphis, James Orange, SCLA field organizer, and journalist Earl Caldwell said the fatal shot was fired from the brush area, not the bathroom. Reporter Kay Black and James Orange both alleged the brush area had been cut and cleared back the morning after the shooting, possibly along with an inconveniently placed tree branch. I learned from Maynard Stiles, deputy director of the Memphis City Public Works Department in 1968, that the pre-dawn clean-up request came from the Memphis Police Department early on the morning of April 5.

A number of suspicious events were confirmed. The only two black firemen were ordered on the night before the killing not to report the next day to their posts at fire station no. 2, overlooking the Lorraine. Black detective Ed Redditt was removed from his surveillance post about an hour before the event. The MPD failed to form the usual security squad of black detectives for Dr King. The emergency TACT support units were pulled back and TACT 10 was removed from the Lorraine to the fire station.

Evidence emerged that the CB hoax broadcast, which drew police attention to the northeastern side of the city, had been transmitted from downtown, near the scene of the killing. A former FBI agent confirmed harassment and surveillance of Dr King by the Bureau, and MPD special services/intelligence bureau officer Jim Smith confirmed Dr King's suite at the Rivermont where he usually stayed was under electronic surveillance by federal agents.

There were increasing indications that members of the Liberto family in Memphis and New Orleans were implicated in the killing. Jim's Grill owner Loyd Jowers seemed increasingly likely to have played a role. Taxi driver James McCraw's earlier claim that Jowers showed him a rifle under the counter in his grill was corroborated by Betty Spates, a waitress at Jim's Grill, who implicated Jowers, her former boss and lover, in the murder, admitting that after hearing what sounded like a shot she saw him run into the kitchen from the brush carrying a rifle. Her sister Bobbi told of having been driven to work by Jowers the next morning. He admitted finding a rifle out the back. She also pointed to some sinister activity going on upstairs on the day of the killing and having been told by Jowers not to take food up to the recuperating Grace Walden, Charlie

Stephens's common-law wife. The death of *Time* magazine stringer and investigative reporter Bill Sartor in 1971 was confirmed to be murder. He was on the trail of the Marcello/Liberto organized-crime connection to Dr King's murder.

In the trial, the prosecution made great play of James's "racism" and that he had supposedly stalked Dr King. Great parts of our evidence were excluded. Betty Spates and her sister were too terrified to testify, and John McFerren fled in fear. In my closing speech, I said the prosecution hadn't introduced a shred of evidence of any motive. I went over the many holes in the prosecution's flimsy case. These included the failure to match the evidence slug to the rifle at the scene, the fact that none of James's prints were found in the rooming house, that the state's chief witness was falling down drunk, the bathroom was empty just before the shot was fired, and there were three eyewitnesses to activity in the bushes and two eyewitnesses who saw James's white Mustang being driven away from the rooming house minutes before the shooting.

I then catalogued strange events surrounding the case, including apparent tampering with the evidence slug, the cutting down of the tree and the bushes, the change of motel and room, the removal of security and standing down of black officers. Could James alone really have arranged these events? The program aired on April 4 1993 – the twenty-fifth anniversary of Dr King's death. The jury found the defendant not guilty.

The silence from media organizations was deafening. No major media outlets reported on this verdict. Despite this, I considered it a success, providing a springboard to open up the case as never before.

3

THE CONTINUING INVESTIGATION: LOYD JOWERS'S INVOLVEMENT

In the trial's aftermath, I began to focus on Loyd Jowers. I wanted to find a way to put on the record the evidence that we had uncovered about his involvement. I thought it would be sufficient to prove James's innocence. To secure his freedom, we also needed to learn as much as possible about what Jowers knew to get to the bottom of the conspiracy in Memphis.

Wayne Chastain, a reporter with the *Memphis Press Scimitar* in 1968 and later an attorney in Memphis, knew Jowers's lawyer, Lewis Garrison. The two frequently discussed the case. Garrison, a man of formidable conscience, told him that his client had dropped hints that he knew much more about the events of April 4 than anyone else and seemed to be looking for a way to open up.

Memphis private investigators Ken Herman and John Billings had worked for me on the television trial. Now they were acting on their own. Herman went to see Garrison about Jowers's involvement in the killing. Garrison somehow learned we had unearthed evidence of Jowers's involvement and told him not to say anything until a grant of immunity was obtained. He undertook to approach the district attorney general to this end also on behalf of Jowers's "heavy" Willie Akins, Betty Spates, Bobbi Smith, and James McCraw. I didn't see how, apart from Jowers, any of the other clients could be charged with any crime. The statute of limitations had run on any criminal acts committed after the crime.

Billings asked his next door neighbor – black judge and founder of the National Civil Rights Museum, D'Army Bailey – to quietly ask the attorney general to review the request for immunity, which would shortly be submitted. I was annoyed Herman and Billings had acted without instructions. They had a continuing legal and ethical responsibility to James, which derived from their association with his defense and myself as his lawyer. They had indirectly tipped off Jowers and Akins to what we knew, and it was quite possible they had put at risk already fearful essential witnesses. If Betty and Bobbi knew that Jowers and Akins had become aware of their cooperation with us, we had little chance of convincing them to cooperate further.

I didn't expect Attorney General Pierotti to approve the request for immunity since he and his office had long been closely associated with the official "solution" of the case. I had no involvement in Garrison's request but was anxious for the truth to come out. It was obvious, however, that Jowers would not reveal what he knew unless some sort of satisfactory immunity or plea arrangement could be obtained.

There were any number of plea bargaining possibilities open to the prosecutor and Garrison. I discovered an alternative route for obtaining immunity. A little-known Tennessee statute provision would allow us to sidestep the attorney general's office and approach the Grand Jury directly and ask that body to hear evidence on the case. Garrison insisted on going the conventional route, believing the story was too big for Pierotti to suppress.

Garrison met with Pierotti on June 3 and laid out the request, stating that his unnamed clients wished to provide specific evidence pertaining to the killing of Martin Luther King in exchange for a grant of immunity from the state and federal governments. Pierotti asked Garrison for a brief statement outlining the evidence. Garrison submitted the formal written request on June 22 1993.

Meanwhile bits and pieces of Jowers's and Akins's story began to be passed on to me, usually through Wayne Chastain, to whom Herman and eventually Lewis Garrison would talk. Supposedly, Frank Holt, a black produce-truck unloader, was hired to do the shooting. We wanted him as a witness in our pre-trial investigation, but Herman couldn't locate him. Jowers also told Garrison that Frank Liberto had given him the contract to murder King, thus apparently independently confirming John Mc-Ferren's story.

Jowers apparently acknowledged having seen James in the Grill on April 4 seated at a table with a dark-haired Latino. This chimed with James's account of meeting with Raul on the afternoon of the killing. Jowers also indicated that the money for the contract came from New Orleans and was delivered to Memphis in a M. E. Carter Produce Company truck. Herman reported that Jowers had confirmed Betty's story about the events of April 4 to the last detail.

There was no indication where and with whom the contract originated. Jowers may have only known local details of the killing, and he wouldn't reveal all he knew until he was granted immunity. Akins, it emerged, only became involved with Jowers about a year after Dr King was shot. While Jowers might have revealed information to him, he did not know him at the time of the killing.

Two and a half months after Garrison met with Pierotti, there was no sign that the attorney general was going to act or even that he was seriously considering Garrison's request. I had therefore begun to think about ways of applying pressure in an attempt to force his hand.

On August 16 (my birthday), I wrote to him, informing him that I was aware of Garrison's petition, calling on him to grant it or make a plea bargain arrangement with Jowers. I pointed out its potential impact, both in setting the record straight and in bringing about the release of a man who had been unjustly imprisoned for almost a quarter-century. The attorney general tried to fob off the request. On September 8, he wrote that he couldn't consider granting immunity until he had "evidence, which can be proven beyond reasonable doubt and to a moral certainty." On September 15, he even denied having anything to consider, saying he had not been presented with "any document requesting formal immunity in the case nor any summary of evidence that might cause him to consider immunity should such an application be made." It became clear he had no intention of considering the request.

On October 4, at the request of Lewis Garrison and Ken Herman,

Wayne Chastain met both men in Garrison's office. Garrison gave him a copy of the actual request for immunity submitted to the attorney general on June 22. Despite Pierotti's letter to me of September 15, the request was indeed a document asking for immunity containing a summary of the evidence on which it was based.

It stated that Jowers (designated as "Witness Green") was approached before the assassination and offered money to locate a person to assassinate Dr King. The funds would come from another city through a local person or persons. Jowers, who had close contact with some persons in the MPD, was advised that he was in a strategic location to assist and that Dr King would be a guest at the Lorraine Motel from a certain date. Jowers was to be provided with a weapon. Jowers located a person to do the job, and funds were delivered to Jowers before the assassination in volumes of large bills. At the time of the shooting, Jowers was stationed close to the assassin, and once the shot was fired, the weapon was passed to Jowers who disassembled it and wrapped it in a covering. Jowers had been advised by other conspirators that there would be a decoy following the assassination.

Betty Spates (designated as "Witness Brown . . . a close acquaintance of Jowers") would state that she was "within a few feet of the location where the shot was fired." Betty would also testify that she saw Jowers with a rifle immediately after hearing the shot. She would state that previously she saw a large amount of money that had been delivered to Jowers. The money was in stacks of large-denomination bills. McCraw, "Witness Black," stated that on the day after the killing, Jowers showed him the gun and told him it was the one used to assassinate Dr King. Willie Akins, "Witness White," would testify that he was asked, after the fact, by Jowers to take care of certain people "who knew too much." Jowers told him he'd received the gun after the killing from the actual assassin.

Bobbi Smith, "Witness Gray," would testify she was aware of the large amount of money paid to Jowers just before the assassination and that she had knowledge of other details about the actual killing. The submission ended with a formal request for immunity for all five people.

Jowers's story, as summed up for Chastain by Garrison, was that he had agreed at the request of produce-man Frank Liberto to hire a man to kill Dr King on his last visit to Memphis, and that he was paid $100,000 which he passed on.

Since I had no doubt that the attorney general would continue to stonewall any action based upon this evidence, I had to take steps on behalf of James. I instructed Chastain as local counsel to approach the Grand Jury on James's behalf. I planned to ask the Grand Jury to subpoena attorney Garrison at which time, if he so chose, he could request immunity for his client(s) in exchange for their testimony. I also formally asked the governor's counsel to ask the governor to hold off on issuing any ruling on our Motion for Exoneration since new evidence was forthcoming. I suggested that the governor could look foolish if he went ahead and ruled against us in light of information that would shortly be revealed.

We delayed our actual submission hoping to maximize the possibility of the members taking our submission seriously. Acting independently we began briefing certain representatives of the American mass media.

By the beginning of December, I was increasingly frustrated. There was no progress on the request for immunity and the media were unwilling to take up the issue and consequently there was no public pressure. On Tuesday evening December 7, I gave Wayne the go-ahead for the Grand Jury submission.

He was to deliver a letter and an affidavit to testify the next day. He rushed it in and, on his own initiative, attached the names and addresses of the people to be subpoenaed. I was concerned that we had provided Pierotti with the names of the witnesses and warned him any contact with these witnesses outside of the Grand Jury room would be closely scrutinized. Earlier, when Betty Spates had tried to come forward and get the truth out to clear James, she was visited unofficially in her home and, the record indicates, then called in officially and interrogated. Frightened off, it took 20 years for her to begin to come around again.

I called Andrew Billen at the London *Observer*, one of England's oldest and most reputable broadsheets. Initially skeptical, Billen had covered the TV trial and had a good working knowledge of the case. He was excited. So was his editor. Convinced no American media entity would break the story, I gave the *Observer* the go-ahead.

I learned from a source that Jack Saltman, the Thames Television producer of *The Trial of James Earl Ray*, was talking to various people, trying to break the story and name the witnesses, whose names I had stipulated from the outset had to be confidential. I was appalled. It was clear that Ken Herman had been working with Saltman for some time and that they had made an arrangement. In confidence, I had disclosed the existence of the "security" witnesses and the nature of their testimony. I believed that my trust was being flouted. Such a disclosure was likely to drive all of the witnesses away, and James would be the loser.

I confronted Herman. Our relationship, which had been strained since the trial, was now severely damaged. I instructed Wayne to add the names of Ken Herman and Jack Saltman to the list of those persons to be subpoenaed. The next day, Thursday December 9, Wayne delivered the names directly to an attendant at the entrance to the Grand Jury room and waited. He was not called. On Friday, the attorney general and his number two were closeted together continually and the local FBI Special Agent in Charge had also been in for meetings. Wayne's request to appear before the Grand Jury was making them anxious. The pressure was building.

Next, I became specifically aware of and increasingly concerned about the "rogue" efforts of Herman and John Billings to locate the man, Frank Holt, whose name had surfaced as the possible shooter. We all believed that Holt was now in the Orlando area. I told them that I would go to Orlando to approach and personally interview Holt if he could be found. I also sent them formal notices asserting my attorney's privilege, on behalf of James, over everything they knew or had connected with the case.

The *Observer* article was released around 10:00 PM on Saturday evening, and I fielded calls for a few hours. Around 2:00 AM Wayne called, saying that the London *Sunday Times* and the *Commercial Appeal* had called him. The Memphis *Commercial Appeal* quoted Pierotti as having denounced both Garrison and me, calling the entire story a "fraud" or "scam." On the morning the *Observer* hit the newsstands, I caught the flight to Orlando. We had an address for Holt supplied by Buck Buchanan, an Orlando private investigator hired for the purpose.

Memphis investigator Cliff Dates met me in Orlando, and we went to

32 North Terry, a small transient boarding house. Herman and Billings were also chasing the story and had got there first. Later, as we drove around, we saw a gray Cadillac approaching. We both recognized Ken Herman in the back, sitting between a black man in a baseball cap and John Billings seated on the other side. I was hindered in my search for Frank Holt by having to spend part of the next two days (December 14 and 15) negotiating with the ABC *Prime Time Live* producers. I had learned that Jack Saltman had sold the story and his counseling services to them.

I saw the program as potentially being useful to the effort to free James, but I was afraid that they might name the witnesses. If Betty and Bobbi were named without their consent and before their statements could be heard in a courtroom, they would probably repudiate earlier statements or not discuss the matter at all. This, of course, is exactly what happened before.

I contacted the ABC producer. Eventually, he promised that only the witnesses they actually interviewed would be named. On the program, which aired nationwide on Thursday December 16 1993, Loyd Jowers cleared James Earl Ray, saying that he did not shoot Dr King but that he, Jowers, had hired a shooter after he was approached by Memphis produce man Frank Liberto and paid $100,000 to facilitate the assassination. He also said that he had been visited by a man named Raul who delivered a rifle and asked him to hold it until arrangements were finalized.

Jowers's "clean-up man" Akins confirmed he was ordered to kill the unnamed "shooter" who ran off to Florida before he could "pop" him.

The producer's promise was worthless. Betty had been surreptitiously filmed leaving her place of work. Though partially obscured, she was recognizable, and she was named.

The next morning I asked Cliff Dates to contact Betty. She was hurt, hostile, and blamed me. She didn't realize that Herman and Saltman hadn't worked with me for eight months. Since she wouldn't talk to me, I sent her a letter explaining the facts.

The morning after the *Prime Time Live* broadcast, there was no news coverage of the previous night's program; not even on ABC. There was a small mention in *USA Today* and the *Washington Post*, which featured Pierotti's new willingness to investigate the case further, though not to reopen it. Here was a confession, on prime time television, to involvement in one of the most heinous crimes in the history of the republic, and there was virtually no American mass media coverage.

I had concluded that the governor would not seriously consider the basis for the motion for exoneration. I filed a petition on James's behalf seeking a trial on the basis of the new evidence discovered during the course of our investigation as well as the sensational public admissions of Loyd Jowers. On the night the program went out, John Billings, who was trying to keep lines of communication open, called to tell me that they had still not found Holt. When they found him, I would be the first to know. I just listened. Earlier that morning, I had learned it was all over Memphis that Holt was the person implicated in the killing.

I was scheduled to fly back to London on Friday December 17. About an hour before the flight I learned that Dwight Lewis of the *Nashville Tennessean* newspaper had left a message on the office answering machine: they had found Frank Holt, and he wanted to get my reaction to Holt's statement. My heart stopped. I called Lewis, who told me that two of the *Tennessean*'s reporters and a photographer had located Holt that day at the men's homeless center on Central Boulevard in Orlando, one of the shelters where I had "hung out" earlier in the week. He would move from shelter to shelter – long stays were not allowed. He apparently said that he had been inside Jim's Grill on the afternoon of April 4 but knew nothing about the assassination. The *Tennessean* had flown him to Nashville, where he took and passed a lie detector test.

The paper published a feature article on their interview of Frank Holt on Sunday December 19. That morning, I learned that Lewis had gone to the airport to put Holt on a plane bound for Orlando. I asked Buck Buchanan to meet the flight and offer Holt a temporary safe house. Though the *Tennessean* had not printed Holt's address, his name and general location were public, and he had publicly refuted all allegations that he was the shooter. I thought his life might very well be in danger.

Buchanan met the plane, and Frank Holt accepted the offer of protection and temporary safe house accommodation until I could arrive to interview him on Wednesday. On Tuesday, Buchanan was contacted by the *Tennessean* and by investigators from Attorney General Pierotti's office. He had left his name at the homeless center the previous week when searching for Holt, and both the newspaper and the Shelby County officials had become aware of his interest.

The prosecutor had had five witnesses under his nose for over six months and had made no move to interview them, yet the *Tennessean*'s story was not even two days old, and Pierotti had already sent a team to another state to search Buchanan out to, as he put it, "shoot full of holes" the story told by Loyd Jowers.

Buchanan met me on my arrival in Orlando on Wednesday December 23, and we took Holt out to dinner. He was a generally placid, almost expressionless man, concerned about his safety, and wanting to leave the Orlando area. The next day, I interviewed Holt for four hours at my motel. Though I questioned him repeatedly, his story never varied. He said that he had left his home in Darling, Mississippi in the mid-1950s and ended up in the Jacksonville area, which he had come to regard as a second home. In the early 1960s, he went to Memphis and eventually took a job at the M. E. Carter Produce Company as a driver's helper, going on deliveries to towns in Arkansas and Mississippi. Occasionally, he would travel to New Orleans to bring back produce to Memphis. This was the job he was doing in 1968 at the time of the assassination.

He had the impression that Frank Liberto, who had his own produce business ("LL & L") also had some interest in M. E. Carter. Occasionally, he overheard conversations between Liberto and the "big wheels" of M. E. Carter, and on one occasion during the sanitation workers' strike, he heard Liberto say, "King is a trouble-maker, and he should be killed. If he is killed, then he will cause no more trouble."

Holt said that he drank beer at Jim's Grill two or three times a week. He recalled going upstairs in the rooming house to visit and drink beer with two friends – "Apple booty" and Commodore. Apple booty had worked the warehouse at M. E. Carter. The last time Holt remembered being upstairs in the rooming house was before Commodore moved, sometime before the shooting. From his description of the layout, it appeared clear that Commodore had occupied room 5B, the room rented by James on the afternoon of April 4, under the name John Willard.

Holt said that on the day before the shooting, he had gone on a delivery run deep into Mississippi and did not return until late morning or early afternoon of the following day. When he reached Memphis, he made the rounds of a few bars and eventually ended up in Jim's Grill late in the afternoon. To the best of his recollection, he was inside the grill at the time of the shooting and could not explain the reference in the FBI report that he was passing the grill on his way to work. He did not recall ever being interviewed by the police or FBI. This could have been explained by Holt's own faulty memory, the passage of time and alcohol abuse.

When asked why Loyd Jowers named him, he was puzzled. "He probably thought I was dead," he said. Holt had left Memphis in late 1969. He had no interest in notoriety and abhorred being linked to the assassination. He seemed credible and a most unlikely assassin. That afternoon, he took another lie detector test and underwent hypnosis. Both the hypnotist and the polygrapher concluded that Frank Holt was not involved in the crime. Late in the afternoon of December 23, I shook hands with Frank Holt and said goodbye. He had, I said, further assisted in clearing his name.

I returned to England believing that Jowers was lying about Holt's involvement and was either covering up his own role as the shooter or was protecting someone else by implicating Holt. Even his claim that he had asked Akins to find Holt and kill him in 1974 was incredible. By that time, Holt had been gone from Memphis for five years.

In 1994, Jowers may have been constructing one of his self-protective stories, for around this time James was about to obtain a *habeas corpus* hearing. When threatened by events over the almost 26-year history of this case, Jowers had always developed such stories.[2] It would take time to discover why.

Breakthroughs, January–April 15 1994

In an interview with the *Tennessean* on January 7 1994, Attorney General Pierotti said that he was going to tell the Grand Jury to go ahead and listen to what Chastain had to say. The foreman, Herbert Robinson, said that even though Chastain "was a pain," they would hear him sometime after January 18 when the new Grand Jury was formed. He was still waiting to be called in 1995. I found this appalling. When James had pleaded guilty on March 10 1969, Attorney General Canale pledged on the record of that hearing that "if any evidence was ever presented that showed there was a conspiracy, he would take prompt and vigorous action in searching out and asking that an indictment be returned . . ."

Fortunately, we had already decided to proceed with filing a petition for trial. I flew to Nashville to meet James who was in good spirits and interested in the possibility of using the imminent petition to obtain declassification of relevant documents, files, and reports.

On Monday January 10, Wayne filed the petition for the trial along with five volumes of exhibits and two video exhibits. We then drove out to Jim Lawson's old church, Centenary Methodist, where a press conference had been scheduled to call for an independent Grand Jury investigation. When we got there a number of participants including Reverend Lawson, who had flown in from Los Angeles, had already arrived. I briefed the group, which included several prominent church leaders (amongst them the Reverend William Sloane Coffin, whom I had long regarded as one of the most articulate preachers in America), and we answered questions before the two-hour press conference. This focused on the group's commitment that a Grand Jury should independently investigate the murder of Dr King under the leadership of its own foreman and an independent prosecutor not associated in any way with the Shelby County district attorney general. All agreed that he couldn't be regarded as an objective, impartial investigator.

We left the meeting feeling uplifted. Later that day, we learned that the petition had gone to the court of Judge Joe Brown, with the hearing scheduled for the following morning. When we arrived at the Criminal Justice Center, television cameras were already there. During the brief hearing, the judge raised the question of whether or not our petition could prevail because of prior decisions that had been reached on some of the issues, primarily related to overturning a plea of guilty. We argued that those prior decisions were made without the benefit of the new evidence we now sought to produce, which proved James's actual innocence of the crime. The judge asked both sides to prepare memoranda of law on the issues, scheduling a hearing for April 4, the twenty-sixth anniversary of the assassination.

Early that afternoon we met John McFerren, who on April 4 1968 had overheard Frank Liberto calling for King to be shot on the balcony and who promised that this time he would not "chicken out." He recalled hearing from a local man, Tommy Wright, that on Saturday mornings Liberto would meet regularly with a high-level Tennessee state official at his law office in Fayette County. Alarm bells went off. James had found a government business card with the name Randy Rosenson scribbled on the back in the white Mustang before crossing the border from Mexico to California. Raul, who had paid for the car, kept a spare set of keys. Randy Rosenson had insisted that in 1978, around the time of his interviews by HSCA staff, he had been visited by the same high-level Tennessee state official who tried to get him to say that he had been acquainted with James Earl Ray. If Rosenson had known James, then he could have dropped the cigarette pack containing the card himself. If he didn't know James, then someone else had to have left the pack and card behind. James had always stated that he believed the card was linked to Raul. The state and the HSCA had taken the position that Raul did not exist, so any evidence to the contrary had to be a problem for them.

The connection being alleged between Liberto and the official could explain why pressure was put on Rosenson to say that he knew James. McFerren said that another source of information was his lawyer from Jackson, Tennessee, Mr H. Regan. He had told McFerren quietly, years ago, that the same state official "handled" matters and looked out for the interests of organized crime in Tennessee. Retired MPD Captain Tommy Smith confided that various senior officers of the department were regularly on the take back in 1968, but he didn't know any details. He was out of the loop. He also said that the police officers who went to the FBI Academy – N. E. Zachary, Robert Cochran, Glynn King, and others – formed a special clique.

In late January, I was finally able to speak again with Betty Spates. She said that Jowers, Akins, and others were interested in doing a book or movie about the case. They wanted her to change her story to say she saw a black man handing the rifle to Loyd in the doorway of the kitchen seconds after the shooting. Willie Akins came around with a tape recorder and she was supposed to listen to help her get the story straight. When she refused to go along with this farce, Akins told her that she had "blown it" for all of them. They could have split $300,000 if she had cooperated.

Betty totally refuted the story involving Frank Holt and strongly insisted, as before, that when she saw Jowers running toward the back door of Jim's Grill's kitchen there was no one with him. In mid-January, Betty told me that the Tennessee Bureau of Investigation had called her and wanted to interview her. I advised her to see them and answer their questions truthfully. Over the last weekend of January, John Billings told me that he had learned that Pierotti had asked the TBI to conduct an investigation into the new Jowers evidence. He said that they had already spoken to McCraw who was sticking to his story. Billings offered to be interviewed by the TBI, and Ken Herman was also willing to throw new light on the case. Billings was told that the attorney general would have to agree. The impression Billings received was that they wouldn't be interviewed and that by using the TBI, Pierotti was distancing himself from direct responsibility for the investigation while still controlling the inquiry. They were never interviewed.

I wrote to Pierotti offering any reasonable assistance to the FBI investigation of the new evidence. I told him James was interested in being released and not in solving the murder. If released, James intended to leave the country, but while he stayed inside the investigation aimed at establishing his innocence would, of course, continue.

On March 7, 8, and 9, I spent a total of 13 hours with Betty Spates. She agreed to tell me her story from the beginning, adding that she had been racking her brains, trying to remember each detail about what she observed on April 4 1968. I met her in her darkened home on Roland Street. She told the story of her involvement with Jowers and the grill as she had always told it, adding details. There were a few surprises, however, when she related the events of April 4 1968.

Now Betty remembered going over to the grill just before noon on that day and noticing that Loyd was nowhere around. Somewhat nervous, and always insecure in her inter-racial, extra-marital relationship with Jowers, she went back to the kitchen at the rear to look for him. The door was slightly ajar. She was only in the kitchen for a short time when Loyd came through the back door carrying a rifle. The gun had a fairly light brown stock and handle and a barrel that appeared to be of normal length; she did not remember seeing a scope. She said that Loyd did not appear to be in a hurry or under stress. He was almost nonchalant. She was startled and asked, "Loyd, what are you doing with that gun?" He replied, half jokingly, "I'm going to use it on you if I catch you with a nigger." She said, "Loyd, you know I wouldn't do that," and he said he was only kidding, that she knew he'd never hurt her.

He put the gun down alongside a keg of beer and then, as though he had second thoughts, picked it up again, and proceeded to break it down in front of her. He then carried the pieces through the Grill, went out the front door, and turned left, walking several feet to where his old brown station wagon was parked. As she watched through the window, he put the broken-down rifle into the back of the wagon, looking around afterward to see if anyone was watching. Then, he came back inside. She confirmed that during the course of that afternoon, she was in and out of the grill. Although Jowers always discouraged her from being around on Thursdays when his wife would drop by, that Thursday, he seemed especially ill at ease and kept chasing her out. That only made Betty more suspicious that he was cheating on her, and she was in the grill when Jowers's wife came in around 4:00 PM. Mrs Jowers walked straight up to her and called her a whore and told her to get out. Loyd intervened, telling his wife to get out herself and directing Betty to get behind the counter. Sullen and speechless, Loyd's wife stalked out.

After a while, Betty went back across the street returning to the grill to check on Loyd sometime before 6:00 PM. She believed that Bobbi was still there. Loyd, however, was again nowhere in sight. Eventually, she went back toward the kitchen, noticing that this time the door between the restaurant section and the kitchen was tightly closed. Thinking that this was unusual, she made her way into the kitchen, where she noticed that the door leading to the backyard was ajar. Soon after she recalled hearing what sounded like a loud firecracker, and then within seconds, she looked out, and saw Jowers rushing from the brush area through the door carrying another rifle. When she first saw him, he was about 10 to 15 feet from the door. He was out of breath, she said, and white as a ghost. His hair was in disarray, and the knees of his trousers were wet and muddy as though he had been kneeling in the soggy grass or brush area.

When he caught his breath, he didn't appear angry but plaintively said to her, "You wouldn't ever do anything to hurt me, would you?" She said, "Of course I wouldn't, Loyd." Without another word, he moved quickly to the door leading into the grill which opened right next to the counter on the left. In one quick step, with the rifle at his side, he was behind the counter, and she saw him break the rifle down, wrap it in a cloth, and put it on a shelf under the counter and push it farther back.

She remembered that the rifle was distinctive. It had a dark mahogany brown stock, a scope, and a short barrel that made the gun look like a toy. There was something screwed or fixed on to the barrel somehow, fitting over it and increasing its diameter.

In this statement, for the first time, Betty had spoken of two separate instances of seeing Loyd Jowers bringing a gun in from the brush area behind the kitchen. It was worrying that this was the first time she had mentioned a second gun. On the other hand, this account corroborated what McCraw had said all along about Jowers showing him the gun under the counter.

Betty went on to say that a few months after the killing in 1968, she was visited by three people who she believed were government officials. One was black, another white, and the third appeared to be Spanish or Latino. They offered her and her sisters new identities, relocation, and money, for, it was said, their own protection. They refused, supported by their mother, and the men left. Two of the same men returned about five years later. (This would have been around the time that James was being given an evidentiary hearing in federal court.) The offer was repeated and again refused.

Jowers's friend Willie Akins had acted aggressively toward Betty, firing at her and her two sons on one occasion and firing three shots into her sofa on another. She believed he was trying to frighten, not kill her. Betty signed detailed affidavits in support of all of these events. When we filed Betty's primary affidavit with the court, the *Tennessean* published its contents. Shortly afterwards, Attorney General Pierotti leaked a statement taken by the TBI on January 25 that we found distressing. In it, also purportedly under oath,[3] Betty denied seeing Jowers with the rifle at 6:00 PM and further denied having any information supporting James's innocence. When I asked Betty about it, she did not recall giving the specific answers recorded. She said they only asked her to respond to specific points in Ken Herman's statement.

It did appear, however, that she had signed the TBI statement. I obtained a copy. The handwritten statement, dated January 25 1994, appeared to contradict the affidavit she had given me on March 8 1994. However, she said she didn't read it because her glasses were broken. It was read to her, and the investigator wrote as he asked her questions, telling her not to volunteer information but to simply answer questions. She said the men from the attorney general's office and the TBI made her afraid. Betty went out of her way to assure me that she now wanted to testify and to clear her name of any hint of her being a liar.

The April 4 hearing had been put off until April 15. Though the hearing was to focus on the law, I argued the law by substantially elaborating upon and applying the facts. This enabled me to put a long list of suppressed factual evidence and factual discrepancies on the record and of course to be heard by the judge, and the media seated in the chairs normally occupied by the jury.

Pierotti spoke for about 15 minutes as part of the state's rebuttal argument and appeared to be agitated. At the end of the argument, the judge complimented both sides and then, referring to lengthy notes, stated that although the state might be technically correct, requiring him to deny the petition, nevertheless he was going to allow us to put forward evidence. This evidentiary record would be available to an appellate court, he said, as well as to history. In an impassioned reference to the importance of Dr King, he said history compelled him to allow as much information as possible to be placed before the public under the auspices of his court. The state was stunned. Judge Brown said he would not finalize or file any judgment until after the submission of evidence was over. We were elated.

It was an extraordinary result. Judge Brown's ruling could hardly have been more creative. If he had explicitly ruled in our favor and granted a trial or a full evidentiary hearing, the state would have appealed, and considering the inclination of the Court of Appeals and the Supreme Court, he would likely have been overturned. In any event, we would have been off on the appellate trail. By not finalizing any ruling, he kept the matter before him and could thus allow us to call witnesses and submit evidence. We intended, for example, to file a motion asking to test the rifle and the bullets in evidence. Whether or not the judge would go so far as to order a trial at the conclusion of our evidence remained to be seen.

I eventually decided to open up another legal front and sue Loyd Jowers on behalf of James. Jowers had, after all, actually admitted on prime time television that he played a key role in the case, for which James had spent 25 years in prison. Jowers had also publicly admitted that James was a patsy and did not know what was going on. Thus Jowers's acts and his continued silence had resulted in the unjust imprisonment of James.

We filed the complaint for the civil suit against Loyd Jowers, Raul _____, and other unknown parties on Thursday August 25 1994. We alleged that Jowers had participated in the tort of conspiracy, as a result of which James had been deprived of his liberty, and been wrongly imprisoned. We added the newly developed ancillary tort of outrage, which was justified by the very nature and continuation of the wrongful acts. Damages sought were $6,500,000 actual and compensatory and $39,500,000 punitive.

Early on, we decided to depose Jowers, and the deposition took place over a nine and one-half hour period. He had with him a typed clause asserting his Fifth Amendment rights ready for use. Nine hours would pass before he would use it. We began at a gentle pace as I took him from his childhood and early life in a large rural family to his days on the police force, which lasted roughly from 1946 to 1948. After that, he formed his own Veterans Cab Company staffed at first by Second World War veterans. It was during his brief career as a police officer that he met Memphis produce dealer Frank C. Liberto in 1946 or 1947. He said that back in 1946, he knew both patrolman N. E. Zachary and Sam Evans. Jowers supplied details of his own six marriages (three to the same woman).

He recalled Frank Liberto in the late 1940s as a prominent produce man, whose business was located downtown in the market near Central Police Headquarters. Later, the market moved to Scott Street, and Liberto moved his business there.[4] He denied knowing Frank Liberto well although he believed that "Frank," as he called him, did help him get some taxi business from the market.

He said that he didn't see Frank Liberto again until 1965. He refused to acknowledge any business dealings with him. In 1966, he left Veterans Cab and went to work for the Yellow Cab Company as a dispatcher. The next year (1967), he opened a restaurant called the Check Off Inn and opened Jim's Grill in the summer of 1967. He denied the Check Off Inn was a gamblers' haunt.

When he opened Jim's Grill, he hired Betty Spates and her sisters Alda Mae Washington and Bobbi Smith. He bought fresh vegetables from M. E. Carter. They were delivered daily. He said that the back door from the rooming house was boarded up, but he couldn't explain why it appeared to be open in police evidence photographs I showed to him taken shortly after the killing.

Jowers said that, on April 4, he drove a white Cadillac to work. Bobbi Smith worked on the morning of April 4 but left around 4:00 PM. He said Betty Spates did not work at all that day because one of her children was sick. Also, he said that Big Lena and Rosie Lee had gone from his employ months earlier and that he himself had fixed breakfast for the "eggs and sausage" man. Some time prior to Jowers's deposition, I had located Rosie Lee Dabney, and she confirmed that she was waiting on tables in Jim's Grill on the afternoon of April 4. She said she served eggs and sausage to a stranger on the afternoon of the shooting and again the next morning. An MPD report corroborated her story.

Jowers could not identify a photograph of Jack Youngblood, intelligence officer and mercenary, as the "eggs and sausage man," although Wayne Chastain said he did so at an earlier time.

Jowers said he was drawing a pitcher of beer at the time of the gunshot. He confirmed with certainty that the bushes in the backyard had been cut down and he actually drew a line surprisingly close to the building, up to which he said the thick bushes came. He acknowledged that the waitresses probably did bring food up to Grace Walden but denied telling Bobbi not to bring food up to her on the morning of April 4.

He denied driving Bobbi to work on the morning of April 5 or going out to the back or even looking out there on the morning after the shooting. Incredibly, he categorically denied having any relationship with Betty Spates. He did, however, admit to speaking with Betty on December 13 1993, the night the *Prime Time Live* program was filmed, to warn her, he said, that reporters were on the way to her house.

I showed Jowers a copy of the transcript of the ABC *Prime Time Live* program, and he agreed it was an accurate statement. I then entered it into the record. When I began to question him on the statements he made on the program, he invoked the Fifth Amendment. I noted for the record that the transcript had already been agreed to and entered into evidence and that in my opinion the protection of the Fifth Amendment was not available to him. Garrison then agreed to stipulate ". . . that the questions were asked and Mr Jowers gave these answers" (the answers being those responses given during the television program).

Jowers's testimony was extraordinary for the number of untruths he told, many of which were clearly contradicted by other evidence and testimony and some of which were the result of him contradicting his earlier statements. For reasons best known to himself and his counsel, Jowers insisted on deposing Betty Spates. Lewis Garrison served a subpoena on her, and she came along in a hostile frame of mind. Before beginning, I took her aside and explained that Jowers, who had denied having any relationship with her, had insisted that she be called. Gradually, she decided to cooperate, confirming the factual truthfulness of the affidavit she had given to me earlier.

Willie Akins was also deposed and stated that a few years after the event, Jowers admitted that he was involved in the killing. Jowers described his meeting with Raul, who brought the gun to him at the Grill, and Frank Liberto arranging for a delivery of a large sum of money in a produce box included in a regular delivery. The scene was striking. Jowers greeted Akins cordially, and then Akins, under oath, proceeded to directly incriminate his old friend. Akins continued to maintain that years later he had been asked by Jowers to kill Frank Holt. At the end of the deposition, Jowers and Akins went off talking about old times.

Betty's sister Bobbi Smith was also subpoenaed and appeared on December 22. Under oath, she confirmed what she had told me in an informal interview on December 18 1992, two years earlier. Jowers had told her not to bring breakfast upstairs to Grace Walden on the morning of April 4. She usually did this about twice a week around 10:00 to 10:30 AM after the morning rush was over. I had always thought that this was significant because it meant that something was going on up there well before noon that day, some four or more hours before James arrived to rent the room. Bobbi also said that Jowers picked her up on the morning of April 4 and 5, as usual, in his brown station wagon, which he parked just north of the grill in front of the Store Fixtures building.

On the way in on the morning of April 5, Jowers told Bobbi about the rifle being found in the backyard after the killing. She also confirmed that Jowers often spent the night at the Oakview House, where she lived with her mother and Betty in 1969, and that he had a long-standing affair with Betty during all of this time. Finally, she said that she had told the same story to the TBI and attorney general's investigators sent by Pierotti, and she did not understand why they would say that she knew nothing or had retracted her story. They told her not to discuss the matter with anyone.

Subsequently, on Saturday March 11 1995, Attorney Lewis Garrison, with Loyd Jowers present, began to depose James in a small conference room at the Riverbend Penitentiary. Throughout the session, Jowers listened intently as James gave the usual answers to the questions he had heard a thousand times before. As he left the prison that afternoon, Loyd Jowers seemed to be more amenable than ever before to revealing details which I believed would ultimately establish James's innocence.

Jowers agreed to answer some further critical questions about the killing through his lawyer. There would be no recordings of his statement, and the attorney Lewis Garrison would take the follow-up questions to him for his response. On March 14 1995, the process began in Garrison's 400 North Main Street office while he provided some new details of the conspiracy. Much of what he said confirmed information obtained previously from Betty Spates, Betty's sister Bobbi Smith, and taxi driver James McCraw.

At the outset Garrison stressed the Holt story was not concocted by his client, but had to acknowledge Jowers went along with it for a while. He was uncertain whose brainstorm it was but believed it originated with Willie Akins and Ken Herman.

Jowers contended that in March 1968, he was first approached not by Liberto but by a local businessman who dealt in securities and bonds and whom he had come to know from his gambling activity with Frank Liberto. This man told him that because of the location of Jim's Grill, he was going to be asked to provide certain assistance to the carrying out of a contract to assassinate Martin Luther King. He would be paid handsomely.

Sometime between March 18 and March 28, soon after this conversation, Jowers was approached directly by produce man Frank C. Liberto, to whom he admitted that he owed a very large debt. For some time, I believed that the debt was a gambling loss. More recently, I have come to believe that it was more sinister. I believe that Liberto got rid of the body of a Mexican Jowers killed after finding him in bed with Betty. This debt would be forgiven, and he would receive a large amount of money if he would help. Specifically, Liberto said: $100,000 would be delivered to him in cash in the bottom of an M. E. Carter vegetable produce box. The money came from New Orleans as did the contract on King's life, and:

- He would be visited by a man who would bring him a rifle – and leave it with him for pick-up at the right time. (Upon consideration, it is not clear that this was the murder weapon.)
- There would be a patsy or decoy to distract attention.
- The police – some of whom were involved – would be nowhere in sight.

Jowers agreed. As Liberto said, a man did come to see him. Jowers thought that he introduced himself as "Raul" or "Royal," and appeared to have a Latin/Indian appearance. He was about 5 foot 9 inches in height and weighed approximately 145–155 pounds. He had dark hair and appeared to be between 35 and 40 years old.

They discussed the plans for the killing. Raul told Jowers that his role would be to receive and hold the weapon on the day of the killing until it would be picked up. After the shooting Jowers would have to take charge of the actual murder weapon and keep it concealed. Jowers was also expected to keep his staff out of the way at all times. He confirmed Bobbi's story that he instructed her not to follow her usual practice of taking food up to Grace Walden.

On the morning of April 4, sometime around 11:00 AM after the rush was over, Raul, according to plan, came into Jim's Grill, bringing with him a rifle concealed in a box which he turned over to Jowers to hold. Jowers said that Raul told him that he would be back later that afternoon to pick it up. Jowers put the gun under the counter and carried on with his work. He next admitted that he went away to take a rest sometime around or after 1:00 PM when the lunch crowd had gone. When he returned to work, it was around 3:30 PM. Sometime later, Raul returned briefly and took the gun from him and went back into the kitchen area with it. Jowers claimed to be uncertain as to whether he remained in the rear of the grill, or went upstairs by the back stairway. (According to James's recollections, Raul was upstairs off and on during the afternoon. It therefore seems more likely that Raul took the gun upstairs to room 5B and concealed it there.)

Jowers said that sometime before 6:00 PM he went out into the brush where he joined another person. He did not provide any more details except to admit that immediately after the shot he picked up the rifle which had been placed on the ground and carried it through the back door of Jim's Grill. As he ran into the back of the grill, he was confronted by Betty who, as she had said, stood near him as he broke the gun down, wrapped it in a cloth and quickly put it under the counter in the grill itself. Jowers finally confirmed her recollection of the events was basically correct. He also admitted that the next morning between 10:00 and 11:00 AM, he showed the rifle in a box under the counter to taxi driver James McCraw, thus confirming McCraw's recollection. Sometime later that morning, Raul reappeared in the grill, picked up the gun and took it away. Jowers said he never saw the rifle again and has no idea where it was taken or where it is today. The version of events just laid out was completely at odds with the answers Jowers gave in his deposition. Jowers had altered some of these details, probably to cast his role in a slightly better light. Some years later, he would bring us closer to the complete truth about the events leading up to and taking place on April 4 1968.

4

NEW STRANDS AND CONNECTIONS

H. L. Hunt

Billionaire oilman H. L. Hunt, who had been dead since 1974, had close ties with people and institutions emerging as pivotal players in the conspiracy now unfolding.

I approached his former chief aide John Curington who offered many new revelations on Hunt's close ties to the FBI and the Mafia. Curington had worked for Hunt Oil for 15 years and for nearly 13 of these had worked for H. L. Hunt personally, occupying the office right next to him. He frequently worked 18-hour days, seven days a week, and often traveled with Hunt.

As he explained it, he was basically Mr Hunt's "follow-through" guy. He did whatever was necessary to get a job done. While not directly engaging in the "dirty" work himself, he made the arrangements at the old man's request. According to one of my investigators, at one point he had even referred to himself as Hunt's "bag man," saying that he carried and delivered cash, sometimes in very large amounts, to any number of places, organizations, and individuals in support of right-wing activities. Some went to pay for specific operations.

Curington had participated in many of the illegal activities he detailed and was remarkably frank. While continually referring to documents in an old brown leather suitcase, the then 67-year-old Texan confirmed that a closer relationship than had ever been publicly known existed between his ex-boss and FBI director J. Edgar Hoover which even included a direct-line red telephone in Hunt's desk drawer. Their association went back to the early 1950s. Apparently, they had been poker-playing friends for many years, and their compatible right-wing political views, though differing sexual orientations, made them allies. Hoover had even seconded a trusted FBI agent, Paul Rothermel, to Hunt as his head of security. Rothermel left the bureau in late 1954 and joined Hunt in 1955.

Curington was present at various meetings between Hoover and Hunt when Martin Luther King was discussed. Usually, Hoover came to the old man's hotel room. While the two men shared a dislike for Dr King, Hoover's animosity was more passionate and obsessive, more personal. Hoover regularly provided Hunt with a considerable amount of documentation and material to be used as ammunition against Dr King in his extreme right-wing, daily nationally syndicated *Lifeline* radio broadcasts. King was a favorite and a regular target of *Lifeline* venom.

Curington recalled one meeting in June 1967 in Chicago between Hunt and Hoover in Hunt's hotel room. Hunt told Hoover he could finish King by constantly attacking him on his daily radio broadcasts. Hoover replied that it would not work. He said the only way to stop King would be to "completely silence" him. After King's murder, Hunt acknowledged to Curington that Hoover had won that argument.

In April 1968, *Lifeline* produced a 15-minute daily program, six days a week, on 429 stations in 398 cities across America. Between 1967 and 1968, Hunt spent nearly $2,000,000 on this program alone. Curington revealed that the entire effort, as well as other shadowy often deeply covert political activity, was funded by moneys diverted by Hunt from H. L. H. Products, Inc.

Curington ran this company, which the "old man" had established as a front for funding such political activity.[5] He also acknowledged that his boss and Hoover shared many of the same friends, including several kingpins of organized crime. Not only was Hunt close to gamblers Frank Erickson (to whom he once owed $400,000) and Ray Ryan (who at the same time owed him a large amount), but he associated with Frank

Costello, the mob's liaison to Hoover. Hunt's top-level mob ties also included Carlos Marcello and Dallas boss Joe Civello.

In politics, Curington noted that Sam Rayburn, the former speaker of the House of Representatives, and his protege Lyndon Johnson were both life-long close political assets of Mr Hunt. Curington also said that H. L. Hunt's daily liaison with President Lyndon Johnson on political matters was former FBI agent Booth Mooney, who was personally close to the President. Mooney not only delivered communications between Johnson and Hunt but also wrote over half of the *Lifeline* broadcast tracts, including many of those attacking Dr King.

On April 5, the day after Dr King's assassination, Hunt told Curington to make arrangements for him (Hunt) and his wife to travel to a Holiday Inn resort hotel in El Paso, Texas. For whatever reasons, the old man wanted to be away and inaccessible in the aftermath of the killing of Dr King. Curington said that on the evening of the assassination shortly after the shooting, Hoover called Hunt and advised him to cancel his anti-King *Lifeline* programs, which were to be aired that evening and the morning of April 5. After that call, Curington said he was called to Hunt's home and told to put together a team of secretaries to call the radio stations.

By the end of our session, I concluded that John Curington, 25 years later, still appeared to be in awe of the man who, he said, moved on an entirely different level from "the rest of us."

James's last parole hearing

A parole hearing for James was set for May 25 1994. This would be the first time he appeared before the board. Such hearings are largely confined to a review of conduct during time served. They are not concerned with any determination of guilt or innocence. I had no doubt that the decision would be made on purely political grounds and had already been taken. Consequently, we decided to use this hearing as a forum to focus on James's innocence.

I challenged the board to act independently of the governor who appointed them and who had publicly expressed his wish that they deny parole and also to disavow the previous statements of the board's former executive director, who said James would not be paroled unless he admitted guilt. Parole was denied. James was told he could apply again in five years after he had served a full 30 years.

At a post-hearing press conference in response to a question about the testing of the rifle, Pierotti made the extraordinary statement that he didn't know if James was guilty and he didn't have to prove it. So much for the requirement that prosecutors shall be primarily concerned with justice.

I was more convinced than ever that our best hope lay in Judge Brown's courtroom. Judge Brown had been pressing us for some time to submit our draft order for the testing of the rifle and the bullets in evidence. I believed it likely that once the judge granted our request the state would appeal his order and seek a delay pending review. This, of course, is what ultimately happened with our efforts resulting in a May 8 1995 Criminal Court of Appeals ruling endorsing the judge's action.

The Whitlock/Liberto story

Around 10:30 PM on the evening of June 4 1994, I received a call from Memphis cab driver Nathan Whitlock, who had known Frank Liberto in the 1970s and who, I heard, had been told by Liberto himself that he had paid to have King killed. Whitlock usually drove a cab at night, and on that evening, he was driving a limousine. I rode with him, so we could talk. He told me about his conversation with "Mr Frank" some 16 years before. He said that his mother LaVada had owned a restaurant that lay on the route between Liberto's home and his LL & L Produce Company business. Nearly every day, the produce man would stop in there for breakfast in the morning on his way to LL & L and for drinks in the afternoon on his way home. Nathan said that when he had had a few drinks, Liberto took to bearing his soul to LaVada. She would often leave her post at the bar, sit down at a table, and talk with him. One day, as the congressional committee's work was being reported on the television in the restaurant, he told her he had arranged for the killing of Martin Luther King. Nathan said that when his mother told him about this, he became upset that Mr Frank would involve his mother in this "gangster" talk.

Nathan played guitar and used to travel, but in between trips he would help out in the restaurant, where he would often serve beer to Mr Frank. Nathan said Liberto wanted to appear like a big shot around him. He showed off a thick roll of bills and a jade, diamond, and gold ring purportedly given to him by Elvis Presley. They became reasonably friendly.

Another customer of the restaurant once quietly advised Nathan to be careful since Liberto was in the Mafia. Nathan, who was about 18 at the time, once asked Liberto if indeed he was in the Mafia and what the Mafia was anyhow. Liberto told him that the Mafia was a group of businessmen who "took care of business." He added that as a youngster he used to push a vegetable cart with Carlos Marcello in New Orleans. At the time, this meant nothing to Nathan because he didn't know who Marcello was.

Upset about Mr Frank's conversation with his mother, he decided to confront him. One afternoon in 1978, just before Nathan was scheduled to go away on a trip, Liberto came in and ordered a beer. Nathan engaged the 300-pound produce dealer in conversation and then asked him directly if he had killed Dr King. He said Mr Frank looked as though he was going to be sick to his stomach. He immediately asked Nathan if he was wired. The boy thought Liberto wanted to know if he was on drugs, which he denied. Then, Liberto said, "You've been talking to your mother, haven't you?" Nathan admitted that he had, and Liberto then told him, "I didn't kill the nigger, but I had it done." Nathan then said, "Well, that SOB is taking credit for it," (referring to James) to which Liberto responded, "Oh, he wasn't nothing but a trouble-maker from Missouri." He added that James was a "front man," a "set-up man."

Then, Nathan said Mr Frank turned on him, saying, "You don't need to know about this," and after jumping to his feet and drawing his right hand back as though to hit him, he said, "Don't you say nothing, boy," and glared at him. He stomped around, thinking for a minute or so and then said, "You're going to Canada, aren't you?" Nathan said he was. Liberto became quiet, and Nathan went to the back of the restaurant to take care of something. When he returned Liberto's beer was still on the table, but Mr Frank was gone. He never saw Liberto again, but during his trip, in early 1979, his mother sent him a letter stating that Frank Liberto had died.[6]

Sometime later, Nathan would tell this story directly to the attorney general, after which he was interrogated by members of his staff. He said they tried to break down his account, but he stuck to his guns. Later, both Nathan and his mother told their stories under oath. John McFerren had been vindicated.

On June 5 1994, Wayne Chastain and I met for the first time with Willie Akins, Jowers's old friend and enforcer. In a three-hour session, he discussed how he had come to know Loyd Jowers and how he gradually learned about Jowers's involvement in the killing. He confirmed acts of violence against Betty but said he never took a contract on her life and never meant to kill her.

Jowers had only recently begun to open up to him about the King case. When the BBC documentary aired in the United States, in which Earl Caldwell spoke about seeing a figure in the bushes, Jowers called Akins. He said "Big N [Jowers always called him that, which he said stood for Big Nigger], you know that figure in the bushes he talked about – that was me." He said that on one occasion, Jowers told him that the person who could do him the most damage was the chauffeur. He was referring to the long-missing Solomon Jones.

Akins continued to pay lip service to the story about him being asked to get rid of Frank Holt. My sense was that Akins had pieced part of the story together but that Jowers certainly had not told him everything. He was clearly lying about some things, but Akins's information only added more corroboration to Jowers's involvement. The question still remaining, however, was whether or not he had been out there alone and whether he himself had pulled the trigger. I increasingly believed that the answer to both questions was no.

The hedge

Back in London in September, we came across a photograph in the *Commercial Appeal*'s pictorial history, *I Am A Man*. It was a shot of MPD officer Louis McKay guarding the bundle allegedly belonging to Ray in Canipe's doorway. It was taken pointing south toward the fire station and in the background in the upper right was a hedge running down to the sidewalk between the parking lot and the fire station. Although there had been rumors of a hedge in that spot, we had never seen any photographs of it. On checking the evidence photographs from the attorney general's office, this hedge did not appear standing in any of the evidence photos. Then I came across a photograph of the hedge cut down to its very roots. From all of the other photographs, one would have never known that a hedge had ever been there. This was highly significant. The official investigators had contended that on leaving the rooming house, James had seen a police car parked up near the sidewalk, which caused him to panic and drop the bundle. There was no police car in this position. Even if there had been, the hedge would have obstructed the view and made the official story untenable.

Here was evidence that at the time of the killing, a hedge was there. Sometime shortly afterwards (probably the next morning when the bushes at the rear of the rooming house were cut), it was cut to the ground, and all trace of its existence obliterated. At the TV trial, Hickman used a photograph which showed a police car in clear view pulled up to the sidewalk.[7] That photograph and others like it must have been staged, taken after the scene had been physically altered. In fact, the staged photographs were clearly taken later since the billboard advertisements were different from the ones in place on the day of the killing and the day after.

Art Baldwin's account

On October 15 1994, I drove out to the Shelby County Correctional Center and finally met with Arthur Wayne Baldwin, the government informant who worked closely with the Marcello organization in Memphis. He said that he now sympathized with James. He volunteered having heard that James was assisted in escaping from the prison in June 1977 and that he was not supposed to be brought back alive. It seemed to me that some things never change. He told me about two contracts on

James's life, with which he was involved. The first came from the "Memphis Godfather" who in 1977 told him that the people in New Orleans wanted this matter cleared up once and for all. Ray was supposed to have been killed in Memphis, but it had been botched.

Baldwin was not keen to get involved but did not want to offend the Man. He had been present on other occasions when the Godfather talked to Frank Liberto on other matters. He said that Liberto was treated like a "puppy dog" and ordered about in brutal fashion. Baldwin said he offered the contract to Tim Kirk. It went nowhere. The approach from the Bureau came some months later.[8]

Under the proposed scheme, he and a state official would go to Brushy Mountain prison with transfer papers for James under the pretext of moving him to Nashville. They would arrive around 3:00 AM and take him. Baldwin was expected to kill James en route. They would then bury the body. James would go out of the Brushy Mountain population "count," and since Nashville was not expecting him, he would not be missed for some time. The transfer papers at Brushy Mountain would then be pulled. Baldwin said he became uneasy when he could not get answers to questions concerning how long they expected the story to be kept quiet and what the ultimate explanation was to be. He began to believe that perhaps he and even the official were to be killed as well as Ray. He pulled back.

He said they offered him lifetime immunity from all prosecution. His Nashville control FBI agent also knew about the scheme and had heard the two agents discussing other efforts to get rid of James. Both the mob and the government wanted him dead. They believed that it was only his continued presence that kept questions about Dr King's assassination alive.[9] Baldwin was willing to take a lie detector test. His candor surprised me. It was obvious that he was fed up with being used by the government. His disclosure was the first time that I had heard the details about the Memphis Godfather's involvement in the case although Mafia protocol would have required that Marcello process the contract through his Memphis boss and not deal directly with a local lieutenant like Liberto.

James's former attorney, Jack Kershaw, revealed that at an earlier time, an offer of money and parole had been made through author William Bradford Huie, who had collaborated with and funded James's first attorney Arthur Hanes. James would have to admit his guilt. James rejected it out of hand. Shortly afterward, Jerry Ray (James's brother) received a telephone offer for James from Huie with a substantially greater sum on the table. That attempt was recorded and transcribed.

After James had rejected these approaches, a more lethal scenario involving Art Baldwin was introduced.

Another Marcello scenario

Some time after telling me his story about Frank Liberto, Nathan Whitlock told me about a rumor of an earlier King murder contract put out to a member of a family named Nix who lived in Tipton County, Tennessee. Nathan said he understood that Red Nix had been given a new car and a rifle and paid $500 a week to track and kill King. If he succeeded, he was to get $50,000. He thought the offer came from Frank C. Liberto. Red had been killed not too long after Dr King was shot. At Nathan's suggestion, I met with Red's brother, Norris, and Bobby Kizer who jointly owned and ran the New Moon night club in East Memphis. They confirmed that Red was given a new car and was put on a payroll for a job. "He was after someone all right," said Norris Nix, "but I don't know who." They believed that Tim Kirk, who was a friend of Red Nix, would know who hired Red and offered to ask him to tell me what he knew. Tim, they said, could free my client.

I was surprised. I thought I knew everything Kirk had to say. Eventually, I visited Tim Kirk again to ask him about the Red Nix murder contract. He said with certainty that the contract was put out by Carlos Marcello, not Frank C. Liberto. It was sometime in mid-1967. He said Red knew Marcello and undertook various jobs for him. A car had indeed been provided. Here was another indication directly linking Marcello to a contract on Dr King. Based on his experience, Nathan Whitlock had formed the impression that Liberto had also been behind the Nix contract. Kirk said there was no way. It came directly from New Orleans and Carlos Marcello.

More than ever the trail of the Memphis contract that resulted in Dr King's death led to New Orleans and pointed toward the involvement of the Mafia organization of Carlos Marcello. Marcello had not just given his approval but had taken on the job and had attempted to subcontract it on more than one occasion – the last time successfully through his Memphis associates which included the Memphis Godfather and Frank C. Liberto.

Louie Ward's account

For a number of years, there had been rumors about a Yellow Cab taxi driver who saw someone jumping down from the wall just after the shooting. In autumn 1994, a driver came forward. At first, he tried to tell his story to the attorney general, but he encountered a total lack of interest. He contacted Garrison after reading an article about the case. Garrison passed his number on to me.

On November 5 1994 Louie Ward told me a story he had held back, out of fear, for 26 years. On the night of April 4, around 6:00 PM, he was parked near the corner of Perkins and Quince. Suddenly, he heard the dispatcher come on the radio, obviously responding to a driver's call about an emergency. (Any driver could only hear the dispatcher's side of conversations with other drivers.) He heard the dispatcher say that he would send an ambulance and then, in response to something else, the dispatcher said he would send one anyway and call the police. From what he had heard, Ward learned that the emergency was the shooting of Martin Luther King. He also realized that the driver was taking a fare to the airport.

Ward went straight to the airport and met up with the driver who told him his story. Ward said that the driver, whom he knew as Buddy and whose full name he could not recall, was in his early sixties, and driving car 58. The driver said that he had gone to the Lorraine shortly before 6:00 PM to pick up a passenger with an enormous amount of luggage. As they finished loading up his taxi in the Lorraine parking lot, the driver turned to look at the area of dense brush and trees opposite the motel. His passenger quickly punched him on the arm in order to get his attention and (so the driver later thought) distract him from looking at the brush, saying, "Look up there – Dr King's standing alone on the balcony. Everybody's always saying how difficult it would be to shoot him since he is always in a crowd. Now look at him.''

At that precise moment, the shot rang out, and the driver saw Dr King get struck in the jaw and fall. The driver said he grabbed his microphone and told his dispatcher that Dr King had been shot. The dispatcher said he would call an ambulance, and the driver said that considering the wound he didn't think it would do much good. Then Ward said the driver told him that, immediately after the shot, he saw a man come down the wall empty-handed, and run north on Mulberry Street and get into a black and white MPD traffic police car which had stopped in the middle of the intersection of Mulberry and Huling. At that point, the driver told the dispatcher to tell the police that one of their units had the man. Meanwhile, the passenger was becoming irritable, saying that they had to leave immediately because otherwise the ambulance and other cars would box them in, and he had to make the plane. They left.

Ward heard the driver repeat the story to three MPD officers at the airport and observed a second interview being conducted later that evening in the Yellow Cab office by other policemen. After that evening, Ward said he never saw Buddy, the driver of car 58, again. Days later, he returned to the Yellow Cab office for the first time after the killing and asked after Buddy. Three or four of the drivers in the office told him that they understood he had fallen or had been pushed from a speeding car from Route 55, on the other side of the Memphis–Arkansas bridge, late on the evening of April 4.[10]

5

RAUL AND THE GRABOWS

On October 31 1994, as a part of our discovery in the civil suit against Loyd Jowers, Raul _____, and others, I prepared to take the deposition of Glenda Grabow. She had known a person named Raul in Houston, Texas in the 1960s and came to learn of his involvement in Dr King's killing. She had contacted Lewis Garrison in autumn 1993, after reading about Loyd Jowers's request for immunity. Garrison had brought Ken Herman into his first meeting with her in 1993. Glenda Grabow and Lewis Garrison both believed he was still working as my investigator.

I had been denied access to Glenda. However, Lewis Garrison finally gave Chastain and me her name and telephone number, adding that Herman had told him categorically that she would not talk to us.

We drove out to where Glenda Grabow and her husband Roy lived, a few hours from Memphis, and they appeared pleased to meet us. After that first meeting in Garrison's office, they only met with Herman and former Thames Television producer Jack Saltman. They had wondered where the lawyers were since they had come forward to help free an innocent man.

Glenda told me her story. In 1962, when she was 14 years old, she met a man who went by the nickname of "Dago." Years later, she learned his real name was Raul. (I have used the pseudonym "Pereira" for his family name.) As she walked to school each day, she passed a small gas station on the corner of East Haven and College Boulevard. Dago didn't seem to work at that station but just sat around in front. Since he was friendly to her and she was having a difficult time living with her aunt and uncle, where a pattern of abuse had been established over a number of years, she was happy to know him. She recalled that he was about 5 feet 9 inches tall, a bit wiry, and weighed 155–160 pounds. His hair was dark with a reddish tint, and she thought that he would have been around 30-years-old. When she was 15, she met and married Roy, who, by his own admission, drank continually and stayed out a good deal.

Soon after they were married, Glenda and Roy moved to a small house near the gas station and only saw Dago occasionally, and between 1966 and 1970 he disappeared from the area.

In 1969 or 1970, she and Roy came to know a man called Armando. With Roy gone much of the time, Glenda was very lonely. She began to spend more and more time with Armando and his friends, and she appears to have been exploited by them and some of their associates. Armando did not drive, and she frequently drove him places. One of the places they visited was the rented house of Felix Torrino on the corner of 74th Street and Avenue L. At Torrino's house, some time in 1970, she recalled seeing Dago again. At that time, Armando told her Dago was his cousin and that his real name was Raul Pereira. He said that they immigrated to the United States from Brazil or Portugal.[11]

Over time, Armando and Torrino independently told Glenda that Raul had killed Martin Luther King. They even told her some details, mentioning some bushes and trees at the rear of the rooming house. Raul, they said, had leaned on and broken a tree branch while carrying out the killing. When she heard this, she was shocked. Raul did not know Glenda knew his link with the assassination, and his cousin thought it should stay that way.

Glenda became increasingly close to this group between 1970 and 1978, knowing that they were involved in different illegal activities including gunrunning, forging passports, and making pornographic films. She assisted in passport forging and gunrunning. When a shipment of guns was arriving from New Orleans, she would drive down to the Houston ship's channel, go on to the docks, and allow the boxes to be loaded into the trunk of her car.[12] Though she never asked questions, she heard the men comment it was safer to ship the weapons around the coast than to deliver them by road.

This story chimed with British merchant seaman Sid Carthew's account of being approached in the Neptune bar in Montreal. Sid Carthew now lives in West Yorkshire, England, but in 1967 and 1968 he was a merchant seaman. He frequently traveled to North America. In Montreal, he would frequent the Neptune Tavern, a hangout for merchant seamen near the docks. It was in that bar on two occasions that he met a man named Raul. Carthew tried to contact me after seeing the television trial in England, getting nowhere until he contacted the General Council of the Bar in London, which gave him my address. He said that Raul approached him at the Neptune sometime in early 1967 and struck up a conversation about guns for sale. Carthew had a passing interest, and Raul said he would sell him some Browning 9mm handguns. He quickly turned off, however, when it became clear that Carthew wanted four weapons, not four boxes. Sid Carthew described Raul as being about 5 feet 8 inches tall and weighing approximately 145 pounds. He had a dark, Mediterranean-like complexion, and dark brown hair. Carthew remembered him saying that the guns were stolen from a military base and that the price included the fee for the master sergeant who organized the supply and who, according to Raul, would deliver them himself to his ship in exchange for cash. I couldn't believe my good fortune.

Glenda said during this period Raul Pereira lived or at least spent a good deal of time in a second-floor apartment in a house on Navigation near 75th Street close to the docks. Though Raul did drive, she frequently drove him and Armando wherever they wanted to go. She recalled dropping Raul off at the Alabama movie house, where he would often go to meet with Houston associates of Carlos Marcello. Roy said Marcello owned a number of movie theaters in Houston, and Glenda thought some pornographic film-making was going on at the Alabama. Glenda actually saw Marcello in Houston on a couple of occasions with Armando, Raul, and their friends, at a fruit stand on Navigation and in a bar next door. She said that on another occasion, it was arranged for her to spend time with Marcello at a house in the area.

One day in the early 1970s, around 1:00 PM, she drove Armando over to Torrino's house, where the usual group had gathered. Her car keys were on a ring, which had a plastic viewfinder containing miniature photos of John and Robert Kennedy and Martin Luther King. She put the keys on the table, and someone picked them up, looked into the viewfinder, and then tossed it to Raul. Glenda said when Raul saw it, he became angrier than she had ever seen him.

She remembered him shouting, "I killed that black son of a bitch once, and it looks like I'll have to do it again." He dropped the keys on the floor and stamped on the plastic viewfinder. Then, he grabbed her, put a gun to her head, forced her into a bedroom, and raped her. She left Torrino's house that afternoon shattered by the experience. Her husband pressed her to tell him what was wrong, but fearful he might do something they would regret, she didn't.

From then on, although she still associated with the group, she tried to keep her distance from Raul who behaved as though nothing had happened. She recalled that in 1978 and 1979, two of Roy's brothers got into trouble and were prosecuted. Glenda and Roy asked Houston attorney Percy Foreman to defend them. Foreman became attracted to Glenda and offered her a job in his office. He was trying to impress her and even gave her an original sketch of himself, which he personally signed on June 22 1979.

After a while, she learned that Foreman had been James Earl Ray's lawyer. He told her that one day white Americans would learn that Ray was a "sacrifice" or had to be "sacrificed" for their welfare. He even told her that he knew Ray was innocent, but that it didn't matter. Glenda, who had been harboring the terrible secret about who she believed killed Dr King for some time, decided finally to unburden herself. Shortly afterwards, Foreman told her he had spoken with Raul Pereira. To her horror, he appeared to have known him for some time. Thereafter Foreman called her at home several times a week to talk to her about Raul and tell her to be careful. She had the impression that he spoke regularly with Raul and was trying to take advantage of her plight to get her into bed. She was afraid of alienating him but wasn't interested and tried to keep her distance.

Finally, at one point in 1979, Foreman told her that if she and Roy did not leave Houston, they would be dead within the year. They prepared to leave and put their house up for sale. In a matter of weeks, she was driving on the expressway, and a wheel simply fell off her car, nearly causing her to be annihilated by an 18-wheel tractor-trailer. Every lug nut came off – they must have been deliberately loosened. The Grabows left town, returning only to sell their house. They had no further contact with Armando or Raul Pereira. Glenda executed an affidavit, which set out her story in detail and also said that she knew James Earl Ray was innocent and she was prepared to testify in court on his behalf.

When I returned to England, a Houston area lawyer confirmed in a lengthy telephone conversation that in the 1960s and 1970s Percy Foreman had become the foremost lawyer for organized crime figures. Former mob lawyer Frank Ragano, who had represented Carlos Marcello and Santo Trafficante, had previously told me about Foreman's role as a lawyer for prominent mob figures.

I heard a rumor that Raul Pereira lived in the northeast. I began a computerized state-by-state, name and residence check and cross-referenced search. It was a long shot that the man might be using his real name but there was always a chance. A number of people with that name surfaced. I arranged for credit and other checks on them. By a process of elimination the list gradually reduced. The search was completed in early June and one person remained who satisfied the basic criteria.

He appeared to be a relatively successful businessman, nearly 61 years old. He jointly owned his home, which was in a middle-to-upper-middle-class neighborhood in a city in the northeast with his wife. He had a 25-year-old daughter and a son of 33.

Raul, I learned, owned another property on the same street where his import/export business was located in one of the city's poorest areas. He was reportedly a member of the local Portuguese American society and had no criminal record. From immigration records I learned that he had entered the United States from Portugal through New York City. His social security number had been issued in New York between 1961 and 1963 and he first appeared in his city telephone directory in 1965. If this was James's Raul then for at least twenty years he had clearly led a double life.

James wrote to say he had received a letter from Saltman advising him that he and Herman had confronted Raul. It was obvious that Herman and Saltman wanted to develop a commercial production based on Glenda's story. Raul had been hostile, taken photographs of the pair and got his Portuguese-speaking wife to ask them to leave. I arranged for a surveillance team to photograph this Raul Pereira. I needed to show it to Glenda and also to determine whether this was the same man Herman and Saltman were chasing, whose photograph I had seen at Jowers's deposition. On seeing the photographs, I was virtually certain it was.

I decided to call Herman. He put Saltman on and they confirmed the visit and the hostile reception. Raul would not come to the door. His daughter spoke to them, lying in response to even the most simple and apparently non-threatening questions. Giving no indication of where the man was or the man's identity, they both assured me that the man that they had found was Glenda's Raul. When I expressed skepticism designed to draw out information, they jointly confirmed to me that the birth date and social security number of the man in the older photograph were identical to those of the man they had recently visited who was in the more recent photographs.

I spoke immediately with Glenda. She told me that prior to Herman and Saltman's visit to Raul, they arranged a telephone conversation and she spoke to Raul Pereira at his home, with family members participating on extensions. When Raul spoke she knew it was the Raul Pereira she had known in Houston because he pronounced her name distinctively. Despite what became hysterical denials of knowing her and ever being in Houston, she said she had no doubt this was the man. (She did not, at that time, tell me that she had herself spoken to Raul in a private conversation on April 20 1995 and that the conversation had been revealing.)

It was obvious that Raul Pereira had by then been well and truly alerted, and I was concerned that he might flee. This, of course, would allow the state to continue to contend that he was not the right man and that James's Raul never existed. In addition, since Herman and Saltman said they did not have enough to satisfy their television producers I was apprehensive about what further action they might take which could induce him to flee.

We had little choice but to promptly join Raul Pereira as a party in the civil action against Jowers. We prepared a summons to go along with the original complaint in which he had been named and a notice of deposition. It said Raul entered into a conspiracy with others to kill Dr Martin Luther King Jr.

I learned from private investigator Bob Cruz that a source of his inside the Immigration and Naturalization Service (INS) told him Raul Pereira had come into the United States on December 11 1961, and that his INS file had been transferred in October 1994 to Memphis, Tennessee. The source commented that there was no apparent reason for sending the file to Memphis, and it would only be transferred at the request of another federal agency.

With time of the essence, I arranged a meeting with Glenda and Roy in Memphis on the weekend of June 24 1995.

Glenda executed an affidavit, in which she stated she recognized Raul from a 1960s photograph and also recognized the facial features of the man in the 1994 photograph. She further stated she had talked to Raul Pereira by telephone and that she was positive this was the Raul she had known in Houston because of his inability to pronounce her name correctly (he always called her "Olinda") and that based on her identification she understood we were preparing to bring him into the law suit against Loyd Jowers and others.

On Monday at 7:45 AM, we met with Bob Cruz who had organized surveillance. He reported the mother and daughter had already gone out, apparently leaving Raul at home alone. Before approving the final arrangements for service I needed to be absolutely certain that this was the same man being looked at by Saltman and Herman. I decided to call Raul myself. I adopted a sympathetic tone, saying that I believed that he may have been harassed unjustly and I wanted him to know that though these people had once been associated with me as a lawyer in the case, they were no longer working with me. He ponderously took down Chastain's and my details. He spoke with a fairly heavy accent and did not appear to be flustered. It was difficult to tell how much, if any, of Raul Pereira's language problem was feigned since we were able to communicate.[13]

He seemed puzzled that I knew about his "problem" and confirmed that he had been bothered by some people and that this was upsetting him and his family. He expressed surprise that things thirty years old were being raised now and he denied ever being in Houston. I asked him to meet with Chastain and me privately in order to try to clear up any question of his involvement, and he asked me to call him back that evening after 7:00 PM when he would have had a chance to talk to his wife and "kids." I agreed and we held off any attempt at service that day.

At 7:15 PM, his daughter answered and said, in effect, that her father did not have to prove anything and his word denying any knowledge of the events would be good enough. She confirmed that a man named Saltman had appeared at their front door wanting to question her father and she said that she told him that if he published or released any information about her father they would sue him.

My impression was that she was well trained and intelligent. Mr Pereira knew what he was doing by putting her forward. Toward the end of the conversation she said that they might ask their lawyer about talking to me, though she would not give me the lawyer's name. At that point I concluded that we would have to serve Raul Pereira.

The man I have called Raul Pereira was served on July 5 1995 and made a party defendant in the *Ray v. Jowers* lawsuit. Then I arranged to acquire all the information Ken Herman and Jack Saltman had obtained about him. This included the passport photograph and a spread of six photographs including it made by Ken Herman for showing to witnesses. Sid Carthew traveled to London from Yorkshire. I placed the spread of six photographs on my desk. He instantly put his finger on the photograph of Raul's face and exclaimed "That's him, that's the one all right."

Affidavits were obtained from Glenda Grabow, Sid Carthew, and James, identifying Raul from the spread of photographs.[14] Glenda then gave me her phone bill, evidence of her first call with Raul which she made on April 20 1995. It confirmed that they had spoken for six minutes. She also provided me with a summary of that conversation where it was clear he knew who she was.[15]

Raul was represented by two large, prestigious law firms – unusual for a person of his purportedly modest means. He denied our allegations. Ultimately, on January 16 1997, Circuit Judge Holder, who was presiding over the civil action against Loyd Jowers and Raul Pereira, ruled that the case could not go forward until and unless the Criminal Court set aside Ray's guilty plea.[16]

On January 12 the Grabows called. They told me that the day before their house had been shot at four times by people driving by. Glenda was shaken and they planned to leave for a couple of days. Glenda also decided to reach out to Jesse Leeman Wilburn, an uncle who had worked at the gas station where Raul hung out in the early 1960s.

Her relationship with her uncle, known as "Bobby," had become strained and unpleasant. Now, when they met it was clear Bobby's wife did not want him going to court. However, when alone with Glenda, Bobby identified Raul, picking out the same photograph that had been selected by Glenda, her brother, Sid Carthew, and James.

Bobby told them that once a week, a man who appeared to be a law enforcement officer would come by and visit Dago. He was always dressed in a dark suit, white shirt, cowboy boots, and black Stetson hat. He carried a .38 snub-nosed Smith and Wesson pistol in a shoulder holster. The two would talk each time for around half an hour. Dago would also be visited by others who did not work at gasoline stations or come from Houston. Bobby confirmed that Dago often sold guns in and around the station.

6

THE CONSPIRACY DEEPENS

Earlier, in late July 1993 to be precise, I had widened the focus of my investigation. I met with Steve Tompkins, the former *Commercial Appeal* investigative reporter who had spent 18 months researching a front-page piece on the role of army intelligence in surveying and infiltrating black organizations and civil rights groups. It had been published on March 21 1993. Army intelligence had spied on Dr King's family for three generations. The article noted that there was an extraordinary fear in official circles about what would happen if Dr King was allowed to lead masses of American poor into Washington that spring. It stated that army intelligence was ". . . desperately searching for a way to stop him . . ." The article also noted in passing, and without comment, that there was a Special Forces Alpha 184 sniper team in Memphis on the day of the killing.

I wanted to learn whether Tompkins knew anything about the King killing, and if so, whether he could open up some doors for me. Since Dr King had been under army surveillance, I wondered if the killing had been seen and even photographed. Tompkins had gone to work for the Governor's Economic Development Department. He had confirmed the presence in Memphis that day of a number of army intelligence operatives. I needed to know their roles and, if possible, who they were. He would not give me their names, but he did offer an observation that surprised and chilled me. He had stumbled on certain information, which he was unable to print because of the lack of corroboration.

He had come to believe that after talking with a former Special Forces soldier now living in Latin America, in addition to surveilling Dr King on April 4 1968, the army in Memphis was implicated in the assassination. The nervous ex-soldier had showed up with an AK 47 rifle, which he kept near throughout the interview. This man was the only member of the army unit whom Tompkins was able to interview. He believed that another member had been shot in the back of the head in New Orleans. The ex-soldier told Tompkins that he decided to leave the country after his New Orleans comrade was killed. He said it appeared that a "clean-up" operation was under way and that he had better get out.

This important information greatly complicated the picture. It was imperative that I investigate it as far as I could. Tompkins warned me that, if publicly questioned, he would deny telling me the information. As we parted, he said he was relieved to be away from the Special Forces, stating, "Most of these people are the dregs of humanity, real slime. They'd kill you, your mother, or your kids as soon as look at you. You have to be very careful."[17]

Tompkins said these people would want to be paid for their time and want the money in cash before the meeting. They would not volunteer information but always answered his questions truthfully.

A couple of the Special Forces "grunts" (non-commissioned officers) would likely cooperate. In addition to covert operations relating to domestic turbulence in 1967, they had been involved in gun running activities into New Orleans. The operations were coordinated by a master sergeant, and the sales were made to Carlos Marcello's operation and delivered to barges in a cove bordering property owned by Marcello. A man named "Zippy" or "Zip" Chimento handled these transactions for Marcello. The soldiers were given the name and phone number of Joe Coppola, who was connected with the Louisiana Highway Patrol, in case they had any trouble transporting the guns by truck. When I checked, I learned that Zip Chimento was in fact a confidant and associate of Marcello, and Joe Coppola was the commissioner of the Highway Patrol.

During this time, much to Steve Tompkins's surprise, he had received a telegram from the Special Forces soldier he had previously interviewed, who I will call Warren and who now lived in Latin America. The message was simply that "... he now knew who Dr William Pepper was" and that he was prepared to answer any questions I would put to him through Tompkins. Under no circumstances would he meet directly with me. The date he set for the meeting, outside of the United States, was the last weekend in March. Tompkins was willing to go as a consultant and put my questions to Warren, who he said had never lied to him, although, on occasion, he would refuse to discuss a matter or say that he did not know.

Based on what Tompkins had told me about Warren, I knew that he and his partner, who I will call Murphy, had vital information. Tompkins said that though I would have the names and personal details about Warren, Murphy, and perhaps others, one of the conditions would be that I agree not to name them. Without that understanding, there could be no cooperation. If I broke my word on this issue, he thought it likely that both of us would be killed. I agreed to the condition, which did not apply to participants who had since died. Tompkins would give a statement, and his reports would be written and detailed.

On the morning of November 9 1993, I met with Steve in his office in the Tennessee State Capitol Building. He had prepared a chronology of events for me, which I was eager to analyze and discuss. He had printed it out before he left the office the previous night. He looked everywhere but couldn't find it. Since he had left it on top of a letter he had written on behalf of his secretary, he was convinced that his office had been entered and the file taken. I had recently had a similar experience in Birmingham when my address/appointment book had disappeared. On that one occasion I registered in my own name. It has never turned up. It was an ominous indication that a closer look was being taken at my activities.

The role of the army and the other cooperating government agencies in the assassination of Dr King has been one of our nation's deepest, darkest secrets. I have only been able to uncover it by piecing together the accounts of Warren and Murphy with those of other participants, people who were in strategic positions with access to information, and analyzing relevant army intelligence documents, files and other official records which have never been made public.[18]

Military organization[19]

In 1963 the 101st Airborne was deployed at the racial riots in Oxford, Mississippi. Major General Creighton V. Abrams, the on-scene commander, wrote a highly critical assessment of how army intelligence had performed. It stated: "We in the army should launch a major intelligence project, without delay, to identify personalities, both black and white, and develop analyses of various civil rights situations in which they become involved". His report received serious attention from the army intelligence machine in place in 1967 and 1968.

In 1967, Military Intelligence formed part of the US Army Intelligence Command (USAINTC) based at a military compound based at Fort Holabird, Maryland. By 1968 the Investigative Records Repository (IRR) was housed in a huge two-story steel room, containing more than seven million brown-jacketed dossiers on American citizens and organizations. They included files on allegedly subversive individuals, who, according to army intelligence, were "persons considered to constitute a threat to the security and defense of the United States." There were files on the entire King family.

USAINTC took control of seven of the eight existing counterintelligence or US Army Military Intelligence Groups (MIGs) in the Continental United States (CONUS) and Germany. The eighth MIG – the 902nd – was under the command of the army's Assistant Chief of Staff for Intelligence, who from December 1966 until July 1968 was Major General William P. Yarborough, the founder of units known as the Green Berets. By 1967, the MIGs employed 798 army officers and 1,532 civilians including 67 black undercover agents. Of this total force, 1,576 were directly involved in domestic intelligence gathering, and of these "spies," some 260 were civilians.[20]

The MIG officers were responsible for eye-to-eye surveillance operations which included audio and visual recordings of people and events designated as targets. Dr King was a target and throughout the last year of his life was under surveillance by one or another MIG team. Closely related to the USAINTC structure at the time was the separate intelligence office under ACSI Yarborough.

In addition to controlling the 902nd MIG, he supervised the Counter-intelligence Analysis Board (CIAB). This analyzed a wide range of MIG-produced intelligence and forwarded reports directly to the ACSI. The 902nd MIG was a highly secretive organization, carrying out some of the most sensitive assignments. Warren had always refused to discuss the 902nd, saying anyone interested in the "90 Deuce" should dig a deep hole.

Intelligence gathering was also done in 1966 by the 20th Special Forces Group (SFG), headquartered in Birmingham, Alabama as part of the Alabama National Guard. The 20th SFG provided small, specialized teams for "behind the fence" covert operations, made up of reservists from Alabama, Mississippi, Florida, and Louisiana, which also came to provide an organizational cover for some of the most sinister and talented "retired" Special Forces operatives. The Ku Klux Klan had a special arrangement with the 20th SFG, who trained Klansmen in the use of firearms and other military skills at a secret camp near Cullman, Alabama in return for intelligence on local black leaders.

The US Strike Command (CINCSTRIKE) was the overall coordinating command for responding to urban riots in 1967 and 1968. It included liaison officers from the CIA, FBI and other non-military state and federal agencies. Its headquarters were at MacDill air force base in Tampa, Florida. ACSI and USAINTC commanders were primary leaders in developing CINCSTRIKE strategy for mobilizing forces required for defensive action inside CONUS.

The United States Army Security Agency (ASA) carried out all "non-eye-to-eye" or electronic intelligence surveillance (ELINT), employing expert wiretappers, eavesdroppers, and safecrackers. Telephone monitoring and wiretapping were used against Dr King when he stayed at the Rivermont Hotel on March 18 and 28 and at the Lorraine Motel on April 3 and 4 1968. The Psychological Operations section (Psy Ops) was used for highly sensitive and technical photographic surveillance and reports.

The CIA, whose director at the time was Richard Helms, and the FBI led by J. Edgar Hoover, worked alongside this multifaceted army structure, which had vastly superior manpower resources, particularly black operatives which the CIA and certainly the FBI were lacking. The National Security Agency (NSA) and the Office of Naval Intelligence

(ONI) contributed the task force under the umbrella of the coordinating intelligence body – the United States Intelligence Board (USIB) chaired by Richard Helms.

Warren and Murphy had been active in covert Special Operation Group (SOG) missions in Vietnam. They were hardened, highly skilled veterans; Warren was a sniper. Both were from the 5th SFG in Vietnam, and part of a Mobile Strike Force Team involved in cross-border covert operations in 1965 and 1966. They were reassigned in 1967 as reservists to the 20th SFG, with Camp Shelby, Mississippi as their training base.

Throughout 1967 they were deployed in 902nd covert operations as members of small specialized "Alpha team" units in a number of cities where violence was breaking out. They were issued with photographs ("mug books") of black militants in each city they entered. In some instances particular individuals were designated as targets to be taken out (killed) if an opportunity arose in the course of a disruption or riot.

During this time, army intelligence published the green and white mug books on black radicals, which contained photographs, family history, political philosophy, personal finances, and updated surveillance information in order to facilitate their identification by army commanders and intelligence personnel. The units were deployed when riots flared up in Tampa, Florida, Detroit, Washington, DC and on reconnaissance in Chicago.

The Memphis mission

In successive sessions, Warren and Murphy set out the details they knew about the Memphis deployment. They were part of an eight-man "Operation Detachment Alpha 184 team" – a Special Forces field training team in specialized civilian disguise. The unit consisted of the following: captain (as CO), a second lieutenant, two staff sergeants, two buck sergeants, and two corporals. I learned that the colonel in charge of the 902nd, John Downie, had previously selected a team from the roster of the 20th SFG, provided at the request of the ACSI's office and sent to him on October 23 1967.

A two-man reconnaissance unit of the Alpha 184 reconnaissance team which included Warren entered Memphis on February 22 through the Railways Bus Terminal, completed reconnaissance on the downtown hotel area, and mapped egress routes to the north of the city. (The "hoax" automobile chase at the time of the assassination took place in the northern section of Memphis and concentrated attention on this area of the city.)

The team leader was apparently given the final orders for the deployment at 7:30 AM on March 29. Warren and Murphy stated that the team was specifically briefed before departing from Camp Shelby for Memphis at 4:30 AM on the morning of April 4 1968. During the half-hour session the team was left in no doubt as to its mission. On the order they were to shoot to kill – "body mass" (center, chest cavity) – Dr Martin Luther King Jr and the Reverend Andrew Young.

They were shown "target acquisition photos" of the two men and the Lorraine Motel. The team's pep talk stressed how they were enemies of the United States who were determined to bring down the government. Warren said that no one on the team had any hesitancy about killing the two "sacks of shit." Immediately after the briefing the team left in cars from Camp Shelby for Memphis, carrying the following weapons in suitcases: standard .45 caliber firearms, M-16 sniper rifles with 8-power scopes (the closest civilian equivalent would be the Remington 30.06 700 series. James was instructed to buy a Remington 760); K-bars (military knives); "frags" (fragmentation grenades); and one or two LAWS (light anti-tank weapon rockets). It appeared they were prepared for all contingencies.

They were dressed as working "stiffs," similar to those day laborers who worked down by the river near President's Island. The team leader arranged for Warren and Murphy to meet with a senior MPD officer who they believed was attached to the MPD's intelligence division and who told them that their presence was essential to save the city from burning down in the riot which Dr King's forces were preparing.

Warren later identified Lieutenant Eli Arkin from a photograph as being the officer they met. He was also the MPD's chief liaison with Special Agent William Lawrence, the local FBI field office's intelligence specialist.

Some time after noon Warren and Murphy met their contact down near the railroad tracks. Warren named the man, whom he called a "spook" (army slang for CIA). The contact took them to the roof of a tall building that dominated that downtown area and loomed over the Lorraine. Their guide provided them with a detailed area-of-operations map, pictures of cars used by the King group, and the "Memphis police TAC" radio frequencies. The roof was on top of the Illinois Central Railroad Building, which lay diagonally southwest of the Lorraine. They were in position by 1:00 PM and remained on their rooftop perch for over five hours as did (though they did not know it) the Psy Ops photographers who had been on the roof of fire station no. 2 photographing the activity at the Lorraine and the surrounding area. In their two-man sniper unit Warren was the shooter and Murphy the "spotter" and radio man. Murphy's job was to relay orders to Warren from the coordinating central radio man as well as to pick out or "spot" the target through binoculars.

During the course of that afternoon, Warren reported that he had spoken over the radio with an MPD officer whose first name he believed was "Sam" who was the head of the "city TAC." (This had to be Inspector Sam Evans, head of the MPD tactical units.) Warren said that Sam provided details about the physical structure and layout of the Lorraine. He also told Warren that "friendlies were not wearing ties." Warren took this to mean that there was an informant or informants inside the King group.

For the balance of the afternoon, he and Murphy waited.[21]

Finally, near what Warren termed the "TTH" (top of the hour – 6:00 PM) King came on to the balcony, having spent nearly two hours in his brother A. D.'s room 201 and then returning to 306 around 5:30 PM. Warren recognized his target, Andrew Young, putting on his coat, and took aim, holding him in his sights. Radio man Murphy waited to relay the order to fire, which they believed would take place if a sudden disturbance erupted. The order didn't come, and as usual in such circumstances the seconds seemed like hours. Warren kept Andy Young in the cross hairs of his scope, and then, he said, just after TTH, a shot rang out.

It sounded like a military weapon, and Warren assumed that the other sniper unit had jumped the gun and fired too soon because the plan was always for a simultaneous shooting. He said he never knew where the other sniper unit had been placed, but they would also have been above the target and at least 300 yards from it. A less well trained soldier hearing that shot might have fired, but Warren said he had to have the direct order before he would pull the trigger.

Murphy asked for instructions, and there was a long silence. Then the team leader came on and ordered the team to disengage in an orderly fashion and follow the egress routes assigned to them out of South Memphis where they were located. Warren and Murphy packed up and went down the same stairs they had climbed more than five hours earlier. They went across Riverside Drive and down to the river, where a boat was waiting.

The team leader joined them and they quickly went some distance downstream to a prearranged point where cars were waiting. He ordered complete silence for the return trip. Only some of the team went out this way. Warren said his immediate impression that the other team had "screwed up" continued until later that evening when he heard that some "wacko civilian" had apparently done the shooting.

He said he believed that it was entirely possible that the Alpha 184 team mission could have been a backup operation to an officially deniable, though jointly coordinated, civilian scenario. Warren said that he had seen the team leader on only two other occasions after April 4, and he refused to talk to him about what had happened.

As non-commissioned officers, Warren and Murphy would only have been told what they needed to know in order to carry out their particular task on the day. Warren stressed that April 4 was the first time he had been in Memphis, and that he had not participated in any reconnaissance activity. Though their operation was a military one, so far as he knew there was some inter-service cooperation since they were coordinating with Tennessee National Guard units and "NAS" – the Millington Naval Air Station.[22]

Warren had heard about one other time when a 20th SFG unit had almost "taken out" Dr King. This was during the Selma march in 1965. Warren said the sniper, who was also a member of the Memphis Alpha 184 team, claimed that on that occasion he actually had the SCLC leader "center mass" in his sights awaiting the order to fire, which never came because Dr King turned sharply away at the opportune moment and was then closely surrounded on the march.[23]

Steve Tompkins told me that there was one soldier on both the Selma 20th SFG team and the April 4 Alpha 184 team in Memphis. His name was John D. Hill ("J. D."), a buck sergeant who was murdered in 1979. On October 16 1994 I made contact with Jack Terrell, who knew J. D. well. He was a former covert operative converted most prominently with the Iran–Contra affair. At various times, he reported directly to the National Security Council. His testimony before the Senate hearings incriminated Oliver North, who he believed was involved in drug and money laundering operations in order to finance the illegal intelligence operations against the Sandinistas in Nicaragua. Jack Terrell had been used by ABC as a highly credible source. I believed he had vital information that could confirm and provide independent verification about the military presence in Memphis around the time of the sanitation workers' strike. Terrell was one of those bright, initially idealistic, and patriotic warriors who almost inevitably reach a point where they can longer swallow the corruption, deceit, and sheer criminal activity that often characterize official but deniable covert operations. His story was more than I hoped for. Because of the compatibility of the details with those emerging from other sources, it swept away any lingering doubts I had about the plot to murder King and cover it up.

J. D. had shared with Terrell what he personally knew about the King assassination plan. When I initially raised the subject of J. D.'s involvement in the killing of Dr King and asked Terrell whether J. D. had ever discussed the operation with him, he sighed, and was silent for a while. He said the subject had come up, but he was reluctant to open up this can of worms since it could lead to the two of us being killed. He uttered to me the familiar phrase, "You don't know who you're dealing with."

I told him that by now I was getting the idea, but I had as a client an innocent man who had served nearly twenty-six years in prison and that even though his innocence was becoming ever more obvious the state had spurned every face-saving opportunity to free him. Consequently, I had little choice but to solve the case conclusively and free him.

Terrell then said that in the mid-1970s J. D. appeared to want to shed some baggage about his past. He told Terrell about an assassination mission he had trained for over a period of many months, to be carried out on a moment's notice. He was in training with a small unit selected for the mission because they were all members of a Mississippi unit the 20th SFG. He said that J. D. was a member of the 20th SFG which Terrell came to learn that, though officially a Special Forces reserve unit, actually was used for a wide range of plausibly deniable covert special or "behind the fence" operations inside and outside of the US. There would be no record kept of their deployment for sensitive "behind the line" duty and operations. Hence, when investigative journalists enquired, they would find no offense records.

J. D. told Terrell that on April 4 the main body of the Alpha 184 team arrived in cars from Camp Shelby, which was their staging base and the training home for the 20th SFG reservists. He said that all weapons, material, and immediate orders for the Memphis mission were generated from the base, although the actual preparation for a triangulation shooting had been previously practiced at a site near Pocatello, Idaho. At an early stage the scenario called for a triangular shot at a moving vehicle in an urban setting. At the time no official details were provided about the mission and the men believed it was to be directed at an Arab target.

J. D. said that he soon learned that the mission was to be executed in Memphis, Tennessee. He believed that some of the team had gone to the city earlier. J. D. identified the sites to Terrell: a rooftop, a water tower, and a third-story window, with the team expecting to have to fire upon and hit their targets (and there were more than one) when they were in a moving car entering or leaving the motel parking lot. The team knew that the King party was going to dinner that evening, and they didn't believe for a minute that Dr King would appear on the balcony in such an exposed position. They believed they were going to have to work for the kill.

The weapons that Terrell said J. D. told him were carried by the team were in line with the list provided by Warren. Terrell said it was obvious from the way J. D. spoke that something went wrong and that they had to leave unexpectedly and quickly. Some members of the team were flown out from West Memphis.

Terrell said he had always had reservations about J. D.'s death. The official account made no sense to him. J. D. was allegedly shot to death at point blank range by his wife, some time after midnight on January 12 1979. She apparently fired five bullets from his .357 Magnum into a closely confined area of his chest. He was dead before he hit the floor. It had, said Carson, all the signs of a professional killing. He had known J. D.'s wife and did not believe that she had the strength or the capability to handle the large firearm with the precision described.

Terrell believed that J. D., a heavy drinker, might have begun to talk to others about the Memphis operation. Warren had said that he had left the country because he believed a clean-up process had begun within a year of the assassination and that if he returned to the United States he would be "immediately killed." I obtained a copy of the court records relating to J. D.'s death and confirmed that there was no indictment for his murder. J. D.'s wife was released and lives today in another town in Mississippi.

I asked Terrell to check out some details and he reluctantly agreed. Just before we ended, he said, "This meeting never took place." I agreed. "You have to be very careful," he said. "They'll drop you where you stand." Terrell faxed a note a couple of weeks later. It confirmed what he told me and provided further information. J. D.'s team was positioned on a Tayloe Paper Company water tower. Terrell wrote that J. D. confirmed that something had gone wrong and the mission was aborted. They disengaged, were picked up and driven out of South Memphis to West Memphis Arkansas airport where they were placed on a small aircraft and flown to Amory, Mississippi after releasing their weapons and other gear to the logistics officer who remained behind. They apparently dispersed at that point, J. D. returning to his home in Columbus, where he learned Dr King had been assassinated.[24]

Warren said that he had heard "scuttlebutt" (rumors) that the 111th MIG had a black agent inside Dr King's group. Using an intelligence source, I asked for a check to be completed on Marrell McCollough who I had previously confirmed from two independent sources had gone to work for the CIA in the 1970s. The report bore fruit. McCollough was not who he appeared to be. He had been in the regular army between February 1964 and December 1966 and was a military policeman (an

"MP"). Then on June 16 1967, he was reactivated and hired as a Military Intelligence informant and attached to the 111th MIG headquartered at Camp McPherson, Georgia.

McCollough therefore had ultimate reporting responsibility to the 111th MIG, though he was deployed to the MPD as an undercover agent, and officially reported to MPD Lieutenant Arkin.[25]

Warren, whom I had come to believe was credible and reliable, also said that a photograph of the actual shooting from the brush area existed and that some time after the event he had seen it. Warren provided the name and address of the now retired officer who supposedly had a copy of the photo and agreed to approach him. The former Psy Ops officer whom I call "Reynolds" agreed to have contact, but initially he insisted on the same procedure that had been used with his Latin American buddies. My questions would be carried to him by Steve Tompkins. The meeting was set for early December 1994 in the coffee shop of the Hyatt Regency Hotel in Chicago.

Reynolds was about 5 feet 10 inches tall, 160–170 pounds, with gray, short cropped hair. He said that in Vietnam he had been assigned to the 1st SOG based in Can Tho and that he worked for the 525th Psychological Operations Battalion. Reynolds said that he and his partner (whom I will call "Norton") were deployed to Memphis on April 3 as a part of a wider mission they believed was under the overall command of Colonel Downie of the 902nd MIG, for whom he had worked on a number of assignments. They carried the necessary camera equipment and were armed with standard issue .45 caliber automatics. Norton also carried a small revolver in a holster in the small of his back. They were ordered to be in position on April 4, and on that day they arrived before noon and went directly to fire station no. 2 where the captain, Carthel Weeden, gave them access to the flat roof. They took up their positions on the east side of the roof. From that vantage point they overlooked the Lorraine and were well placed to carry out their mission, which was to visually and photographically surveil the King group at the Lorraine Motel and pick out any individuals in photos who might be identified as a communist or national security threat. They had an unobstructed view of the balcony in front of Dr King's room, 306. My colleagues and I long wondered why the army would want to take photographs of the events unfolding on that day.

I have come to believe that the main reason for the photographing was very likely to enable Downie and the relevant army counterintelligence officers not only to be able to identify everyone in the vicinity of the crime scene but also, in particular, to have a clear picture of what they were doing immediately before, at the time of, and immediately after the assassination. This photographic intelligence would certainly give them a lead start in being able to take whatever steps were necessary to suppress observations which could potentially jeopardize the operation.

Then, on New Year's Day 1996, Steve Tompkins received an unexpected telephone call. It was purportedly from Colonel John Downie of the 902nd Military Intelligence Group. I had tried to locate him for three years concluding that his little-known unit, based inside the office of the Assistant Chief of Staff, played the primary organizing and coordinating role in the assassination. He was now living outside the United States, and said he had found my earlier book *Orders to Kill* remarkably accurate, though it gave him too much responsibility for the operation. He insisted he was only an officer in a chain of command following orders. He wanted to correct my impression of his role so the history of these events would be accurately recorded.

He called Steve again on January 28 and suggested they should meet in Southampton, Bermuda on March 9. He asked for a modest good faith sum, up front, to offset his expenses for as many meetings as I deemed necessary. In addition, he asked for one Krugerrand at the beginning of each meeting. This was the same procedure Warren had used.[26]

Steve traveled alone to the meeting. The next morning there was a knock on his door. Downie introduced himself. He stood almost six feet tall, weighed around 185 pounds and appeared to be in his mid-sixties. He was pleased that Steve had arrived alone and reiterated he would not meet with me. He said I was not in danger, since my earlier book had been buried and no one would believe my story. Surprisingly, he said he had met me in Vietnam when I was a journalist. He stated he had been legally dead for a number of years, and was living under a new identity.

He said he would provide all the details possible, but explained, in true military style, that he would have been outside the loop in some aspects of planning and implementation. Five meetings took place over the next eighteen months. The information this man provided gradually served to corroborate that provided earlier by other military and government personnel.

Downie confirmed he played a key role in coordinating the task force consisting of the various military units in Memphis during the week of April 1, up to and including April 4. However, he contended that while he met ACSI Yarborough on a regular basis, his orders were passed through a trusted civilian associate. The emissary, whose name I had never heard before, was a retired army intelligence officer who had served at Fort Bragg under Yarborough. Though the operation came under the jurisdiction of the ACSI's office it was handled indirectly through this trusted loyal colleague.

Downie said the Memphis operation seemed to have been put in motion following a meeting that took place about a week after the riot in Detroit which he attended with Yarborough and others. Dr King's popularity with urban blacks, his opposition to the Vietnam War, and his determination to bring impoverished masses to the nation's capital all helped seal his fate. Downie confirmed Warren and Murphy's account of the Memphis mission, even such details as "friendlies not wearing ties." He said the 902nd began to plan the killing of black community leaders as early as 1963 and 1964 when it seemed cities might get out of hand. He said the unit was still in existence.

Downie provided details that revealed for the first time the relationship between the Marcello crime organization and the 902nd. They were jointly involved in an extensive gun running venture. Weapons stolen from army bases and armories were delivered to the Marcello organization which arranged for their sale in Latin and South America and elsewhere. The proceeds were split equally, and the 902nd used this "black" money for covert operations. The operational link between the army and the mob was, apparently, a now deceased 20th SFG captain in New Orleans, who died in a suspicious car crash. I recalled Warren's account of running guns from Camp Shelby to New Orleans where they were delivered to Marcello's man Zip Chimento. I also recalled Glenda Grabow's description of Raul and his associates picking up guns which were delivered by water and unloaded at Houston docks.

Downie also tied two other people to this activity. One was a senior Mossad agent working in South America who acted as a senior liaison to the US military and CIA. The second was an officer of the 111th MIG based at Fort McPherson in Georgia. Downie urged us to stay away from these individuals.

Eric S. Galt

As for James, Downie said that he was one of many minor crooks with an army history who were used as "patsies" in various operations. Downie said he too had seen photographs of the shooter taken at the time of the killing. It was not James. He said that though James would not have been aware of it he had been assisted and guided in Canada. He said that there was an identities expert used by both Yarborough and Helms at the time James was provided with the Galt identity. James had not known the source. He always tried to protect the person who gave him the Galt name, believing it was someone who was trying to help.

He began to use it in late July 1967, having just entered Canada. This was around the time of the Detroit riots and heightened army concern over Dr King. At one point during my investigation of the involvement of the army, a source placed a photograph in front of me. It was a full frontal head shot of Eric St Vincent Galt – the man whose identity James had assumed and used for most of the time between July 18 1967 and April 4 1968. I was told not to ask any questions because it had come from and was part of an NSA file. I learned that Galt, the executive warehouse operator at Union Carbide's factory in Toronto, had Top Secret security clearance. Galt had worked for Union Carbide of Canada Ltd., which was 75 percent owned by Union Carbide Inc. of the US since the early 1980s. The company was engaged in high-security research projects controlled by the US parent. I learned that in August 1967, shortly after James assumed the Galt identity, the real Eric Galt met with Colonel John Downie's aide. They met again in September.[27]

Somehow James had acquired the name of a highly placed Canadian operative of US army intelligence. He began using the name on July 18 1967, around the time the real Eric Galt was meeting with Downie's aide. Though James likely obtained the other aliases by himself, there was little likelihood that he had accidentally chosen the Galt identity. His manipulation now appeared to involve not only elements of organized crime but also the specific, senior level, highly covert military intelligence group, the 902nd MIG whose involvement could be traced back at least to July 18 1967, when he began to use the Galt identity.

At the time, Galt appeared to me to be a critical link, facilitating the use of James Earl Ray as a patsy by this covert part of army intelligence and using the task force structure involving the 20th SFG, the FBI, and the other associated and collaborating members of the government and intelligence community involved with the assassination of Martin Luther King. Providing the patsy with an identity with Top Secret clearance was a means of securing and protecting him from problems before he was needed. Any routine police check would come up against a protected file, and the result would be that the government agency (in this instance the NSA and the army through the ACSI's office) could control the situation and instruct any law enforcement authorities to let the patsy go.

It was a highly classified secret that the NSA became involved in the effort to locate James after the assassination. It has never been revealed in any official investigation. Frank Raven, the NSA's officer, received the watch lists from the rest of the law enforcement and intelligence community and acted upon them. He received a direct order to place Ray's name, along with several aliases, on the watch list. Unusually, the order came from the office of the Secretary of Defense, Clark M. Clifford, who has no recollection of issuing it. Raven said that he tried to object to the order on constitutional grounds but was told that ". . . you couldn't argue with it – it came from the highest level."

It now appears that army intelligence was involved in the task force through the presence of the 111th MIG on the ground in Memphis and the 902nd MIG which coordinated the operation.[28] From at least July 1967, James acquired the identity of one of the 902nd's assets with Top Secret security clearance. This may have prompted the subsequent unconstitutional involvement of the NSA using the "watch list" to locate him.

It appears likely or at least possible that the order which was routed through the Defense Secretary's office found its way there from the office of the ACSI. An operation of mind-boggling complexity was emerging.

By summer 1997, John Downie had disappeared, perhaps concerned that word had got out about his contact with me via Steve Tompkins. This relatively brief communication provided me with further confirmation that the account of a military backup presence was basically correct. It provided a tantalizing glimpse behind the Pentagon's closed doors where the assassination of Martin Luther King was viewed as one event in a much larger context.

Steve Tompkins continued to meet with Warren during the period that Downie's story began to unfold. On January 27 1996 Warren confirmed that his target, Andrew Young, was in the Lorraine parking lot at the moment Dr King was shot. On August 17, Warren turned over the remaining 20th SFG rosters he had. One name leapt from the Mississippi list. It was the man who Jack Terrell, best friend of Alpha 184 team member J. D. Hill (shot dead in 1979), had said was the briefing officer for the Memphis mission attached to the Mississippi contingent. Terrell had said no one was quite certain exactly who he worked for.

When I obtained the photograph of Raul, included in the spread of six, I asked Steve to make a trip and show it to Warren. Warren instantly picked him out. He identified him as the person he had seen with Marcello's man Zip Chimento when they were picking up guns delivered from Camp Selby to New Orleans. Warren said Raul went by the name James R. Richmond and always insisted on using the initial "R". This clearly placed Raul in the frame of the gun running operations conducted by the army and the Marcello organization.

At 6:01, the fatal moment when the shot rang out, Reynolds quickly snapped four or five photos following Dr King as he fell to the balcony floor. Reynolds said Norton almost instinctively swung his camera from the parking lot to the left and, focusing on the brush area, caught the assassin (a white man) on film as he was lowering his rifle. He then took several shots of him as he was leaving the scene. Reynolds said that though Norton had caught the assassin clearly in his camera he personally only saw the back of the shooter as he left the scene. They hand-delivered the pictures to Downie but Norton kept the negatives and made another set of prints, seen by both Reynolds and Warren. They both categorically stated that the sniper in the photograph was not James Earl Ray.

In February 1997 ABC News's *Turning Point* program decided to do a documentary on the King assassination. It planned to focus on the King family, my investigation and quest for a trial, and James Earl Ray's terminal illness. From the outset, we all cooperated. I persuaded Terrell to be interviewed. In the hour interview he told them what he had learned from his best friend "J. D." Hill, and about the presence of the Alpha 184 team in Memphis on April 4 1968 and their mission. I had been informed that the leader of the eight-man team was dead. With the co-operation of the army, however, ABC News located him alive and living in Costa Rica. With no prior notice, they brought him, along with General Henry Cobb who commanded the 20th Special Forces Group, into an interview with me. I was surprised and told them I had obviously been given wrong information about the team leader's death.

Cobb and the team leader denied not only that the Alpha 184 was in Memphis, but that it even existed in 1968. They insisted that the Alabama contingent of the 20th SFG never trained at Camp Shelby and was never in the city of Memphis. Cobb insisted the unit could not have been involved in such an operation without his knowledge.

I asked a Birmingham private investigator to check out certain details about the team leader's activities in the city and was provided with a copy of his criminal record. He had a conviction for negligent homicide and served one year in prison in Alabama before leaving for Costa Rica. The *Turning Point* program did not reveal this to viewers.

During the course of the program, the idea that the Alpha 184 team was in Memphis to control riots was advanced. This explanation had eventually been raised by Warren in his sessions with Steve Tompkins who came to believe it. Though I gradually came to have a different view, it made no sense to me in the context of events at the time. This was before I came to see the riot as a possible excuse for opening fire and it seemed to me to be well established that riot control planning involved the use of numbers of officers on the ground, not a couple of snipers perched above the fray. Snipers are used to kill people, not control surging masses. It was also inconceivable to me that a riot could have been anticipated late that afternoon when the only activity was to be Dr

King and some of his group leaving the motel to go to dinner at Reverend Samuel "Billy" Kyles's house. This was before I realized the significance of the eviction of the Invaders from the motel just before the killing. The idea that this armed, militant group might react violently to this insulting, unexpected rejection was not unreasonable.

I provided ABC with other documentary evidence of the presence of the team in Memphis and the identity of the team leader. Since I had given my word, it would not be made public. I could not allow the material to be used in the program or even have any reference made to it.

The documentary was aired on June 19 1997. It included the interview with the team leader, myself and General Cobb. It did not include the interview with Terrell or the corroborative information he provided to confirm the presence of the team in Memphis and its mission to kill Martin Luther King. The program did, however, consider a number of other issues which pointed to a conspiracy and the involvement of the government.

Soon after the program Terrell left the country. He told me later that he had been threatened, and had no doubt the government had somehow obtained a copy of his interview. He was furious but offered to help me in any way he could.

Steve Tompkins told me that there was a thick defamation file on General Cobb at the offices of the Anti-Defamation League of Bnai Brith. Steve had seen the file and suggested that I review it. I attempted to locate the file but was not successful, meeting denials that it existed.

7

NEW ALLIES, REVELATIONS, AND UNTIMELY DEATHS

James Earl Ray's terminal illness

In December 1996, I learned that James was terminally ill with cirrhosis of the liver, apparently from long-term undiagnosed hepatitis C. It came as a great shock. On December 21, he was rushed to Nashville Memorial Hospital where he lapsed into a coma and was listed as being in critical condition. Media reports began circulating that he was near death.[29]

I immediately began to explore the range of treatment possibilities, speaking with traditional Chinese medicine specialists at hospitals in Changsha, China and TCM Klinik in Kotzingen, Germany. I also conferred with Dr Roy Calne at Cambridge, who is one of Europe's leading transplant surgeons. I concluded that only a liver transplant could save James's life.

By December 28 James began to show a marked improvement, but his doctor stressed this was short-term. On New Year's Eve James was sent back to the Lois de Berry Special Needs Center where he'd been since his disease had become advanced earlier that year. When I received his medical file it was clear that he had been diagnosed as having hepatitis C as early as 1994. James had not been told and neither had his family.

News of the illness generated extensive media interest in the case. It was initially focused on James's imminent death, but it gave me the opportunity to discuss the case, my long-term investigation, and James's innocence.

On January 6 1997, Jerry and I visited James again at Nashville Memorial Hospital where he had been taken after a relapse. There was some obvious short-term improvement but he was still disorientated.

In the midst of James's health crisis, on January 19, I was saddened to learn that Wayne Chastain was having an operation for cancer and would need four months to recuperate. He had never mentioned having the disease. Memphis attorney Jack McNeil would sit in for Wayne as local counsel since he was taking over a number of Wayne's files. During that period James was in and out of hospital and lapsed into critical condition twice.

Meanwhile, I began to discuss the possibility of James being accepted as a candidate for liver transplant at the University of Pittsburgh Hospital's Thomas E. Starzl Transplantation Institute. I discussed the criteria for James's admission with Dr John J. Fung, head of the Division for Transplantation. He was candid and compassionate. It was clear he believed inmates should not be denied equal access to medical care. His unit had carried out liver transplants on a number of prisoners. This was unheard of in Tennessee.

One of the criteria for admission to his program was that an out-of-state applicant had to be rejected by his or her state's center. The relevant center in Tennessee was located at Vanderbilt Hospital. Dr Rao, James's doctor in Nashville Memorial Hospital, was convinced they would not accept James on their list. I asked him to make a formal application. He did, and on March 7 he was told that James did not meet the criteria. The road seemed clear to Pittsburgh.

John Fung said he would need James to be admitted as an in-patient for three days for tests and assessment. On April 23 I wrote to the Commissioner of the Tennessee Department of Corrections. I asked Jerry and Dr Fung to do likewise, requesting his permission for James to travel to Pittsburgh. Costs would be paid for privately. On May 13 the Commissioner wrote back refusing our request, stating that he had no statutory authority to grant it.

I immediately began to prepare a motion and a proposed court order, and went to Pittsburgh to meet with Dr Fung. I came away highly impressed with his sensitivity and willingness to help. It was clear that most people admitted to his program received a transplant. If we could arrange for James to be admitted he could well survive. Finance would be a problem, but we agreed to explore alternatives.

While in Pittsburgh, I sent final documentation to a much-improved Wayne Chastain in Memphis. Dr Fung, Dr Rao, and James's brother Jerry sent affidavits in support. Wayne filed the motion papers in the Court of Chancery in Nashville, Tennessee, which had jurisdiction, and a hearing was set for June 16.

The attorney general argued against our petition on the grounds that under Tennessee law our petitioner did not state a claim for which relief could be granted because the Commissioner for Corrections had discretion to decide requests for medical furloughs.

I maintained that James's federal constitutional rights under the Eighth Amendment's prohibition of cruel and unusual punishment required that the state enable him to receive the medical care necessary for him to live. I thought that the issue had been settled 21 years earlier with the US Supreme Court case *Estelle v. Gambel*. Not for the first time in relation to James, a Tennessee court refused to follow the law of the land.

If James would not be allowed to go to the University of Pittsburgh Hospital for evaluation, the hospital would have to come to him.

As a consequence of their insurance restrictions the Tennessee authorities were able to perform all but two of the tests required by the Pittsburgh Hospital. I agreed to pay for the last two tests. They were completed in late September 1997. The Pittsburgh Hospital admissions committee reviewed the results the next month. In accordance with their criteria James was declared eligible for a transplant and was placed on their list. The announcement of his admission was formally made at a press conference in November.

Enter the King family

On January 15 1997 I learned that Martin's daughter Yolanda King had called the Reverend Jim Lawson's office wanting my telephone number. I left a message for her. Then, on January 27, Martin's nephew Isaac Farris called. He worked with Martin's son Dexter King at the King Center, had read my earlier work *Orders to Kill*, which set out the results of my investigation through 1994, and was moved to encourage the family to come forward. He had been particularly impressed by the image I had developed of his uncle which showed him to be a leader for social, economic, and political justice and change and not just a civil rights icon. It had, he said, become clear to the family that James Earl Ray's days were numbered. The family feared that when he died, the possibility of a trial, at which witnesses could provide evidence of what really happened, would be lost forever.

They wanted to come forward with some impact, sooner rather than later, and were working on their own strategy.

In early February, Dexter confirmed to a *New York Times* reporter that the family was now going to support a trial for James. I was elated; the significance of the family's involvement cannot be overestimated. The *Times* story broke on February 4 1997 and Isaac called and asked if I would meet members of the family as soon as possible. A meeting was set up for February 10 at Isaac's house.

It lasted from 7.30 PM until 4 AM. I talked Dexter, Isaac, and family friend and advisor Philip Jones through the evidence I had amassed over nearly 20 years. They were astounded at the results and the meeting was highly emotional. It was clear they had already decided to help.[30]

They called a press conference for February 13. All the family were present. In the glare of the national media, with impressive grace and with Dexter as primary spokesperson, they announced their support for a trial for James Earl Ray. The call was made not – as some of the media were to distort – for James to be given one last chance to tell all he knew, but in order for there to be an opportunity for witnesses to testify under oath and be subjected to cross-examination.

Over the succeeding months the family, Dexter in particular, came under attack. Incredibly, financial gain was put forward as the motive for wanting to learn the truth about how Martin was killed. Naïveté was also cited; it was alleged that I had manipulated or even hypnotized them into supporting James.

The media continually sought to undermine the strength of the family's commitment to a trial. Distortions abounded. Take the *New York*

Times coverage on February 20 of our motion to test the alleged murder weapon. Drummond Ayers Jr reported Mrs King's testimony. He wrote:

> Mrs King, speaking after years of silence about Mr Ray's legal maneuvering, took the stand this morning, and acknowledging the incongruity of her appearance on his behalf and behest, said, "We call for the trial that never happened."
>
> Then, her voice urgent and cracking with emotion, she warned that "the tragedy would be compounded" should Mr Ray go to his grave without being pressed one final time in court to tell all he knows about what happened just down the street at the Lorraine Motel on April 4, 1968.

This was a gross distortion of what she actually said, which was:

> We call for the trial that never happened . . . If we fail to seize this fading opportunity for justice to be served, the tragedy will be compounded by the failure of the legal system.

Nowhere in her statement did she refer in any way to James being pressed to tell anything.

In the article, Ayers very clearly gave the same standing to his disinformation as he did to Mrs King's actual words. In the light of this article and the seemingly intractable position of the *New York Times* we decided to meet their editorial board.

The deputy editor attended with two others. They were attentive and asked a number of questions, but we came away believing there would be no change in their position.

In fact, the paper subsequently published an op-ed piece by David Garrow viciously attacking Dexter and the family, alleging they had betrayed Dr King's legacy. For nearly a generation now, Garrow has surfaced wherever there is a move to open up the case. Though an historian who has written extensively on the FBI COINTELPRO activities against Martin, he has never himself investigated the assassination but is one of a long list of publicists who have vigorously supported the government's position.

On March 17, I met with Dexter and Philip Jones. They came to the conclusion they should now move to the next level. Dexter would continue to call for a trial – but also state his belief that James was innocent. I believed it was now essential that Dexter had to become increasingly knowledgeable about the details of the case. If anything should happen to me he would be in a position to supervise any succeeding lawyers, and the integrity of the process would be assured.

Dexter wanted to have a face-to-face meeting with James. It was set for March 27 and took place in the conference room of George McGhee, the Health Services' Administrator.

I introduced James to Dexter and they sat down with the media present for nearly half an hour. At one point Dexter asked poignantly, "Did you kill my father?" James answered, "No, I didn't" and then went on to urge Dexter to examine the files for himself. Dexter replied that he believed him and so did his family and then pledged that "We will do everything in our power to see that justice prevails."

The next two months were filled with media appearances. Dexter and I became convinced that whenever possible we should do live interviews; taped sessions could be distorted through editing.

On the evening of April 14, Dexter, Isaac, and I met with Andrew Young, who in 1968 was executive vice president of the SCLC and a close friend of Martin King, and who had always believed James was the shooter. That evening, after detailed questioning about my investigation, he changed his mind and agreed to take part in a press conference and help in any feasible way.

On April 18 Dexter called to say he'd had a brief but good meeting with Walter Fauntroy, the former chairman of the congressional sub-committee responsible for the King investigation. Walter confirmed his continued belief in James's innocence. He was prepared to say so in the most effective way.

Earlier that day we met with Congressman John Lewis, a leader of the Student Non Violent Coordinating Committee at the time of the killing. He tentatively agreed to join forces with the group of leaders we were putting together to press for a trial.

In just three short months, from early February to May, the King family's involvement had boosted the profile of the fight for justice for James and the truth about Dr King's killing. We knew however that we had to prepare ourselves for further media attacks.

In succeeding months, negative pieces did appear against the family and Judge Brown, and, of course, me. The result was to stiffen the family's resolve to get to the truth. Their support for a trial never wavered and neither did their commitment to support a grant of immunity for anyone involved in exchange for information about the assassination. This posture would eventually lead to one of the most historic and revealing meetings ever held in the thirty-year saga.

The last judicial proceedings

Meanwhile, the effort to secure a trial for James, years after he was bounced into entering a guilty plea by his lawyer Percy Foreman, continued in the courts.

The new Tennessee post-conviction relief statute made it even more difficult than hitherto to set aside a guilty plea. Petitioners now had to submit scientific evidence of actual innocence. The restrictive require- ments of the statute raised serious constitutional issues, but we did not have two or three years to test it.

On June 26 1996, I had appeared in Division IX of the Shelby County Criminal Court before Judge Brown. I argued that since we were facing the burden of having to develop scientific evidence, we should be allowed to test the rifle. We had to demonstrate that there was new technology available now which had not been available to us when the rifle was originally tested by the state.

Since then, there had been significant advances in forensic technology. Electron microscopes could now give vastly enhanced magnification of the particular individual markings which each rifle imposes on bullets fired through its barrel. This would enable us to closely compare the markings on the test-fired slugs with each other as well as to the markings on the death slug. With this new equipment, it might finally be possible to exclude the rifle in evidence from being the murder weapon.

We were, however, in the classic Catch 22 situation. The law required that we submit scientific evidence as proof of Ray's actual innocence, but we could not do so unless we were allowed to conduct firearms identifi- cation tests.

I asked Judge Brown to reconsider our motion and grant us the opportunity to meet our statutory burden.

After a highly contentious hearing, the judge ordered a continuance until September 6 so that we could provide a specific plan for a scientific testing of the weapon and the death slug.[31]

The firearms testing and analysis would be conducted by a three-man panel of experts – all nationally respected professionals – Robert Hathaway, Marshal Robinson, and George Reich.[32] In order to conduct this analysis a two-stage process was proposed. The first involved the conventional use of a comparison microscope to compare the markings on the test-fired slugs with those on the death slug.[33]

The motion was finally heard in Judge Brown's court on February 20 1997. I put on two of the three firearms experts, Robert Hathaway and Marshal Robinson, and Tony Owens of Cam Scan Inc, who described the scanning electron microscope which in the second and final stage, would allow for a vastly increased magnification of cosmetically designated individual markings on the test-fired slugs and the death slug.

Next, I called Coretta Scott King and her son Dexter. They wanted to address the court as members of the victim's family. The motion before the court was, of course, directly related to the application for the guilty plea to be set aside and a trial ordered. Incredibly, Assistant Attorney General Campbell objected to their testifying. The judge, affirming the court's growing respect for victim's rights, overruled the objection. Coretta Scott King was first on the stand. Asked if she had anything to tell the court, she said she did, turning in the witness box to face the judge. Her statement was moving. At one point she said:

Most importantly, for the sake of healing and reconciliation, I appeal to you on behalf of the King family as well as millions of Americans concerned about the truth and justice in this case, to expeditiously set and conduct a trial for Mr James Earl Ray.

Dexter took the stand next and followed the tone set by his mother. The testimony of Martin's widow and son were incredibly moving and provided some highly charged emotional moments. There were no questions for either witness from the state.

At the end of the hearing that afternoon, the judge ruled we should be allowed to test the rifle. He stated that he would ask the Court of Appeals to lift its stay so the testing could begin. It was then up to the Court of Appeals. On April 9, the court lifted its stay and ruled that the trial judge could order the testing of the rifle by the petitioner. Celebration was premature. We had underestimated the state's determination to prevent or control the testing of the alleged murder weapon.

On April 15, the state filed a motion with the administrative judge of Shelby County Criminal Court requesting that the matter be transferred out of Judge Brown's Division IX court and referred back to the original trial court Division III. Apparently, Judge Brown was furious. He insisted that the matter was properly before him and was going to remain in his court in accordance with the Court of Appeals ruling. The administrative judge backed down and allowed the matter to remain in Division IX.

The first-round test firing and examination resulted in an inconclusive finding by the panel of experts. It also revealed the possible reason for the result. The scanning electron microscope showed that a plating or coating of the bore was taking place after each test firing. Apparently, the heat generated by the action caused some melting of the copper jacketing and the residue plating was left behind. This made it impossible for a true "signature" of the rifle bore to be engraved upon the test-fired bullets. Instead, differing individual markings occurred. Even with this finding, however, the results also revealed that there was a common "start" or "reference" point on twelve of the test fires which was not present on the death slug. In light of the results, we filed a motion to be allowed to continue the tests in conjunction with a special cleaning process following a specific number of test fires.

This motion was before the court when in bizarre fashion, Judge Colton (Division III – the trial court division in 1969) appointed a "special master" with subpoena and investigating powers.

On the eve of our court hearing on the motion to continue testing, the Attorney General obtained an injunction against our hearing and Judge Colton's Order and then filed a formal application against both judges seeking to prevent any further proceedings in the case. It occurred to me that Judge Colton's actions had given the state the basis for that appeal, enabling the proceedings in Judge Brown's court to be "piggybacked" into the injunction.

The Appellate Court heard arguments on the issues on September 5 1997 with the state attorney general representing the Shelby County district attorney general and me arguing on behalf of our motion and the propriety of Judge Brown's actions. The packed courtroom included Dexter King representing the family. Later that afternoon the three judges unanimously permanently enjoined Judge Colton, holding that he had grossly exceeded his jurisdictional authority.

Accepting my arguments the court upheld Judge Brown's authority to control the evidence and allow the testing to continue, if he found it to be necessary. To have done otherwise would have sanctioned an unprecedented incursion on the functioning of a trial court whereby the trial court judge's traditional control over evidence in front of him could be removed. In a separately foreboding manner, the judges asked the assistant attorney general if the state was asking for the removal of Judge Brown from the case. At that time, she said no.

We won, but there was a caveat. The court also ruled that the state should not pay for the firearms testing. The petitioner would have to foot the bill. By the time of the ruling, those total costs were approximately $30,000.

The rifle in evidence would never again be tested. Months passed following our victory in the Court of Appeals, but no hearing was held. In light of his own previous questions from the bench, it was clear that Judge Brown believed that a specialized cleaning process, regularly implemented after minimal firing, would yield the scientific results necessary for him to grant a new trial, in that the markings on the experimental test-fired slugs would match each other and yet be distinguishable from the markings on the death slug. I sensed that he had already concluded that the rifle in evidence could not have been the murder weapon, but understandably, given the hostility of the Tennessee Appellate Courts to any possibility of opening up the case, he wanted to have the strongest scientific case possible for his ruling. There was also the intervening factor during this period of Judge Brown being offered a substantial television contract and he was involved in those negotiations.

Eventually, the opportunity to carry out the retesting would be taken from him. The district attorney general soon filed a motion asking him to recuse himself. He denied the motion, and the state appealed. Ruling on the papers submitted, without oral argument, in the darkness of night, as it were, the Court of Appeals overturned his ruling and removed him from the case basically on the grounds that he had ceased to be impartial. Horrendous, but par for the course of Tennessee justice for James Earl Ray. James Earl Ray's last chance for a trial had ended.

Loyd Jowers – continued

From early 1997 I began to have discussions with Loyd Jowers's lawyer, Lewis Garrison, about the possibility of Jowers meeting Dexter King and myself and setting out everything he knew about the killing.

The main impediment to such a meeting was Jowers's fear of being indicted, convicted, and going to jail for the rest of his life. To overcome this, Dexter, on behalf of the family, and I agreed to give undertakings that we would support a grant of immunity for Jowers if he told us everything he knew about events leading up to the killing and the murder itself. I had no doubt Jowers was out in the brush area at the time of the killing and that he knew who actually pulled the trigger. The rub, of course, was that he could have fired the shot himself. In any event, I argued he would be far better off with the support of the family, who were only interested in the truth and were not trying to seek retributive justice.

Jowers agreed to meet. But he kept backing off. The "investigation" of Judge Colton concerned him for a while. Then certain newspaper reports, focusing on his involvement, chilled his cooperation. Garrison received inquiries about our planned meeting from a Memphis *Commercial Appeal* reporter with contacts in the attorney general's office. This led Garrison and me to believe that his phone was still being tapped. Then, at the request of the district attorney general, the Tennessee Bureau of Investigation began to interview witnesses and visited members of Jowers's family, telling them they were going to indict him. This seriously panicked Jowers, who threatened to leave the country.

Finally, a meeting was arranged. Dexter and I met up with Jowers and
Garrison at the Sheraton Inn in Jackson, Tennessee on October 27 1997.
Over three hours, the truth, as known first hand by Loyd Jowers, or at
least, some of the truth, which he had kept bottled up for thirty years,
gradually came out. Jowers continued to be fearful and tried to hedge his
statements. I was able to interrogate him with Attorney Garrison prompting him to confirm facts they had discussed since 1993.

I asked Jowers to begin at the beginning. He said he first met Memphis
produce dealer Frank Liberto when he was in the Memphis Police
Department (MPD). He was told by another officer – John Barger, who
acted as an unofficial mentor to the young Jowers – that Frank Liberto was
a Mafia operative, who could do a lot for a cooperative young policeman.
When Jowers left the MPD and went into business – first running clubs
and then bars and restaurants – the relationship continued. He learned
early on that Liberto was into a variety of illegal activities, including
gunrunning, drugs, prostitution, and gambling. Jowers would help handle
money for Liberto, who would hand over a bundle of bills and instruct him
to deliver the "package" to a particular person. He performed this task a
number of times over the years. So when Liberto came to him in early
1968 and once again asked him to receive a bundle of money and turn it
over to a man named Raul, who Liberto described in some detail, he was
not surprised. When he received the money in a vegetable box, Jowers put
it in a disused stove in the kitchen at Jim's Grill, which is where Betty
Spates remembers seeing it. When Raul turned up a day or two before the
assassination Jowers gave him the money.

I placed a photograph spread of six pictures in front of Jowers. He
picked the photograph of the man I have called Raul Pereira, who was
also identified as Raul by Glenda Grabow, her brother Ross Wilburn, Sid
Carthew and James Earl Ray. Jowers wryly commented that Raul's very
distinctive face was not easily forgotten.

It is important to keep in mind that Jowers has, in the past twenty
years, for understandable though self-serving reasons, given inconsistent
accounts of what happened in and around Jim's Grill on April 4 1968.
This would emerge as a main criticism of him in the June 2000 Department of Justice limited investigation report, discussed below. Now, he
said he recalled that after Frank Liberto approached him there was at

least one, and probably up to three meetings in Jim's Grill to prepare for the assassination. While he maintained that he did not sit in on these planning sessions, he remembered them taking place and recalled most of the participants. They included his old, now deceased friend John Barger – by then an MPD inspector – and undercover police officer Marrell McCollough, whose military intelligence role was unknown to Jowers. At an earlier time, Barger had brought McCollough to the grill and introduced him as his new sidekick. In his 1977 testimony to the HSCA McCollough had denied any intelligence role at the time of the assassination. Now with the CIA, McCollough was interviewed in April 1997 by an ABC *Prime Time Live* producer. He confirmed he knew Loyd Jowers. When asked about Jowers implicating him in the King assassination he said he had no comment and put the phone down. Local contacts have attempted to get McCollough to talk to me without success.

Another MPD inspector who Jowers said was at the planning sessions has had a high profile in the case from the outset. He is still alive. The fourth participant was MPD officer Lieutenant Earl Clark, who died in 1987. Clark ran the MPD firing range out at the Armour Center and was regarded as perhaps the best shot in the force. Jowers also confirmed something I had learned some years ago – Clark was exceptionally close to Frank Liberto. Jowers said Liberto had told him that the police would not be around at the time of the killing and they had a "fall guy" in place. Jowers had previously told Attorney Garrison that he received the murder weapon from Raul the day before the killing and gave it back to him near the actual time of the assassination. He had also said he did not leave the grill for a night or two before the killing.

In our session he stated that the weapon was picked up by Earl Clark on the afternoon of the killing. Jowers said that he was instructed to go out through his kitchen into the brush area just before 6:00 PM and wait. He had the impression someone in Dr King's group was going to get Dr King out on the balcony around that time.

After the shooting, he was to take the gun and keep it until it was picked up by Liberto's man the next morning. Liberto, he said, made it clear to him that the weapon was his "personal property." The following morning, a "Mexican" employee of Liberto's came to the grill, drank coffee and waited until customers had left. He then picked up the gun and took it away. Jowers never saw him again. At other times, he had said that Raul picked up the weapon.

While he continued to deny that Betty Spates was there on the afternoon of the killing, he effectively confirmed her account. His attorney, Lewis Garrison, noted that Jowers had, for some years, essentially validated her story. Betty Spates, as noted earlier, remembered two rifles. Jowers brought one in from the brush area around noon on the day of the killing and broke it down in front of her. She saw him carrying the second gun into the kitchen seconds after the fatal shot.

Jowers confirmed Betty's recollection that he placed the murder weapon under the counter. Taxi driver James McCraw always insisted that this was where he had seen it on the morning after the killing, though Jowers previously denied showing it to him. Jowers admitted being in the brush area with the shooter and taking the rifle "still smoking" from the assassin and running inside with it. Jowers made this crystal clear. He even said that he attempted to flush the extracted cartridge shell down the toilet off the kitchen and that it stopped it up. Though never emphatic, he indicated that the other man out in the brush area, the actual assassin of Martin Luther King Jr, was the MPD's best shot – Lieutenant Earl Clark. He said that the shooter passed the rifle to him and then took off. Jowers was too busy making tracks himself to notice where he went but seemed to recall that he headed back toward the building. I have now come to question not Clark's involvement – I believe that he was totally involved and was one of the people out in the bushes at the time of the shooting – but the allegation that he pulled the trigger. I had always been uneasy with Jowers's less than completely positive statement of Clark's responsibility. There was an ever-present hedge. Now I believe that I know why.

As for Clark, in a sense I had come full circle. I had strongly suspected him of being the assassin in 1988 and 1989. When I interviewed his former wife, Rebecca, in 1992 she gave him what appeared to be an cast-iron alibi. She insisted he had been at home off duty and asleep at the time of the killing and that when he was called in over his police "walkie talkie," she had to drive to the cleaners to pick up his uniform. She seemed believable. She had been divorced from Clark, who had remarried, and therefore had no reason to stand up for him. However, she was still raising his son who sat in on our interview and who had obviously been very attached to his father.

I began to question Mrs Clark's credibility in 1995. Taxi driver McCraw told me that on the night of the shooting, he had picked her up in downtown Memphis and taken her miles away from home. McCraw had also made it clear to me that Clark, a Jim's Grill regular, had openly boasted that he would kill Dr King when he came to town. I had dismissed it as so much racist talk. But in 1995 McCraw told me he had seen Clark emerge from the south side of the rooming house around 6:20 wearing his MPD uniform. Jowers recalled him wearing light-colored civilian clothes at the time of the shooting.[34]

There were, and continued to be, inconsistencies about these and other details, but the scenario was coming together. The facts have been there, capable of discovery from the beginning. The first glimpse of the Liberto connection surfaced with John McFerren's courageous report of the fat man screaming down the telephone to his shooter, "Shoot the son of a bitch when he comes on the balcony." This was further confirmed by his own admissions to the Whitlocks, ten years later. There were other independent corroborating sources. But it would take the courage of Betty Spates and James McCraw to force Loyd Jowers to come forward in 1993, offering to tell all he knew in return for a grant of immunity. The reluctance of the authorities to hear what Jowers had to say was understandable, given how far up the line the conspiracy went.

The Marcello/Liberto/Memphis assassination operation provided the government with a plausibly deniable alternative to the use of its own trained professionals who were waiting in the wings and ultimately not required. We have seen that organized crime frequently fulfills this need and insulates federal, state, and public officials and agencies from responsibility for a variety of illegal acts. The underlying financial arrangements, even commercial collaboration, such as gunrunning and drug dealing joint ventures, which finance the illegal covert operations, rarely come to light. When they do surface, massive damage limitation and cover-up operations are mounted. The assassination of Martin Luther King was a tragedy for the American people. The shameful truth behind its execution and subsequent cover-up is a searing indictment of betrayal and abuse of power.

James dies

During the last stage of James's life, as a part of the Shelby County district attorney general's investigation, I agreed to allow the two lead investigators Marvin Glankler and seconded MPD officer Tim Cook to interview James. My former investigators Ken Herman and John Billings, while not trusting Glankler, initially believed that Cook was trying to get the truth out. I was skeptical, but in the interests of not giving the state the opportunity to say that he did not cooperate with them, I agreed to allow this access, and the visit took place in the Lois DeBerry medical unit at Riverbend.[35] Jerry Ray was also present.

After some initial conversation, Cook began to lean heavily on James to admit his guilt. I had difficulty believing what I was hearing. Would they never learn? He took the line that he could quickly arrange for James to be released and allowed to die outside of the prison in the bosom of his family. He got nowhere. James had not professed his innocence and fought for a trial for 30 years to finally give in to the shameful entreaties of a Memphis Police Department officer. In a brief exchange with the officer near the end of his visit, I learned that Lieutenant Earl Clark's partner, hunting buddy, and friend John Coletta was a member of Cook's family, by marriage; an intriguing coincidence.

James died on April 23 1998, the 31st anniversary of his escape from Jefferson City Penitentiary. I was in London and immediately left for the United States. I agreed to do a *Today Show* interview at Heathrow Airport just before leaving. Author Gerald Posner was to follow me, but there was an understanding that I would have an opportunity, however briefly, to rebut his comments. In response to a question, I noted that I could name some 18 individuals who had significant information and that Posner had not spoken to any of them. After that challenge, Posner claimed that James had made a secret tape recording before he died, probably admitting his guilt. He accused me or Jerry of having and hiding the tape, indignantly calling on me to surrender the recording, stating that the American people had a right to know. It was, of course, an outrageous lie, but I was not given the promised opportunity to reply. Even with James dead, nothing had changed.

Post-mortem events

James's death left us with one last option to have the evidence tested under oath in a court of law – a civil action against Loyd Jowers. Jowers, of course, had voluntarily revealed and discussed his involvement in separate meetings with Dexter King and myself and with Dexter King and Ambassador Andrew Young. These sessions were the culmination of his attempt to obtain immunity from prosecution which had begun in 1993 when he learned that we had uncovered enough evidence for him to be indicted – had there been any official interest in doing so. His account was continually and expectedly dismissed by the attorney general as having been made in anticipation of a book or movie deal. This was arrant nonsense. In fact, as a result of being forced into the open, Jowers had lost everything. Even his wife left him. There was no book or movie deal, and he was, for the very most part, telling the truth.

ABC News convinced him to take a lie detector test, using a former FBI polygrapher, and then announced that he failed. In point of fact, their claims and program notwithstanding, he passed the test. This was revealed by the taxi driver who drove the ABC team to the airport and who overheard their conversation including the lament of the polygrapher who admitted that he couldn't get Jowers ". . . to waver." The same polygrapher would be fined by the relevant Tennessee supervisory body for his conduct of the test. ABC has, also contrary to the law, to this day shamefully refused to provide Jowers with a copy of the transcript and the video of the examination.

Jowers, however, had provided the degree of detail required for a civil action. The family and I discussed the option at length after James's death in the spring of 1998. There were concerns. Would such an action do any good? Would it not bring the media down on the family again? How would it be financed? I could not speak to or resolve many of the personal concerns of the family. They had to bear that burden. I could only advise them that I thought we had a strong case and that the action would provide us with perhaps the last opportunity to test evidence that had never been put to a judge or jury. As to costs, I would not charge and believed that some of our friends would raise funds to help us. Since we would be bringing witnesses from every part of the United States and even England, it was going to be an expensive exercise.

Dexter, who had been out front for the family since they had become involved in 1997 and who had taken the brunt of the attacks, was the most cautious. He knew that if the action went ahead, once again he would bear the major responsibility. Mrs King expressed the feeling that we all had come too far not to complete this effort, which I had begun 20 years before and had kept alive in the face of formidable opposition. We would go to trial.

Wayne and I wasted no time in drafting the complaint against Loyd Jowers and other unknown co-conspirators. Without any publicity, the action entitled plaintiffs the Family of Dr Martin Luther King Jr, Coretta Scott King, Martin Luther King III, Bernice King, Dexter King, and Yolanda King against defendants Loyd Jowers and other unknown co-conspirators, docket kit # 97242TD was filed for trial in Division IV on 2 October 1998.

It would take more than a year for it to get on the calendar. We were scheduled to be first out on November 15 1999, but the judge – James Swearingen – was off and on the bench due to illness, and it was not clear that he would be fit to try the case. At various times, we considered seeking to transfer the case to another judge, but in the end, we waited, and the judge recovered. It could be the last case of his long and distinguished career.

In the interim, on June 7 1999, Wayne died. He had been suffering from pancreatic cancer, and he finally succumbed. I felt a great personal and professional loss.[36]

Don Wilson's materials

Donald Wilson lives in the Chicago area. He is a former FBI agent who joined the Bureau as a young man with a desire to facilitate the civil rights of minority Americans. He became greatly disillusioned, but he had a young family to support and decided to stick it out, eventually retiring after having received a number of commendations from J. Edgar Hoover himself.

In early 1997, Don Wilson contacted the King family and me, providing us with some extraordinary new information. At first, we communicated through his son who was a lawyer in a Chicago law firm. When we eventually met, it was on April 15 in the lounge of the Admirals Club at Chicago's O'Hare Airport. He recounted two incidents. He said that shortly after the assassination, he and another agent were riding in the Peachtree area of Atlanta, and they spotted a person who, they were certain, was the man wanted for the murder of Dr King. The person matched the photograph being circularized of the suspect. Wilson said he and his partner were inclined to apprehend the person they had spotted and radioed the field office for permission to do so. The operator told them to hold on, went off the line for instructions, then came back on, and instructed them to "return to base." Surprised and disappointed, they did as they were told. To this day, Don Wilson finds it strange and unacceptable that they were not allowed to detain the suspect and yet were not given any explanation.

What he told me next was more significant. When the field office received a request from the Atlanta police to check out a white Mustang, which had been parked for some days at the Capitol Homes Housing Project, he went along with a senior colleague to the scene. The suspicion was that the car, with Alabama license plates, had been involved in the King assassination. Wilson said that when he opened the car door on the passenger's side, an envelope and some papers fell out. Instinctively, he said, he put his foot on the papers, bent over, picked them up, and put them in his pocket. The young agent was nervous, thinking that he might have disturbed the evidence at a crime scene. Later, when he had an opportunity to examine the individual sheets of paper, he was shocked and realized that if he turned them over to his superiors, they would never see the light of day.

He kept them hidden for 29 years.

One piece came from a 1963 Dallas, Texas telephone directory. It was part of a page, which had been torn out. The telephone numbers on the page included those of the family of H. L. Hunt, but more significantly, in handwriting at the top of the page, was the name "Raul," the letter "J" and a Dallas telephone number, which turned out to be the phone number of the Vegas Club, which at that time was run by Jack Ruby, the killer of Lee Harvey Oswald.

The second piece of paper contained several names, alongside each of which were sums of money. It appeared to be some sort of payoff list, and at the bottom, it also contained Raul's name and a date for payment. Wilson also said that he had recovered a third piece of paper, on which was written the telephone number and an extension of the Atlanta FBI field office.

The Wilson materials raised the serious issue of the potential collusion of the Atlanta field office, or at least the connection of one or more persons in that office with someone who had access to James's white Mustang. From all that, we knew that the most likely candidate for the FBI liaison had to be Raul. I believed that every effort would be made to discredit Don and his materials.

After considerable discussion with the King family, it was agreed that Don would provide the materials to the Atlanta district attorney, ask them to investigate, and immediately thereafter release the information to the media.

Don and I eventually met with the district attorney who said that he did not have the staff resources necessary for such an investigation, but that he would formally request that the US attorney general institute a full investigation.

The reaction to our press conference was quiet and predictable. The FBI dismissed the materials without even seeing them and attacked Wilson as a fraud, saying that there was no record of him being a part of the team which examined the Mustang. He was not a member of the agent team which had examined the car. He never said he was. He had access to the Mustang in the Capitol Homes parking lot before it was towed to, and examined by others in, the FBI garage.[37]

Don initially made an offer directly to the attorney general to meet with her and show her the materials. When the FBI attacks began, he withdrew the offer. Eventually, he allowed *Atlanta Journal Bulletin* reporter Arthur Brice to come to Chicago and review the original materials. Brice did so and wrote a fair, descriptive story, a rarity in respect of this particular development as well, of course, in respect of any of the new evidence.

Don Wilson's material pointed me in a direction which I did not want to go, toward links between the King and John Kennedy assassinations.

Glenda Grabow had told me how in 1963 she had occasionally seen a man who she only knew as "Jack" with Raul. At one point, in the autumn of that year, she had been intimate with him. It was about a month or two before Roy came out of prison.

She only realized who he was when his photograph was flashed across the world after he had killed Lee Harvey Oswald. I decided not to introduce that element of Glenda's story into our legal submissions on behalf of James. I knew that James's efforts for a trial would not be well served by this linkup. As it was, we were always being depicted as conspiracy nuts. Imagine what our enemies would do with this new information.

Then, along came Don Wilson and his material, on which the name of Raul was written next to the letter "J" and the telephone number of Jack Ruby's Vegas Club. It was problematical in terms of James's interests, but I decided to travel to Dallas in order to interview some former strippers who had worked for Ruby and were around him a good deal.

I met separately with Beverly Oliver, Chari Angel, and Madeleine Brown. Madeleine had not worked for Ruby but was Lyndon Johnson's mistress for years, and, in fact, had given birth to his only son; she also knew Ruby and frequented his main club – the Carousel.

When I put the spread of photographs in front of each of them on separate occasions, each one independently confirmed that she had seen Ruby with the man we had identified as Raul. In fact, Beverly remembered Raul giving Ruby what appeared to be a large amount of cash in what she described as a "Piggley Wiggley" grocery store paper bag.

There was no doubt that each of these women corroborated Glenda Grabow's information that Jack Ruby and Raul knew each other. Don Wilson's materials appeared to fortify that fact.

Prior to James's death, the King family and I discussed the possibility of calling for a new investigation. We believed that what was needed was not another congressional investigation or one conducted by the Justice Department, but rather one conducted by a truly independent body with subpoena power and the authority to grant immunity from prosecution in exchange for information. In reality, we wished for a commission modeled after the South African Truth and Reconciliation Commission.

The family met with President Clinton and explained their wishes. He eventually refused their request and instead asked Attorney General Reno to conduct a limited investigation, which would focus on the new evidence provided by Don Wilson and the admissions of Loyd Jowers.

This was clearly unsatisfactory for it was one more instance of the government investigating itself, but we had little choice but to cooperate with the effort that was to be led by the Justice Department's senior civil rights criminal trial attorney Barry Kowalski.

Kowalski's team moved quickly into high gear as they promptly reached out for Don Wilson. The early contacts were amicable, but it soon turned ominously nasty.

I was in touch with Don off and on during his experience during the summer of 1997. He said that, initially, he was inclined to cooperate and then he learned that the attorney general's team had placed a surveillance officer outside of the bank where he kept the materials in a safe deposit box. A bank officer became suspicious of this lingering person and called the police who came and apprehended him. When the officer flashed the documentation of a federal marshal, Don knew that he was a part of the attorney general's team, and he was livid. He refused to cooperate and became hostile to the attorney general's team's effort to acquire his materials. His life changed drastically after he went public with his story. Before he surfaced he ran a profitable talent agency, representing a number of music groups. After he went public, it all went away. Clients were contacted and told that their careers would not be benefited if Don Wilson continued to be their agent.

His business was ruined. At his age, in order to make a living, he took a teaching job. It got worse. One day after he had left for work his wife was called and told that they had access to her health records and knew about her asthmatic condition, which was aggravated by stress. The caller said that her husband was a liar and that if he didn't turn over the materials, he would go to jail. Eventually, in response to a subpoena, Don gave them the original Dallas telephone directory page and the pay list. Wilson told me in no uncertain terms that these people were no friends of ours or the truth in the King assassination. He said they verbally attacked Dexter King and myself.

I spoke with Barry Kowalski from eastern Europe when this was going on. I raised the treatment of the Wilsons, and he defended his actions saying that they were necessary in order to obtain the materials. He said that otherwise Wilson was not going to surrender the materials to them or, he said, to me.

Shortly afterward, Don told me that his wife was shopping in a suburban shopping area near their home. When she returned to her car, she found the tires slashed. This type of vandalism was unprecedented in that area. They filed a police complaint to no avail.[38] Don was outraged, but he felt powerless and alone, and he began to question the wisdom of coming forward and trying to help. He was concerned about the strain and pressure on Fran, his wife. When we filed the civil action in October 1998, he made it clear that we could not count on his testimony when the case came to trial. By the time the trial date rolled around – November 15 1999 – it was firm. Don would not be moved by any entreaties. I considered him and his story to be a casualty of the attorney general's investigation.[39]

The task force seemed to be attempting to speak to a wide range of people, each of whom had various pieces of information. In November 1999 I learned that the previous June they had obtained what were available of Raul's work records. This was revealed to me when I obtained the same records. Those records, however, indicated a history of extended absences and time off; strange for a simple automobile worker.

The Justice Department team never did speak to Loyd Jowers. Jowers understandably wanted immunity before he would meet with them. While they indicated that they could arrange it with the Shelby County district attorney's office, in fact, an offer never materialized, and they would not be able to interview him. Though they appeared to be close to finalizing their report in the summer of 1999, the trial would come to an end in December without a report being issued.

PART TWO

8

THE TRIAL

We were indeed "first out" in Judge Swearingen's courtroom on November 15 1999. The judge agreed to let one media pool camera in the courtroom along with our own video camera. The media camera, like the media itself, would come and go. (They were nearly always absent, with the notable and sole exception of local anchorman Wendell Stacy who almost lost his job at that time over his insistence that he attend every day. He was eventually fired but won a wrongful dismissal action and has been rehired.)

Jury selection began that morning in the small Division IV courtroom. We discussed moving the case to a larger courtroom, but because of the judge's health needs, it was agreed that the trial would remain in his usual room. The judge disclosed to both sides that he had been a member of the group which had carried Dr King's casket from the funeral home in Memphis after the assassination. If, therefore, either side wanted him to withdraw, he said he would. We certainly had no reason to do so; Defense Attorney Garrison also had no objection.

After almost despairing about finding an acceptable local counsel, I finally was able to obtain the services of Juliet Hill-Akines, a young black lawyer, who had been admitted to the Bar in 1994. Before Juliet agreed, I discussed the possibility with a large number of local lawyers, all of whom turned down the opportunity – usually because they were advised that it would have a negative impact on their careers. Rather than expressing such apprehensions, Juliet took it as a challenge and an honor to be representing the family of Martin Luther King Jr. I admired her decision and was grateful for her independence and courage.

Judge James Swearingen barred the media from the jury selection process. Due to the sensitivity of the case, he was anxious to protect the identities of the individual jury members and, to the extent possible, ensure their privacy. He would issue a further order barring any cameras from being pointed at the jury at any time during the trial.[40]

Since there were five plaintiffs to one named defendant, we had the right to exercise many more exclusions. We used them all since the jury pool – in excess of forty – contained a large number of people who were employed by law enforcement agencies and security firms.

At the end of that first day, a jury of eight men and four women, six of them black and six white, was chosen. The trial would start at 10:00 AM the next morning, and after opening arguments, we would begin the plaintiffs' case with Coretta Scott King as our first witness. On behalf of the plaintiffs, I had drawn together an intelligent, enthusiastic volunteer team.[41]

The trial began on November 16. Opening arguments were finished by the lunch break, and that afternoon we called Mrs King as our first witness. Court TV was there to cover her testimony and provide the pool camera. They would pull out and be absent for most of the trial, returning for celebrity witnesses but missing most of the material evidence as did the rest of the media. In copycat fashion, local regional and national media were absent for most of the trial.

The plaintiffs' case was divided into nine areas of evidence:

- The background to the assassination
- The local conspiracy
- The crime scene
- The murder weapon
- Raul
- The broader conspiracy
- The cover-up – its scope and activities
- The defendant's prior admissions
- Damages

Though many of the witnesses testified to facts with which the reader is already familiar since they emerged in the investigation, discussed earlier, I will summarise the details of the testimony because, of course, they achieve a new status as evidence given under oath in a court of law.

The background

Mrs King led off the group of witnesses whose testimony provided evidence about the historical background and events leading up to the assassination. They offered various perspectives and facts and described the official hostility to Dr King's vigorous opposition to the war in Vietnam and his commitment to lead a massive contingent of poor and alienated people to Washington, where they would take up a tent city residence in the Capitol and lobby the Congress for long overdue social legislation. Dr King's support of the sanitation workers' strike was described by Reverend James Lawson, as was the eruption of violence in the march of March 28 which, Dr Coby Smith of the Invaders testified, appeared to be the work of out-of-state provocateurs.

The role of the Invaders and their sudden departure from the Lorraine Motel were testified to in detail, by former Invaders members Dr Smith and Charles Cabbage. Smith said that the Invaders decided to work with Dr King in the planning of the April march because they had been wrongly blamed for the violence which had broken up the previous march. He insisted that they had conducted their own investigation and became convinced that the disruption was caused by out-of-state provocateurs. He said they had reached a basic agreement with SCLC and Dr King, and in order to facilitate their participation in the planning process, the group had moved into two rooms in the Lorraine Motel. Their rooms were also on the balcony level some doors south of Dr King's room, and he said that they had participated in various planning sessions and meetings with Dr King following his arrival on April 3.

Cabbage described the Invaders' sudden departure within 11 minutes of the shooting. He said that a member of the Lorraine staff knocked on their door. It must have been after 5:30 PM. They were told that they had to leave because SCLC was no longer going to pay their bill. This appeared strange because the bill for that evening's lodging would have clearly been paid, or obligated to be paid, much earlier in the day. Though it made no sense from any standpoint, he said they accepted the order, which he said they were told came from Reverend Jesse Jackson. They quickly packed up their things and began to leave around 10 minutes before 6:00 PM. The timing of their departure was later confirmed by the testimony of MPD Captain Willie B. Richmond (retired), who noted the event in his surveillance report developed from his observation post inside and at the rear of the fire station. Captain Richmond also testified that around the same time, he observed Reverend Kyles knock on Dr King's door. Richmond said Dr King opened the door, spoke with him briefly, and then closed the door. Kyles then walked some distance north on the balcony and stood at the railing. This account, of course, contradicted the story Kyles has told for over three decades, in which he said he was in Dr King's room for about 30 to 45 minutes before the shooting.

At one point when they were being asked to leave, Cabbage said, he observed the Reverend Jesse Jackson standing on the ground near the swimming pool, which was opposite the balcony rooms occupied by Dr King and the Invaders. He said that Reverend Jackson kept glancing impatiently at his watch. (It must be said, however, that the group was running late for their scheduled dinner at Reverend Kyles's home.)

It is more difficult to understand why Jackson would have caused them to be summarily evicted (if he indeed did so) at that hour so near the time of the killing. Reverend Jackson has reportedly stated subsequently that he didn't even remember that the Invaders were staying at the Lorraine.

Cabbage never understood it. In his testimony, he also confirmed that the Invaders occupying the Lorraine rooms were quite heavily armed as was their usual custom because of the hostility of the MPD.

The local conspiracy

The involvement of produce dealer Frank Liberto in setting up the local conspiracy was conclusively established by a string of witnesses. For the first time in the 22 years that I have known him, John McFerren took the stand and testified under oath about hearing, within an hour and a quarter of the killing, Liberto screaming into the telephone to "Shoot the son of a bitch on the balcony," subsequently telling the caller to go to New Orleans to collect money from his brother. John, courageous and forthright, began his testimony by telling the jury about the long history of his family's ascent from slavery and his civil rights activity and harassment in Fayette County, one of Tennessee's most racist areas. As he described the events that took place, he repeated the same story under oath that he first put before the FBI/MPD team who interviewed him for hours at the Peabody Hotel on the Sunday evening following the crime. The federal and local officials dismissed his account in 1968 as did the congressional committee 10 years later. This time it would be different.

The role of Frank Liberto was further confirmed by the testimony of Nathan Whitlock and his mother LaVada Addison who provided details about the admissions Liberto made to them separately in 1978, leaving them in no doubt that he had organized the Memphis hit on Dr King, that there would be no security, the police were cooperating, and that a patsy was in place. In subsequent testimony, Dexter King and Ambassador Andrew Young testified that in their separate interviews with Loyd Jowers, he had told them that some time in March, after Dr King's first speech on behalf of the sanitation workers on March 18, he was approached by Liberto, to whom he said he owed a "big favor." He basically confirmed the story he had told on the *Prime Time Live* program without any mention of Frank Holt being involved. Liberto told him that he would be given $100,000 in a vegetable delivery box and that he was to turn this money over to a man named Raul who would visit him sometime afterward. He told Dexter, Andy, and me that Liberto had told him no police would be around and that they had a patsy. In fact, he said, it all happened in exactly that way. Planning sessions for the assassination were held in his grill involving Lieutenant John Barger (whom he had known from his own early days on the police force); Marrell McCollough, a black undercover officer introduced to him by Barger as his new partner; MPD sharpshooter Lieutenant Earl Clark (who was a hunting companion of Jowers); a senior MPD inspector; and finally, a fifth officer whom he did not know. He said he remembered that there were five because he had to pull up a chair to the four-seater booth. Jowers said that if James was at all involved, he was an unknowing patsy.

Hence, Jowers also confirmed the involvement of Frank Liberto. Along with the testimonial evidence of McFerren, Whitlock, and Addison, and the deceased Art Baldwin's earlier disclosures, Frank Liberto's primary role in the assassination appeared to be clear.

A steady succession of witnesses provided details of the removal of all police from the area of the crime, the failure to put the usual security unit in place as well as the removal of other individuals whose presence in the crime scene area constituted a security risk to the assassination mission.

Firemen Floyd Newsom and Norvell Wallace, the only two black firemen at fire station no. 2, testified that less than 24 hours before the assassination, they were ordered not to report to their regular fire station no. 2 post on the periphery of the Lorraine Motel but to stations in other parts of the city. Newsom and Wallace said that their transfers left their base station short-handed while they were surplus to requirements at the stations where they were sent. The transfers made no sense, and they were given no satisfactory explanation. Newsom said eventually one of his superiors told him that the police department had requested his transfer.

Detective Ed Redditt, a community relations officer assigned to intelligence duty as Willie Richmond's partner on the surveillance detail at the rear of the fire station, testified that he was picked up by Lieutenant Eli Arkin about an hour before the assassination and taken, first, to Central Police Headquarters, where he was ordered, by Director Frank Holloman, to go home because of an alleged threat on his life. His protests were ignored. As he sat, parked with Arkin in front of his house, the news of the assassination came over the car radio. He never again heard about the alleged threat, which was explained as a mistake of some sort. He never received a satisfactory explanation, but it was clear that his primary community relations police duties had caused him to become closely involved with the community, not MPD intelligence. It was understandable that he would not be trusted to be allowed to stay in the crime scene area if dirty work was afoot.

Memphis Police Department homicide detective Captain Jerry Williams (retired) testified that on Dr King's previous visits to Memphis, he had been given the responsibility of organizing and coordinating a security unit of all black homicide detectives who would provide protection for Dr King while he was in the city. They would ordinarily remain with him throughout his visit even securing the hotel – usually the Rivermont or the Admiral Benbow – where he stayed. Captain Williams testified that on Dr King's last, and fatal, visit to Memphis, however, he was not asked to form that security unit. At one point, he was told that Dr King's group did not want them around. There was no indication, of any kind, from any SCLC source that this was true. In fact, Reverend Lawson remembered being impressed with the group on a previous visit and their verbal promise to him that as long as they were in place, no harm would come to Dr King. On April 3 and 4 1968, they were not in place. Testifying out of order, because he had been hospitalized, Invader Big John Smith said that though there was a small police presence at the motel earlier on the afternoon of April 4, he noticed that it had completely disappeared within a half-hour of the assassination.

University of Massachusetts Professor Phillip Melanson took the stand to testify about the removal of the emergency forces' TACT 10 unit from the Lorraine Motel on April 4.[42] He said that Inspector Sam Evans admitted pulling back the TACT 10 unit, which had been based at the Lorraine Motel, to the periphery of the fire station. Evans claimed that the decision was taken pursuant to a request from someone in Dr King's group. When pressed as to who actually made the request, he said that it was Reverend Kyles. The fact that Kyles had nothing to do with SCLC, and no authority to request any such thing, seemed to have eluded Evans.

It would be hard to imagine, on that April 4, a more complete stripping away of not only the available security personnel from Dr King but also a more thorough removal of individuals who were not deemed completely trustworthy or controllable. And it was all set in motion twenty-four hours before the assassination.

To address why Dr King's motel room had been changed, former New York City police detective Leon Cohen testified that early in the morning on the day following the assassination, he learned from Walter Bailey, the manager of the Lorraine Motel, that Dr King was meant to be in a secluded, more secure courtyard room, but that on the evening prior to his arrival, someone from SCLC's office in Atlanta called to instruct that Dr King be given a balcony room overlooking the swimming pool. Cohen, who had moved to Memphis and worked as a private investigator after retiring from the New York City Police Department, testified that Bailey maintained that he tried to talk the person, who Bailey said was a man he knew, out of this decision, but the caller was adamant. Dr King was moved.

At the time of the trial, taxi driver James Milner had known Loyd Jowers for over twenty-five years. He testified that, in fact, in the early to mid-1970s, Jowers had basically told him the same story that he revealed in 1993 about how he became involved with the assassination, how it was planned and carried out, and that the deceased Lieutenant Earl Clark was likely to have pulled the trigger. (Jowers's ambivalence about the shooter's identity was consistent. He definitely pointed in Clark's direction but never positively. Clark was dead. If someone else had been the shooter and was still alive, this could explain Jowers's conduct. But, if not Clark, who? Who, I agonized, could Jowers be protecting? At one point I remembered that he had said there was a fifth MPD officer at the planning sessions in Jim's Grill, but Jowers said he did not know him. Possible? Of course, but not likely that he would not have been introduced to him as he had been to the other stranger, Marrell McCollough. Could this fifth officer have played an ultimately more sinister role? Was he the shooter?)

Another driver – J. J. Isabel – testified that on the occasion of St Patrick's Day 1979 or 1980, he and Jowers drove two chartered buses to Cleveland taking a Memphis group to a bowling tournament. They shared a hotel room, and after a meal and some drinking on the first evening, when they returned to their room, Isabel said he asked Jowers, "Loyd, did you drop the hammer on Martin Luther King?" He said that Jowers hesitated for a moment or two and then replied, "You may think that you know what I did, but I know what I did, but I will never tell it in court."

The value of Milner's and Isabel's separate testimony is, of course, that like Whitlock/Addison and McFerren, they provide corroboration at least of a local conspiracy, as well as aspects of Jowers's story, long before his involvement become an issue.

One of Jowers's former waitresses Bobbi Balfour testified that on the day of the killing, Jowers told her not to carry food up to a tenant in the rooming house, Grace Walden Stephens, who was ill. She said that it had been her regular practice with Loyd's approval to bring food up to Charlie Stephens's common-law wife during her illness, but on that day, Loyd explicitly told her to stay away from the second floor.

Finally, Olivia Catling, who lived, and in 2002 still lived, on Mulberry Street, midway between Huling and Vance about 200 yards from the Lorraine, testified that she was at home preparing dinner for her family when she heard the shot. She knew that Dr King was staying at the Lorraine Motel, and she feared the worst. As quickly as she could, she collected her young children and ran out of her house down Mulberry Street toward the Lorraine. By the time she reached the northwest corner of Huling and Mulberry, the police had already barricaded Mulberry Street with a police car, so she and the children had to stand on the corner. She testified that shortly after she arrived on the corner, she saw a white man running from an alley, halfway up Huling, which ran to a building connected to the rooming house. He arrived at a car parked on the south side of Huling and facing east, got in, and drove quickly away turning left on to Mulberry and going right past her as well as the MPD officers opposite her who were manning the barricade. She was surprised that the police paid no attention to him and did not try to prevent him from leaving the area.

She testified that shortly afterward, she saw a fireman – who she believed must have walked down from the fire station – standing near the wall below the bushes, yelling at the police on the street that the shot came from a clump of bushes apparently just above the area where he was standing. She said that the police ignored him.

Olivia Catling testified that she had never been interviewed by any law enforcement officials. She said that there was no house-to-house investigation. Though she has lived so close to the scene of the crime for 32 years since the assassination, no one had knocked on her door until I did so in November of 1999. She was relieved to finally get it off her chest. She said that she had been so burdened all of these years because she knew that an innocent man was in prison. By the time I met her, James had died, but at least this wiry, clear, and tough-minded Memphian could take satisfaction that at last her story would be heard.

Memphis Police Department homicide detective Captain Tommy

Smith (retired) testified that very soon after the assassination, he interviewed rooming house tenant Charles Quitman Stephens, the state's chief witness against James Earl Ray, and found him intoxicated and hardly able to stand up. It must be remembered that it was on the strength of Stephens's affidavit of identification that James was extradited from England. In actual fact, Captain Smith said Stephens was not in a condition to identify anyone.

The state had always maintained that after firing from the bathroom window, James stopped in his room to pick up his bundle of belongings and fled carrying the rifle and the bundle, eventually exiting the front door of the rooming house, dropping the bundle in the doorway of Guy Canipe's shop. Then, the official story goes, James got into a white Mustang parked just slightly south of Canipe's store and drove away. Stephens was supposed to have caught a glimpse of the profile of the fleeing man.

Charles Hurley testified that while waiting to pick up his wife from work, he parked behind that white Mustang about an hour and a quarter before the shooting. He said that a man was sitting in it and was still there when they drove away. Most importantly, however, he again confirmed, though now under oath, that the white Mustang parked just south of Canipe's store, in which James is supposed to have driven away, had Arkansas license plates. James's Mustang had Alabama plates.

We read into the record and introduced into evidence FBI form 302 statements taken from two witnesses who left Jim's Grill about 20 minutes before the killing. Ray Hendrix and Bill Reed said that late on the afternoon of April 4, they walked north on South Main Street after having looked closely at the white Mustang parked directly in front of Jim's Grill. The car interested them so they took particular note of it. They both confirmed, in separate statements, that as they were about to cross Vance – two blocks north of Jim's Grill – the Mustang turned the corner directly in front of them. The male driver was alone. This would have been about 5:45 PM. This statement was suppressed at the time and never turned over to the defence or revealed to the guilty plea jury a year later.

The crime scene

Olivia Catling was the latest observer to give evidence about the bushes behind the rooming house being the place from where the fatal shot was fired. There was abundant, current, and historical eyewitness testimony, which clearly established this fact and which was introduced into evidence.

Solomon Jones, Dr King's driver in Memphis, told a number of people at the scene shortly after the shooting, Wayne Chastain being one, that he saw a figure in the bushes come down over the wall. The Reverend James Orange could not appear due to a death in his family, but his sworn statement was read into the record. He said that as he turned around from a crouching position in the Lorraine parking area, immediately after the shot, he saw what he thought was smoke (we have since learned that although it had the appearance of smoke, it would have been sonic dust rising from the bushes caused by the firing of the high-powered rifle in the heavily vegetated area.) He said no law enforcement or investigative person had ever taken a statement from him.

Memphis Police Department dog officer J. B. Hodges testified that he arrived on the scene within minutes after the shooting. With the aid of a metal barrel to stand on, he climbed up over the wall and entered the brush area. He described the bushes as being very thick from the edge of the wall for some distance toward the back of Jim's Grill and the rooming house. He said he had to fight his way through the formidable thicket, but that eventually he arrived at a clearing and went to the alleyway, which ran between the two wings of the rooming house. Not too far into the alley, he said he found a pair of footprints heading in the direction of the rooming house. At the end of the alley, there was a door leading to the basement, which ran underneath the entire building. It had rained the night before, and the ground cover was wet, but there was no growth in the alley, and the mud revealed apparently freshly made large footprints – sized 13 to 13½. Hodges guarded his discovery until a cast was made. Those footprints have never been identified or explained. Eventually, I would wonder about the shoe size of the fifth MPD officer at the planning sessions described by Jowers.

As a part of their testimonies related to their questioning of Loyd

Jowers, Dexter King and Andrew Young separately recounted how Jowers admitted taking the rifle from the assassin whom he said had in fact fired from the bushes. An earlier deposition of Jowers's former waitress/lover Betty Spates was read into the record, in which she claimed having seen him carrying a rifle, running from the bushes in through the back door of his kitchen. In this last instance, the defense raised the question of her credibility noting that she had altered her story when questioned by official investigators. As noted elsewhere, this was true, but it was the result of their harassment. The last statement she gave to me under oath was consistent with what she originally told me in 1992.[43]

Former *New York Times* reporter Earl Caldwell could not break prior engagements in order to testify, but the defense agreed to allow a video of his testimony at the television trial on the condition that the cross-examination conducted by former US Attorney Hickman Ewing was also played. We agreed, and the jury saw and heard Caldwell testify that he was sent to Memphis by the *Times* on April 3 with the instructions from national editor Claude Sitton to ". . . nail Dr King." He said he was in his ground floor motel room when he heard the shot, which he said sounded like a bomb blast. In his shorts, he said he ran outside of his room and began to stare at the bushes, from where he instinctively thought the shot must have come. He is certain that he saw an individual crouching in the bushes which, he said, were quite thick and tall. He vividly described the person's posture in cross-examination, coming down from the stand to demonstrate how the person was squatting and rising.

Probably the most powerful single piece of evidence (although the cumulative weight is overwhelming) that the assassin fired from the bushes was provided by the testimony of Louie Ward, who recounted the story of a fellow driver who he always knew as "Buddy" who, when in the process of picking up a passenger at the Lorraine just before 6:00 PM, happened to see, immediately after the shot, a man come down over the wall, run north on Mulberry Street, and get into a Memphis Police Department traffic car, which had been parked at the corner of Mulberry and Huling and which then speeded away. Louie Ward testified that he later learned that the taxi driver had been killed that night, allegedly having been thrown out of a speeding car on Route 55, on the other side of the Memphis–Arkansas bridge. He heard that the body was found the next morning.[44]

The murder weapon

Independent testimony established that the rifle in evidence was not the murder weapon. Criminal Court Judge Joe Brown took the stand under subpoena to share his particular knowledge of the rifle evidence. I qualified Judge Brown as a ballistics expert for the purpose of his testimony about the weapon, and as he moved through his testimony, his expertise was never in doubt. He began by telling the jury that the scope on the rifle supposedly belonging to Ray had never been sighted, which meant that one could not fire it accurately when lining up a target through the scope. We introduced an April 5 1968 FBI report, which stated that the rifle, on the day after the killing, had failed an accuracy test – firing 3.5 inches to the left and 4 inches below the target. In addition, he said that the metallurgical composition of the death slug lead was different from the composition of the other bullets found in the evidence bundle in front of Canipe's while the composition of each of the other bullets matched. He had no doubt the rifle in evidence was not the murder weapon.

In a startling development, Bill Hamblin, deceased taxi driver Mc-Craw's housemate for 15 years, took the stand and testified that for those 15 years, spanning the 1970s and early 1980s, McCraw had consistently told him (but only when he was intoxicated) that on the morning after the shooting (April 5) Jowers not only showed him the rifle that killed Martin Luther King but told him to get rid of it. McCraw said that he drove on to the Memphis–Arkansas bridge and threw it off. In his deposition taken years earlier, McCraw had only gone so far as to say that Jowers had shown him the actual murder weapon on the morning after the killing. If we are to believe that testimony, and there is no reason for Hamblin to lie, but also that Jowers was telling the truth to McCraw, then the actual murder weapon used to kill Dr King has been enmired in the silt of the Mississippi River since 1968.

Hamblin also testified that on one occasion when he and McCraw were renting rooms in a house on Peabody owned by an FBI agent named Purdy, he told the FBI landlord that he should talk to McCraw sometime because he had information about the killing of Dr King. Promptly after that conversation, he said, they were given their eviction notices, and during the 30-day grace period, the MPD harassed them on a number of occasions.

At the time of the assassination, Bill Hamblin was working in a Memphis barbershop – the Cherokee barbershop – and his boss was Vernon Jones. Mr Jones just happened to have as a client the same FBI agent Purdy who some years later would become Hamblin's and Mc-Craw's landlord. The agent had apparently been having his hair cut by Mr Jones for upwards of 10 years, and so they had a long-standing relationship. Hamblin testified that the agent came in for a haircut within two weeks after the killing, and after he had finished, as the agent was about to leave, Hamblin's boss pulled him aside and within earshot asked him who killed King. Hamblin said he did not hear the soft-spoken reply, but he asked his boss about the answer and was told "he said the CIA ordered it done."

Birmingham, Alabama Probate Court Judge Arthur Hanes Jr, who, along with his father, was James Earl Ray's first lawyer, testified that in his preparation for trial, which they had no doubt would result in James Earl Ray's acquittal, he had interviewed Guy Canipe in the doorway of whose store the bundle of evidence including the evidence rifle was dropped. He said that Canipe told him in no uncertain terms that the rifle was dropped about 10 minutes before the shot was fired so it obviously could not have been the murder weapon. Judge Hanes testified that Canipe was prepared to testify for the defense at the trial.

Washington DC attorney James Lesar, who specializes in Freedom of Information Act legal actions, testified that in one such application, he obtained an FBI report concerning tests that had been conducted on the bathroom window sill or, more specifically, on a dent in the window sill which they suspected might have been caused by the assassin resting or pressing the barrel on the old wooden sill. We introduced into evidence the actual report issued by the laboratory in April 1968. Though a prosecutor had alleged to the contrary before the guilty plea jury on

March 10 1969, the report stated that it would not be possible to tie the dent in the windowsill to the rifle in evidence. Thus the Shelby County district attorney general's office knew all along that the window sill evidence was false.

In their testimonies, Dexter King and Andy Young said that the defendant Jowers himself had made it clear that the murder weapon was not the rifle in evidence, but the one he took from the shooter. Jowers also told them that he had tried to flush the spent shell down his toilet, but it stopped it up, and he had to remove it. The silt of the Mississippi River became its final resting place too.

We explored the possibility of recovering the rifle from the river but gave up the idea when we learned that a train locomotive, tanks, barges, and cars had been lost in the enormous deep silt bottom, which was stirred continually by a strong current. It was frustrating to have to accept that even though we believed it likely that we knew the location of the murder weapon, we would not be able to recover it. This disappointment, however, was alleviated by the realization that we had demonstrated through clear and convincing evidence that the rifle purchased by James, as instructed, was not the murder weapon.

Raul

Memphis private investigator John Billings provided the background information on how a photograph of the man we had come to know as Raul was obtained. Ironically he said, a Memphis Police Department officer, who had been assigned to the district attorney general's task force, had obtained the Immigration and Naturalization Service photograph and turned it over to them in an effort to convince them that he was willing to cooperate and work with them in the search for the truth. Eventually, they learned that nothing could have been further from his true intentions, but, in the short run at least, it gave them the photograph taken in 1961 when Raul emigrated to the United States from Portugal. Billing's colleague Ken Herman organized a spread of six photographs for exhibiting to witnesses. Billings testified that, in his presence, when he placed the spread in front of him, James Earl Ray readily identified the man in the spread as being the person who had controlled his movements and given him money and who he had come to know as Raul. As mentioned earlier, James had seen the same photograph in 1978 and, at that time, identified it (with some media coverage), so this was not a surprising revelation.

Glenda Grabow had earlier consistently identified the man in the photograph as the person she had known in Houston from 1963 onward and who, in or around 1974, in a fit of rage implicated himself in the assassination of Dr King just before he raped her.

At the time of the trial, Glenda had injured ribs from an automobile accident and was suffering from internal bleeding preventing her from testifying. Her husband Roy testified instead and confirmed that he had been present when she gave her earlier affidavit statements. Thus, the jury had access to Glenda's story including the details about her relationship with Percy Foreman, his admission that James Earl Ray, though innocent, had to be sacrificed and the fact that Foreman knew – or so he said – Raul.

After Roy confirmed its authenticity, I introduced into evidence a telephone bill for their home telephone which showed, on April 20 1996, a six minute telephone call to Raul's home telephone number. Under questioning, Roy stated that Glenda would not have stayed on the phone for six minutes with this person unless he was known to her. It is hard to imagine anyone keeping a conversation going with a complete stranger for that period of time.

Glenda had some time previously provided me with notes of her conversation with Raul, written, however, after the conversation. Whilst I believe them to be an accurate account of the conversation, I did not think that, in Glenda's absence, we should attempt to enter them into evidence. It is useful however to see them in the context of Raul's denials about even knowing Glenda. The conversation went as follows:

Glenda: Raul?
Raul: Yes.
Glenda: This is Glenda Grabow.
Raul: Olinda.
Glenda: Yes. I was just calling to tell you I was supposed to come to New York.

Raul: Where you at?
Glenda: Houston.
Raul: Houston?
Glenda: When I come to New York, I will call you.
Raul: When?
Glenda: I still don't know yet when. You sell wine now?
Raul: Ya.
Glenda: Do you still deal in guns?
Raul: Ya, I still deal in lots of guns.
Glenda: You do?
Raul: Ya.
Glenda: Have you heard from Jack V—— lately?
Raul: No, not for long time. Why you want to know? Why you
          call me?
Glenda: I will try and talk to you when I get there.
Raul: OK. O ya.
Glenda: I heard your daughter was getting married?
Raul: Ya, she get married. How many you have now?
Glenda: I just have the two girls and they are grown now. Time
          flies. Well I will call back later. When is the best time to
          call?
Raul: My wife get here, or [leave here] at 6:00
Glenda: OK, I will call you when I get there.
Raul: OK
Glenda: Bye.

Glenda's brother, Royce Wilburn, an electrical contractor from Nash-ville, Tennessee who had not discussed the case or his testimony with his sister, testified that the man he knew as "Dago," and whose photograph he picked out of the spread, did indeed hang out, off and on, at a gas station near their home in Houston. He confirmed that his sister and he used to see and talk with the man because the gas station, where he hung out, was between their home and school.

British merchant seaman Sid Carthew in a telephone deposition described how he had met Raul – whom he had under oath previously identified from the spread of photographs – late in the summer of 1967, in the Neptune bar on West Commissioners Street in the Montreal docks area. At that time, he said Raul appeared to be with another person who may well have been James Earl Ray. Carthew said at one point Raul came over and introduced himself (as Raul). Sid, who was identified with the British Nationalist Party, said that the Neptune was a regular haunt of his and his mates when they came ashore following days at sea on the voyage from Liverpool. Someone in the bar must have told Raul about his politics because eventually the conversation came around to the question of whether Sid might want to buy some guns. Sid said he expressed interest, and they began to negotiate. Raul said that their guns were new army (US) issue, and the price reflected the money that had to be paid to a sergeant who was organizing the supply. (To my mind, this matched Warren's earlier account of guns being taken from Camp Shelby or other military installations, trucked to New Orleans, and delivered to Carlos Marcello who organized the sales, with, according to Glenda Grabow, deliveries from Houston.) The deal fell apart according to Sid over the quantity.

Former UK Thames Television producer Jack Saltman, who had produced the 1993 Thames/HBO television trial of James Earl Ray, took the stand to testify that after the trial, when convinced that an egregious injustice had been done, he continued some investigating efforts on his own. He particularly focused on Raul. At one point, he took the spread of photographs to Raul's front door. The jury heard the tape-recorded exchange between Saltman and Raul's daughter who was on the other side of the door. They heard her admit that the photograph was indeed of her father. Her words were effectively that ". . . anyone could get that picture of my father." It was a startling admission for now Raul's own daughter had joined the ranks of all of the others, who had confirmed that the critical photographic evidence was indeed her father.

Both Dexter King and Ambassador Young testified that the defendant Loyd Jowers had unhesitatingly identified the photograph as being that of the man who appeared in his grill to pick up the Liberto cash and leave the murder weapon, a "package," for the actual assassin.

Barbara Reis was very uncomfortable on the stand. Reporters do not like to have to testify in court. She was the primary US correspondent of *Publico*, the largest newspaper in Portugal, and because Raul was Portuguese, her paper was interested in the story. She was covering the trial and in attendance in court almost every day for the first two weeks. Some time earlier, however, she had gone to Raul's home and spoke with a member of his family (whom we agreed not to identify) and that was why we believed that we had no choice but to issue a subpoena for her testimony. She was outraged, but I believed that her evidence was too valuable not to be put in front of the jury. So, under oath, she reluctantly recounted what she had been told during the course of that interview.

She said that she was informed that though these allegations had greatly disrupted their lives and were terrible, nevertheless the family took great comfort from the fact that they were being protected and advised by US government agents who had visited their home on three occasions and who were monitoring their telephones. The government was helping them through those difficult days.

The fact that the government was helping a retired automobile worker in such a fashion was not lost on the members of the jury. Ordinary private citizens are obviously not afforded these services. It is our contention that Raul was and will continue to be protected for services rendered and perceived to be in the national security interests of the state or the special interests which determine what is to be designated as national security interests.

Don Wilson's resolve hardened, and he refused to testify at the trial. Early on, Don had told Dexter King about the events and given him copies of two of the pieces of paper he took away from James's abandoned Mustang. Dexter was, therefore, in a position to identify the materials, the originals of which had been with the Justice Department going through a process of authentication for several months. In the course of his testimony, Dexter recounted how Don Wilson originally explained how when he opened the slightly ajar passenger door of James's car, an envelope fell on the ground, and he instinctively put it in his pocket. The young agent was initially afraid that he had screwed up material criminal evidence by allowing it to become separated from the automobile possibly connected with a crime. Later, when he had an opportunity to consider the materials, he decided to hold on to them, in part because he was in a difficult, if not impossible, position for not having turned them in straight away and also because he genuinely came to believe that the notes would be buried if he turned them over to his superiors at the Atlanta field office. So he retained them – for nearly 30 years – until he decided to come forward in an effort to support the King family and James Earl Ray.

The material did in fact contain the name Raul as well as what appeared to be a list of payments to be made. When shown a copy of the torn page from a Dallas telephone directory with handwriting at the top, in his testimony Dexter King identified the name Raul as he did for a second time on the payoff list.[45]

Glenda Grabow's story about the connection between Raul and Jack Ruby had, in my view, been corroborated, but I eventually decided against introducing into evidence this connection and the link to the Kennedy assassination. I did not want to run the risk of taking the jury down that road. It was, after all, surplus to our main case, and there was always the possibility that the jury would refuse to accept the connection with the Kennedy assassination. I had Madeleine, Beverly, and Chari lined up to travel to Memphis and then did not call them. It was a temptation, which had to be resisted, but it was not easy because I believed these courageous women. Madeleine Brown for example is very credible, and some aspects of her recollections of her life and genuine love for Johnson were compelling. In fact, as I mentioned earlier, she gave birth to his only son. I obtained a copy of Johnson's commitment (through his local lawyer Jerome Ragsdale) to provide support for Steven which continued even after the president's death. That she was able to provide such detail about their relationship was impressive. Of particular note was her recollection of the events of Thursday evening November 21 1963 – the night before the Kennedy assassination. She said she attended a social gathering at Clint Murchison's home. Ostensibly, it was an event to honor J. Edgar Hoover who was a close friend of Murchison, H. L. Hunt, and the other Texas oil giants. The guest list included John McCloy, chairman of Chase Manhattan Bank, Richard Nixon, George Brown, of the Brown and Root construction company, R. L. Thornton, president of the Mercantile Bank, and Dallas mayor Earle Cabell, brother of General Charles Cabell, former Deputy Director of the CIA who was fired by President Kennedy after the Bay of Pigs.

Madeleine told me that near the end of the party, Johnson made an appearance and the group quickly went into Murchison's study behind closed doors. After a while, the meeting broke up. Johnson, anxious and red-faced, came up, embraced her, and with a quiet grating sound whispered a message she would never forget in her ear. "After tomorrow, those goddamn Kennedys will never embarrass me again – that's no threat, that's a promise." She was stunned, but the next day she realized what he meant.

I decided not to take our case in this direction. It was a tactical decision but if, however, I am asked whether I believe that Raul and Ruby knew each other, were associates, and that the same forces were involved with both assassinations, I could only truthfully answer in the affirmative.

The broader conspiracy

We next turned to present the evidence that the conspiracy to kill Martin Luther King Jr extended well beyond Memphis, Tennessee and, in fact, reached into the echelons of power in the nation's capital.

Former Memphis Police Department intelligence officer Jim Smith took the stand under subpoena. His testimony at the television trial had resulted in him losing his security clearance, being put under surveillance, and, eventually, being in fear for his life, leaving Memphis only to find that the FBI had permanently blocked him from ever again obtaining a position in law enforcement. Now, six years later, he returned to Memphis having been transferred there in another line of work. He was uneasy and not willing to testify unless subpoenaed. We served him. He basically restated his earlier testimony that on March 18 1968 he was assigned to assist a two-man surveillance team parked in a van in the area of the Rivermont Hotel. The van contained audio surveillance equipment and two agents – he did not know which federal agency they were from. I had earlier concluded that they were Army Security Agency (ASA) operatives and that they listened in on conversations and activities in the suite occupied by Martin King. He did not, himself directly, participate in any of the surveillance but he observed it and understood what was going on. Back in 1992, I had been able to obtain a detailed description of the location of the microphone placements in the suite. It was so extensive that even if Dr King went on to the balcony his conversation would be relayed to the tape recorders in the van below. In addition to the covert (non-eye-to-eye) surveillance activities of the ASA agents, the court heard testimony from defense witness Eli Arkin, the MPD intelligence officer, that the 111th MIG was on the scene conducting its own surveillance activities. He said that some of them were based in his office.

Military historian Doug Valentine, whose book *The Phoenix Program* included a mention of a rumor that photographs of the assassination were taken by army photographers, took the stand to testify about the military affiliation of the man who provided the Memphis police with the false assassination threat against Detective Redditt, justifying his removal from the surveillance detail at the rear of the fire station. Valentine said that when he interviewed the individual, Phillip Manual (who had been in Memphis on April 3 and 4, ostensibly pursuant to his position as a staff member of the McClellan Committee), he learned that Manual previously – and perhaps then as well – worked with the 902nd MIG. I had gradually come to believe that this little-known unit coordinated the federal agency task force activity in Memphis and also liaised with the non-military side of the operation.

Carthel Weeden, the former Fire Department captain in charge of fire station no. 2, testified in detail about how in the morning of April 4, he was approached by two men in civilian clothes who showed him army credentials and asked to be taken up to the roof of the fire station where they would be in a position to photograph people and activity in the area. Though Carthel was not certain exactly how he carried them up to the roof, it must have been up the outside iron ladder which at the time was attached to the north side of the building near the side door and the fire hose tower. He said that he observed them taking their photographic equipment out of their bag. Carthel testified that he did not notice them again during that day and he just assumed that they completed their various tasks. Carthel also testified that he had never been interviewed any local, state, or federal law enforcement official. The reason for this is obvious. Had he been interviewed, it is quite likely that the investigators would have become aware of the soldiers on the roof. They would then have had the obligation to locate them and the photographs they took. This, of course, would be the path that any serious investigation would have to take. It would be anathema to those efforts which were only set up to conceal the truth. The actual assassin was caught on film, however, lowering the rifle right after the fatal shot.

In his testimony, Professor Clay Carson read into the record portions of documents which I had provided to the King Papers Project, which he directs, at Stanford University. One of the documents was a report from Steve Tompkins after a meeting at the Hyatt Hotel in Chicago with one of the photographers (see Appendix B). Amongst other details was the photographer's confirmation that the assassin was caught on film and that it was not James Earl Ray.

Professor Carson also read the responses to questions I had asked Steve Tompkins to raise with the Green Beret I had referred to as Warren. The exchange, on the record, is set out in its entirety in Appendix C. As can be seen from Professor Carson's testimony, a jury heard for the first time the details of the investigative process Steve Tompkins and I employed in order to reveal the presence and the role of the eight-man Alpha 184 unit in Memphis on April 4 1968. It became abundantly clear from Professor Carson's testimony that the team did not carry out the assassination but were in fact in position to do so. Steve had always maintained that they were only going to be ordered to shoot in the event of a riot. As mentioned earlier that never made any sense to me, given the apparent absence of any possible riot at the time in the area of the Lorraine. However, in his testimony Invader Charles Cabbage acknowledged that the members of his group, who occupied two balcony rooms just south of Dr King's room, were armed. When ordered to leave the hotel, shortly before the assassination (actually leaving within 11 minutes of the event) the Invaders might well have been expected to react violently disrupting the surface calm of the motel. If instead of leaving peacefully, the Invaders had reacted violently that could have created the required circumstances and cover for any military action deemed necessary. In the event, the Invaders left peacefully; the killing was not carried out by the army snipers who were ordered to withdraw from their position promptly after the shooting and leave the city immediately.

Covert operative Jack Terrell desperately wanted to testify in person but his liver cancer became worse and he was not allowed to travel. We had to use his video deposition taken in Orlando, Florida on February 7 1999. It stunned the court. After describing his previous covert activities on behalf of the government he described his close friendship with the 20th SFG Green Beret J. D. Hill who he came to know in Columbus, Mississippi, contradicting the Alpha team leader and 20th SFG Commander Cobb's statements on the ABC *Turning Point* program. He said that J. D. told him that the 20th would train for two weeks every summer at Shelby and that he used to return in excellent physical condition. He said that on one such occasion in 1975, J. D. seemed to want to unburden himself. It was then that he began to spell out the details of a mission for which he had trained and which was to be carried out in Memphis. He said that his unit had trained for a considerable period of time to carry out an assassination against a target or targets who were to be in a moving automobile. He said that snipers were placed high above and a considerable distance away from the target vehicle. They were not told who was the target but suspected it might have been an Arab.

Jack said J. D. told him that on April 4 1968 he and his unit set out for Memphis, still not aware of who the target was to be. In my first session with Jack in 1994, he had indicated that J. D. told him that the team was already in Memphis and had been on three occasions in position – similar to Warren's version – when they were told to withdraw. The discrepancy arose between his 1999 deposition and the statement he originally gave to me in 1994. There may in fact be no discrepancy at all. In his earlier account it was clear that the unit was staying somewhere in the area but outside of Memphis. They would travel to town and take up their positions – water tower, building roof, and window – and then leave at the end of the day. It may well be that when he testified that they were en route to Memphis when told to withdraw he was referring to the last trip in on April 4. When he heard about the assassination, J. D. told Jack, his initial reaction was that another team was also involved and his unit did not get the call. What is incontrovertible, however, is that J. D. Hill was a member of a unit which trained to carry out an assassination on American soil and that the event was to take place in Memphis, Tennessee on or around April 4 1968.

When, shortly afterward, J. D. learned that Dr King had been assassinated on the day of their mission, he realized that this was his unit's mission. Terrell then described the suspicious circumstances of J. D.'s death in 1979 where his wife was alleged – though not indicted – to have put a neat semi-circle of 357 Magnum bullets in his chest after he returned home late at night. Terrell said it was impossible for J. D.'s wife, who weighed about 90 pounds, to have handled the 357 Magnum weapon with such precision.

Terrell went on to describe the three-hour interview he gave to the ABC *Turning Point* program at my request. ABC did not use one second of the interview but soon afterward he began to receive official calls which led him to believe that his life could be in danger. He left the country for several months.[46]

The cover-up

A large number of witnesses testified to the extensive range of activities which caused the truth in this case to remain hidden and justice denied for nearly 32 years. Incredibly, the chronicle of events and actions included murder, solicitation of murder, attempted bribery, suppression of evidence, alteration of the crime scene, and the control, manipulation, and use of the media for propaganda purposes.

Former taxi driver and security officer Louie Ward testified as noted earlier about what he learned from the observation of yellow taxi cab driver Buddy who, when picking up a passenger at the Lorraine at the time of the shooting, saw a man come down over the wall, run north on Mulberry Street, get into a Memphis Police Department traffic car and be driven away. Louie Ward testified that he heard this account directly from Buddy, who was driving car number 58 on that day. He said that Buddy told him this story just before two police officers arrived and were told the same thing. Later that evening Ward said he saw a number of MPD cars parked at the yellow cab offices. He was certain that they were taking a statement from Buddy.

Since he was only a part-time driver, Ward said he did not return to work as a driver for about two weeks. When he did, he asked where Buddy was. He said he was told that he was dead, having been thrown out of a car on Route 55 – on the other side of the Memphis–Arkansas bridge – on the night Martin Luther King Jr was assassinated.

Ward testified that he watched the newspaper for an obituary or death notice, but there was none. Massachusetts attorney Raymond Kohlman testified that he had enquired about any death records in Memphis and the neighboring states and found that there was no record of Buddy's death.[47]

Though we were never able to locate with certainty the dispatcher on duty that night, one person, who Ward believed also knew what happened and who may have been the dispatcher on duty on the evening of April 4, refused to discuss the matter. This same person apparently came into a substantial amount of money after the event and bought a very expensive house, which would have certainly been way beyond both his means as a taxi driver or any apparent family resources.[48]

We had no doubt that Louie Ward was telling the truth. He had no reason to come forward at this point in time and lie. He never asked for anything, and our team concurred unanimously that he was one of the most credible witnesses we put before the jury.

The effectiveness of the cover-up of this side murder event, however, was staggering. There was no police report or statement taken from the driver, in any file, and no death record or report existed. No driver alive, except Louie Ward, remembered or was willing to talk about the incident, although Hamilton Smythe IV, the present manager of the yellow cab company, did acknowledge to Nathan Whitlock that he heard about such an event, but then quickly said only his father could comment. The father, Ham Smythe III, as noted earlier, stated that he did not believe it ever happened.

Maynard Stiles, in 1968, was a senior administrator of the Memphis Department of Public Works. In 1999, he had been retired for a number of years living outside of the city, but he readily agreed to testify about what he did early on the morning of April 5 1968.

The day after the assassination began for Maynard Stiles at 7:00 AM when his phone rang. He said MPD Inspector Sam Evans was on the other end of the phone, and he had an urgent request. He asked Stiles to send a team to completely clean up the area behind the rooming house on South Main Street. The team would work under police supervision, but the basic job was to cut the thick brush and bushes to the ground, and rake them into piles so they could be carted away. Stiles hung up and called Dutch Goodman, who he instructed to pull a team together. Willie

Crawford was recruited along with some others who began working that morning.

Stiles said that he checked on the progress in late morning, and he recalls that the job was so extensive that it took his men more than one day to complete.

So far as he was concerned, he was cooperating with the police. It was not his job to question the decision to clean up the area. For all he knew they were looking for evidence. In fact, a cardinal rule of criminal investigation was contravened. An area which was part of the crime scene was not only not sealed off preventing intrusion but also a clean-up crew was brought in for the express purpose of drastically altering the entire physical setting itself so that it could never be examined, considered, and analyzed as it was at the time of the crime.

Where potential evidence was stumbled upon or acquired it frequently was ignored or suppressed – this was the case with the two FBI 302 statements given by William Reed and Ray Hendrix, which we put into evidence. They were the two men who left Jim's Grill about 20 minutes or so before the killing and spent some time looking at James's Mustang before walking north on South Main Street. Just as they reached Vance, about two blocks away, they saw the white Mustang, driven by a dark-haired man, turn the corner in front of them. These observations, in fact, corroborated James's account of how he left the scene several minutes before the shooting in an effort to have the flat spare tire repaired. In other words, they constituted an alibi but were kept from the defense and suppressed.

Also suppressed were critical scientific reports known to the prosecution at the time. First, that the dent in the bathroom windowsill, which the state contended had been made by the murder weapon, could not have been proved to have been made by a rifle. Secondly, that the death slug removed from Dr King's body could not be linked to or matched with the rifle in evidence, and that this alleged murder weapon had failed an accuracy test on the morning after the shooting because it had never been sighted in.

Though this evidence was noted earlier, it is important to focus on it here in terms of the cover-up. Near the end of his tenure as James Earl Ray's lawyer – he was replaced by Mark Lane in 1977 – and during the early period of the investigation by the House Select Committee on Assassinations, Jack Kershaw testified that he was asked to attend a meeting in the offices of a Nashville publishing company. The meeting was held in a large conference room, and those present included author William Bradford Huie. He didn't recognize any of the other persons, but he said that two of them appeared to be government types.

He was asked to take an offer to James Earl Ray. The offer consisted of a sum of money (in this instance $50,000), parole and an opportunity for a new life if James would finally admit that he was the killer. Kershaw said he listened, challenged Huie at one point in terms of the reason behind, and the feasibility of the arrangements but agreed to take them to his client. He said James rejected the proposal out of hand.

James's brother Jerry took the stand to testify how, some time later, he was personally contacted by author Huie who made the same offer except that this time the amount of the offer had increased to $220,000. James was still having none of it.[49]

The jury heard evidence of two other more sinister cover-up efforts to put an end to James Earl Ray's protestations of innocence and request for a trial. Former congressman and HSCA King subcommittee chairman Walter Fauntroy testified that after James Earl Ray escaped with a number of other inmates in 1976, they learned that the FBI had immediately and uninvited sent a SWAT team consisting of upwards of 30 snipers to the prison. Their information was that this unit was there not to help capture Ray but to kill him. Fauntroy said that at his urging HSCA Chairman Stokes called Tennessee Governor Ray Blanton and asked him to intervene in order to save their main witness and Blanton's most famous prisoner. Blanton promptly took a helicopter to the prison and ordered the FBI out of the area, thus saving James's life, for he was captured non-violently shortly afterward.

April Ferguson who later became a federal public defender was, in 1978, Mark Lane's assistant. She testified that their office was contacted by an inmate, named Tim Kirk, at the Shelby County jail. When she and an assistant went out to interview Kirk, he told them that he had been asked by a Memphis Mob-connected topless club owner Arthur Wayne Baldwin to put out a contract on James Earl Ray. Kirk, who had some lethal connections at the Brushy Mountain Penitentiary, could have organized the hit but he became suspicious. Baldwin did not reach him that first time, and he had to return the call. When he did call back, he realized that the number was to a suite of rooms in a hotel near the Memphis airport, where a suite of rooms was kept by the local US attorney's office and the FBI and used to interview witnesses and for other purposes. He thought that he might have been set up, and so he decided to contact Ray's lawyer. Another effort to silence James was aborted.

Half a day was occupied with the testimony of Attorney William Schapp, who we qualified as an expert on government use of the media for disinformation and propaganda purposes. After providing the jury with a survey of these practices by governments throughout history in a detailed question and answer exchange, Schapp introduced the court to these practices of the United States government in other cases, or issues, where intelligence and/or national security interest were believed to be involved. A number of examples were cited. One, for example, involved a CIA propaganda story that was spread all over the world and widely believed for some four years, that Cuban troops fighting in Angola had:

1) raped Angolan women
2) were tried and convicted of these crimes
3) were executed by the victims.

In fact none of the above was true. The story was revealed by the agent who promulgated it to be false and to have been totally concocted at the CIA station in Zaire and disseminated through the extensive world-wide agency network. Schapp revealed that the agency alone – not to mention its counterparts in the rest of the American intelligence community – owned or controlled some 2,500 media entities all over the world. In addition, it has its people ranging from stringers to highly visible journalists and editors in virtually every major media organization. As we have seen and were indeed experiencing every day of the trial, this inevitably results in the suppression or distortion of sensitive stories and the planting and dissemination of disinformation.

Schapp then turned to the coverage of the King assassination and examined the extraordinary universal media hostility against Dr King when he came out against the Vietnam War, and the same reaction against his family when they decided to advocate a trial for James Earl Ray. Cited were specific examples of media distortion and blatant lies, which characterized the media coverage of the case and James Earl Ray's alleged role for over 30 years. Particular mention was made of the totally baseless *New York Times* front-page-column piece reporting on alleged investigations by the FBI, the HSCA, and the *Times* of the 1967 Alton Illinois bank robbery. This piece was far worse than distorted or slanted reporting, since the investigations did not take place and the Ray brothers were never even suspects as the *Times* article stated. It was a domestic example of the type of pure fabrication similar to the story about the Angolan rapes.

Schapp explained that a Harvard neurologist had helped him to understand the power of the neurological impact upon human cognizance, intellectual functioning, and reasoned decision making when the same story is told over and over again. That impact makes the story a kneejerk part of the people who are exposed to it. Even if they are convinced on one occasion by powerful evidence to the contrary, the next day will usually find them reverting to the long-held belief, which has became a part of themselves – often integral to their very identity. Nothing less than some sort of intense deprogramming experience with ongoing reinforcement is required.

After analyzing the powerfully comprehensive control of the media by the forces who control American public policy and examining their identical policy and coverage in terms of the assassination, the systematic brainwashing of Americans in respect of this case became abundantly clear to the court, jury, and those present. Bill Schapp's analysis and testimony highlighted the absence of the media in our courtroom. In effect by not being there, they proved his point. As noted earlier, only one local television journalist stayed.

Considering all of the aspects of the cover-up in this case, the ongoing media role is the most sinister precisely because it, if not powerfully controverted, as was done with the trial, perpetuates the lies and disinformation from one generation to the next, for all time.

The defendant's prior admissions

The defendant Loyd Jowers had made a number of admissions over the years, which, taken cumulatively, constituted powerful evidence of his knowing involvement in the assassination. A number of witnesses took the stand, each with a particular piece of the picture of Jowers's role.

Taxi diver James Milner, who met Jowers in the early 1970s, recounted how he came to work closely with Jowers during 1979 and 1980, seeing him about eight hours a day. On one occasion during this time some twenty years ago, he testified that Jowers told him that Dr King was killed not by James Earl Ray but by a law enforcement officer and that he knew all about it.

Milner said that after Jowers told him that Dr King was actually killed by a law enforcement officer, he added that "You can take that to the bank." After that admission over 20 years ago, Milner said that in 1998 he carried on a long-distance telephone relationship with his friend over a period of around three months. During these conversations, Milner testified that Jowers essentially told him what happened. Milner said he asked Jowers if he pulled the trigger, and the response was, "I was involved to a certain extent, but I did not pull the trigger." He said Jowers stated that Frank Liberto sent him a large sum of money in a produce box. He took it and put it in an old stove. Then, the man he knew as Raul picked it up. Loyd told him that the assassination was planned over two days in meetings in his cafe attended by five men – only three of whom he knew.[50]

Milner said that Jowers told him that Frank Liberto instructed him to be at his back door around 6:00 PM where he would receive a "package." He was there, heard a shot, and then took the "still smoking" rifle from his friend Earl Clark. Then, he tried to flush the cartridge shell down his toilet, but it stopped it up. When he retrieved it later that night, he threw it in the Mississippi River. The next morning, Jowers said, Raul picked up the rifle.

As noted earlier, J. J. Isabel testified confirming his earlier statement that he and Jowers each drove a chartered bus to Cleveland, shared a hotel room, and after dinner and beers (with Jowers having more than a few), sat on their beds talking. Isabel said Jowers confirmed his knowledge about Jowers's involvement in the assassination. Isabel said Jowers's response gave him pause. He dropped the subject and never raised it again.[51]

Bobbi Balfour (Betty Spates's sister, previously Smith), one of Jowers's waitresses, testified that on the morning of the day of the assassination, Jowers instructed her not to bring food upstairs in the rooming house to Grace Walden Stephens who was bedridden and recuperating from an illness. Grace and Charlie Stephens's room was right next to the one rented by James Earl Ray in mid-afternoon, and which appears to have been used by Raul for setting up James. Ms Balfour also testified that Jowers picked her up and drove her to work the next morning. On the way, she said, he told her that the police had found the murder weapon out behind the cafe.

Betty Spates's story, which first surfaced in 1992, was put into evidence as a rebuttal witness through her deposition and her earlier affidavits, in which she stated that she was standing at the back door of the cafe's kitchen around 6:00 PM on April 4 1968 when she saw Loyd running from the bushes carrying a rifle. His face was white as a sheet, and the knees of his trousers were wet and muddied. Rushing by her, she said he broke down the rifle; then wrapping it in a cloth he carried it into the grill, where he put it under the counter. For all of the intervening years, Betty Spates thought Loyd himself was the assassin because she didn't see anyone else out in the bushes.

Defense counsel Garrison attacked Spates's credibility quoting from a statement she gave to the Shelby County district attorney general's and FBI investigators, in which she denied seeing anything. She had subsequently told me that she felt threatened by the two official investigators. We intended to call defendant Jowers at this stage of the proceedings, but after the first week of the trial, his health deteriorated preventing his return to the courtroom. Consequently, we read portions of his deposition into evidence. That evidence included the statements discussed earlier that he confirmed he made in a December 16 1993 television interview with Sam Donaldson on his *Prime Time Live* program, in which Jowers admitted that he became involved in facilitating the assassination at the request of Memphis mobster Frank Liberto, to whom he owed a big favor. As noted earlier, he was told that there would be no police around and that a patsy was in place.

The most critical testimony and in terms of evidence damning admissions by Loyd Jowers came from Ambassador Andrew Young and Dexter King.[52]

Both testified that Jowers admitted being approached by Frank Liberto. Jowers would receive a lot of money, which he was to turn over to a person named Raul, who would visit him and who would leave a rifle with him.

He said these events took place, and subsequently there were meetings in his grill where the assassination was actually planned.

The testimony revealed that Jowers said that on the day, Earl Clark collected the rifle from him within an hour of the killing. The next time he saw it was when he took it from the shooter when it was still smoking after the shot.

Jowers insisted that he didn't know who was going to be killed and contended that he did not actively participate in the planning sessions.[53] Both Dexter King and Andrew Young testified that on this point, they didn't believe him. They agreed that he appeared to be an old man wanting to relieve himself of a great burden, but that he didn't quite seem able to bring himself to be completely truthful as to his role and the extent of his knowledge in front of the victim's son.

The interview session conducted by Dexter King and Andrew Young was tape-recorded, and that recording authenticated by Ambassador Young was introduced into evidence in its entirety.

Damages

The King family did not bring the action for the purpose of obtaining a large damage award against Loyd Jowers or his co-conspirator agents of the City of Memphis, State of Tennessee, and the Federal Government. The family decided to request only nominal damages in the amount of $100 toward the funeral expenses of their loved one. Three of the five family members testified with great dignity. Mrs King, Dexter, and Yolanda, each in her or his own special way, told the jury what it meant to lose Martin King as a husband and a father. From their perspectives, the jury and the court had a unique opportunity to focus on the personal loss to young children of a loving, caring, and playful father, as well as the sudden absence suffered by their mother as she was traumatically separated from her lifetime partner. One began to get a glimpse of the burden of being the close family of a man, a human being, who becomes a legendary, heroic figure in life, then mythologized, and perhaps beatified if not sainted on earth. (At the time of writing, Martin King has been declared a Martyr by the Vatican – the first step toward sainthood.)

The case for the defense

Defense counsel Garrison called this case the most important litigation he had tried in his 40 years of practice. He had, however, been placed in a most difficult position by his client's admissions which were driven by a desire on the one hand to obtain immunity from prosecution (which began in 1993) and on the other to unburden his conscience in his waning years. The defense therefore took the position that Mr Jowers had no liability, but if he did, it was minuscule compared with that of the co-conspirators who were agents of the city, state and federal governments. The strategy was to minimize Jowers's involvement, and consequently, it made little sense not to acknowledge the role played by the alleged co-conspirators.

Therefore, throughout the presentation of the plaintiffs' case, defense focused on eliciting evidence from relevant witnesses on cross-examination, which tended to minimize his client's involvement though not that of the co-conspirators.

At the conclusion of the plaintiffs' case, the defense moved for a dismissal on the grounds that the plaintiffs' wrongful death action had been filed outside of the one-year statute of limitations.[54] After extensive oral argument, the judge denied the motion.

The most hotly disputed defense motion, and the last before Lewis Garrison opened his case, was for a mistrial based upon the inability of his client to attend the trial and assist with his defense due to his deteriorating health condition.[55]

The judge was unhappy with the language of a doctor's letter in support of this motion, noting that it did not explicitly state that Jowers was unable to attend court or testify. The court denied the motion for a mistrial, and the defense moved on with its case.

First, he called Reverend Samuel "Billy" Kyles. In response to questions put to him on direct examination, Reverend Kyles described his civil rights experiences in Tennessee and the events surrounding the sanitation workers' strike and Dr King's visit. He said that they were all under surveillance and he referred to the Redditt–Richmond surveillance operation which was conducted from the rear of the fire station. He said that he learned that one of the black officers (he was referring to Willie B. Richmond) engaged in that activity was so troubled by it that he became an alcoholic, left the police force, and died, implying that he committed suicide. He gave his usual account of how he went into Dr King's room about an hour before the assassination, spending the last hour of Dr King's life with him. He described their conversation or "preacher talk." He gave an emotional statement of how he had come to believe that it was God's will that he had been present when this great man died. He said, inexplicably, that Dr King did not die using drugs or from engaging in some other criminal activity but because he was there to help the garbage workers. He described how a little old lady came to one of his speeches and told him how she just wanted to shake his hand because his hand had touched Dr King. Thus, he considered himself blessed to have had this experience. When Lewis Garrison surrendered the witness, Kyles was riding high with his credibility intact.

I had decided that my associate Juliet Hill-Akines would conduct the cross-examination of Reverend Kyles. She focused on how he drew pleasure from women, such as the one he described, reaching out to him, and seeking to touch his hand. Then, her questions dealt with Willie B. Richmond indicating not only that he was alive but also that he had testified at this trial. Kyles was surprised. She then walked him through a previous statement Kyles had made which refutes his claim to have been in Dr King's room. He had said he simply knocked on the door, had a few words with Dr King who then closed the door, and Kyles walked over to the balcony some way down from the room.

Reverend Kyles said that statement was simply not true. He could not explain, however, why Richmond would lie about these simple facts. Then Juliet played a videotape of a speech he had given on the thirtieth anniversary of the assassination. In it, he described again how he spent Dr King's last hour on earth with him and Reverend Abernathy in room 306. Then, as he described how he and Dr King stood together on the balcony at the railing, he seemed to get carried away as he said ". . . only as I moved away so he could have a clear shot, the shot rang out . . ." The jury and the judge looked stunned.

Juliet played the tape three times, so it became very clear that Kyles had, in fact, somehow admitted stepping aside so that a shooter could get a clear shot. When she asked him who he was thinking about getting a clear shot, he said he supposed it would have been James Earl Ray. At one point during cross-examination, Kyles mouthed silently to her "You should be ashamed of yourself." When he was dismissed, he walked behind the attorneys' chairs and asked Garrison – "What did you get me into?" Garrison replied "I just called you as a witness." Yolanda King was in court that day and had the very uncomfortable experience of sitting through Reverend Kyles's testimony.

Next, the defense called Frank Warren Young from the Shelby County criminal clerk's office. He brought with him the original transcript of the record of the guilty plea hearing and authenticated it so that it could be placed in evidence and in the record. The defense thus ensured that James Earl Ray's guilty plea was in evidence for the jury's review.

On cross-examination, I asked him to look at the first pages of the transcript and observe whether or not James Earl Ray had been put under oath by Judge Preston Battle (required practice during a guilty plea hearing). He had not been sworn. I next asked him to read James's interruption of the proceedings when he stated that he had never agreed with Ramsey Clark or J. Edgar Hoover that there had been no conspiracy and he did not want to do so now.[56]

As their next witness, the defense called former MPD lieutenant Eli Arkin. Arkin, who was a senior intelligence officer, confirmed that he had picked up Detective Redditt at the fire station and eventually, after the meeting in the MPD Central Headquarters, on director Holloman's instructions, took him to his home. Shortly after they arrived, the assassination took place.[57] Eli Arkin's confirmation of the presence and activity of the 111th Military Intelligence Group in Memphis added to the defense's mitigating claim.

The first wife of Lieutenant Earl Clark, Rebecca Clark, was called as the next defense witness. Prior to her testimony, she had asked for a copy of her deposition to review and was provided with it. Mr Garrison established that her husband kept a large collection of guns and that he was an expert shot. She said that she got off work at 4:00 PM that day and that it took her about 10 to 15 minutes to get home, so she arrived home around 4:15 PM. She then said she believed that her husband got home about an hour or so later and lay down for a nap which lasted 30 to 40 or 45 minutes until a report came over the police walkie talkie radio, which he had left on the dining room table for her to monitor.

When word of the assassination came through, she woke him up, and he told her to go and get his clean uniform from the cleaners before they closed. She set out for the cleaners which was about 15 minutes away, and he took a bath. When she returned, he left.

Attorney Garrison raised the fact that the kind of walkie talkie she was talking about was not available during those times. She couldn't comment on that. On cross-examination, I came back several times to the question of whether she was lying to protect her dead divorced husband and her children. She denied that she would lie for that purpose. One major problem with her alibi for her former husband was the timing of the events, and the conflict between her earlier recollections in her deposition of April 1999 and her current story.

In her deposition, she had clearly stated that she usually worked until 3:00 PM, but on that day, she worked until 4:00 PM. She also stated that her husband came home "fairly soon" after she had arrived. She set the time of his unannounced arrival at some 10 to 15 minutes after her own. She also indicated that he was not asleep very long when the announcement came on the radio. In court, she now remembers that he could have arrived as much as 45 minutes after her, putting his arrival at or around 5:00 PM, and that his nap could have lasted for quite some time – an hour or more.

It appeared to me that she was trying to cover up for an unexplained period of an hour, which may have meant both she and her husband came home earlier and that he left well before the assassination.

Attorney Garrison read portions of a "John Doe November 5 1999" telephone deposition into the record. The witness, who contacted Garrison, declared that he was involved in the assassination of Martin King, and that he was present when a $400,000 contract for the killing was put out by Walter Reuther, the leader of the United Auto Workers' Union. He contended that Reuther was being pressed by Hubert Humphrey and Lyndon Johnson because of Dr King's anti-war activity, and that Carlos Marcello cooperated but was not directly involved, and James Earl Ray was not even there, having left for Atlanta.[58]

The defense had subpoenaed Marvin Glankler, the investigator in charge of the Shelby County district attorney general's last investigation, and retired judges James Beasley and Robert Dwyer who were assistant attorneys general in 1968, prepared the state case against James Earl Ray and in Beasley's case actually presented the state's evidence to the guilty plea jury. Garrison said that initially they told him they would be pleased to take the stand and defend their work and the case against James.

By early December, close to the time they were due to take the stand, their positions had changed. A motion to quash the subpoena was filed on their behalf by the state attorney general. The motion was argued out of the presence of the jury; the judge denied the motion and ordered the former judges to appear.[59]

Garrison attempted repeatedly to draw information from Glankler on the attorney general's investigative report, which was published in 1998. He was met with continual objections from the Tennessee assistant attorney general who was there to represent the state, the Shelby County district attorney general, and, of course, Investigator Glankler. The state lawyer was up and down like a jack in the box. His intention was clearly to limit Glankler's testimony to the maximum extent possible. He basically contended that the report should speak for itself, and since Glankler did not write it, he could not comment on it. Garrison was able to extract the facts that the district attorney general's office began an investigation in 1993 and ended it in 1998, that he, Glankler, was the chief investigator, and that the investigation may have included statements taken from some 40 witnesses.

On cross-examination, I took a different tack. I asked Glankler if he had interviewed 25 named witnesses, the evidence from all of whom had already been heard by the jury. I asked him about each one in turn. Of the 25, he had interviewed only two. He had not even heard of most of the others. The negative impact on the credibility of the district attorney general's investigation and report was evident in the expressions of disbelief on the jurors' faces.

The defense next called LaVada Whitlock Addison, Nathan Whitlock's mother, and, as noted earlier, she testified in detail about the time in her cafe when her regular customer Memphis produce man Frank Liberto told her that he had arranged the killing of Martin Luther King. She said that she ran the little pizza parlor – which was between Liberto's home and his warehouse in the Scott Street market – between 1976 and 1982. On the day in question, she said they were sitting together at two tables pushed together, and something came on the television about Dr King. (The congressional hearings were being televised in 1978.) Liberto leaned forward toward her and said, "I had Dr Martin Luther King killed." She said she recoiled and told him, "Don't be telling me anything like that. I don't want to hear it. I don't believe it anyway." She said this was the only time he ever mentioned it to her though she saw him many times afterward.

Attorney Garrison read large portions of James Earl Ray's deposition into the record, which basically set out James's story and the history of his involvement from the time he escaped from prison in 1967.

After the Spates rebuttal evidence, discussed earlier, was concluded, defense counsel Garrison renewed his motion for a mistrial, based upon his client's absence from court. This was denied promptly, and he then filed a motion for directed verdict, which he argued was justified because the plaintiffs did not meet the required burden of proof. I argued that the evidence adduced on behalf of the plaintiffs was overwhelming and that though we had met the standard we decided not to move for a directed verdict in the case because we wanted it to go to the jury. The judge denied the motion, and closing arguments began.

Meanwhile, the attorney general appealed Judge Swearingen's denial of the motion to quash the subpoenas served upon judges Beasley and Dwyer to the court of appeals and the court promptly overturned the ruling and ordered the subpoena quashed. Judges Beasley and Dwyer were spared the inevitably uncomfortable task of defending the state's investigation and justifying certain representations made on March 10 1969 to the guilty plea hearing jury.

The closing arguments

Over a period of nearly two hours, I took the jury through the evidence, step by step, reminding them that the King family had brought this trial because the initial investigation was badly flawed and had not been remedied by any subsequent official local or federal investigation. I reminded them that the truth had been covered up for 31 years but that in this courtroom, even though the media had been absent most of the time and the outside world had not learned about the evidence or even heard about the trial, the truth had been revealed. As Martin King had said, "Truth crushed to earth shall rise again" – and so it did.

During the last half-hour, with the use of computer graphics, we took the jury through the last 21 minutes of Dr King's life and the 11 minutes immediately following the killing. Lewis Garrison contended that if his client had any liability, he was at worst only a small cog in the conspiracy which took Martin Luther King's life. He tried to focus the jury's attention on the city, state, and federal government as well as on James Earl Ray.

The jury instructions

By late morning, we were finished and the judge instructed the jury. He gave the standard instructions, defining direct and circumstantial evidence, advising them that they and only they must decide questions of fact and how much weight to put on the various aspects of evidence which had been laid before them, while he would determine the law. He reminded them that they must find for the plaintiffs if they found that the plaintiffs' allegations were proved by a preponderance of the evidence, in other words if the allegations were more likely true than not. On the issue of damages, he reminded them that they were bound by the parties' stipulation that the damages should not exceed $100 – a payment toward the funeral expenses.

Finally, he told them that he had prepared a jury verdict sheet, which contained those questions to be answered.

1) Did the defendant Loyd Jowers participate in a conspiracy to do harm to Dr Martin Luther King? If yes,
2) Did you also find that others including governmental agencies were parties to this conspiracy as alleged by the defendant?
3) What is the total amount of damages to be awarded to the plaintiffs?

The case went to the jury just before lunch.

The verdict

It took the jury about one hour to decide. After nearly four weeks of trial and some 70 witnesses they found that:

1) YES – Loyd Jowers participated in a conspiracy to do harm to Martin Luther King.
2) YES – Others including governmental agencies were parties to this conspiracy as alleged by the defendant.
3) The total damages to be awarded to the plaintiffs is $100.

The judgment

The issue of comparative liability was agreed to rest with the judge. Based on the evidence before him, Judge Swearingen apportioned liability as follows:

30 PERCENT – defendant Loyd Jowers
70 PERCENT – all other co-conspirators.

9

THE AFTERMATH AND A POST-TRIAL SUMMARY

The media

For a period of about 12 hours, there was a window of factual coverage of the results. The verdict was reported, however irregularly, around the world. Mr Garrison and I spoke to the media for the first time, and I participated in the family's press conference on December 8 at the King Center. All four family members addressed the media including Bernice who spoke out for the first time. Her eloquence was moving. Here, at last, was a family who had finally had an enormous burden lifted from them. Each family member expressed this relief as well as their feeling of being vindicated for their struggle to bring out the truth. In response to the questions about what was next, so far as we were concerned that was up to others. The truth had emerged from the trial. A jury had effectively exonerated James Earl Ray and found that a conspiracy existed which included agents of the City of Memphis, the State of Tennessee, and the Government of the United States. In fact, the judge had apportioned 70 percent of the liability on those official co-conspirators. We doubted that there would be any prosecutions – although even in the year 2000, some could be developed – and we also had little expectation that the attorney general's report would embrace and reflect the truth which had been revealed by the trial.

In a private very emotional meeting, the family expressed their gratitude to me for the long-term effort I began in 1978. I commended their courage for unlike the other prominent American families victimized by assassination, Martin King's family did not recede into the shadows and refuse to ask questions. Instead, they came forward even though they were attacked and maligned and suffered financially as a result of their quest and courage.

The spins

Within 24 hours, the mighty Wurlitzer of the powerful private and public interests involved was in full volume. Analytical pieces suddenly appeared criticizing the judge, the defense counsel, and the jury. The trial was diminished in importance, and journalists blandly asserted that nothing had changed. To counter the inevitable spins, the closing arguments and the summary of the plaintiffs' case went up on the web site of the King Center, and arrangements were made to put the entire transcript on the site (thekingcenter.com).

A leading publicist of the government's position and the official line, Gerald Posner, was everywhere at once. On one television show after another and with a nationally syndicated op piece, he insisted that the King family had been duped and that the trial was a farce. I was able to publish a strong rebuttal of his banal generalizations only in the *Washington Post*. The *New York Times* allowed me 200 words to respond to a 1,000-word piece by a former US assistant attorney general.

What was ludicrous about all of the criticism, of course, was the fact that none of the critics had attended the trial or heard the evidence. Of all the media professionals commenting on the case, only Wendell Stacey, the local Memphis anchorman, at the risk of his job, attended court every day. At the end, he repeatedly said he was totally convinced that the jury was right and that he had never been so ashamed of his profession.

Though the lockstep media conformity was expected by all of us, it was nevertheless sad to see it at work again. In the end, the predictable performance of the media had been heralded by the testimony of William Schapp as he laid out the practice of government manipulation and use of the media for propaganda purposes. The King assassination and the search for the truth were a national security matter, and as such the mass, and reputable fringe, media would be effectively controlled in all aspects of coverage.

New evidence

After the trial, Mrs Clark's alibi for her husband Earl began to fall apart. Two critical aspects of her story were more closely examined. Our post-trial research on the availability of walkie talkies for MPD officers in 1968 confirmed that there were no walkie talkies (as we know them) in use at that time. There was, however, a much bulkier unit, which was issued to a limited number of officers, and Lieutenant Clark could have had such a unit. It has alternatively been described as being the size of two bricks standing side by side or a lunchbox. Former police officer and private investigator Jim Kellum told me that that unit might well have been referred to as a "walkie talkie." We had to clear up the point if at all possible.

I asked Reverend Jim Douglas, an Alabama minister who sat through the entire trial taking copious notes, if he would mind going to Memphis and having a non-threatening word with Mrs Clark now that the trial was over. He agreed and on a weekend in February 2000 he visited with her in her home. She confirmed that the "walkie talkie" her husband had which had been sitting on their dining room table was a little larger than a television remote control. No such unit of that size was in use at the time by the MPD.

In her deposition taken on April 23 1999, over seven months prior to the date she testified at trial, Mrs Clark stated that on the afternoon of April 4 1968, she arrived home from work at about 4:15 PM, and her husband arrived a short time later – perhaps around 4:30 PM. She said he lay down to take a nap on the living room sofa and asked her to monitor the police "walkie talkie" which was on the dining room table. She said he was not asleep for very long, perhaps 30 or 40 minutes, when the word came over the radio that Dr King had been shot. She woke him instantly, and he told her to go and get his clean uniform from the cleaners (they used Dent Cleaners, on Broad Street, which gave MPD officers a discount) while he took a bath. She said that she drove the 15 to 20 minutes to the cleaners from her home on Barron, picked up the uniform and returned home, the whole trip taking about half an hour. Her husband then left in the MPD car in which he had driven home. She said he would not have been home over an hour and a half.

Toward the end of this deposition, Mrs Clark stated that she could not be 100 percent certain that she woke up her husband as a result of hearing about the assassination rather than because she heard him being called back to work.

The obvious problem posed by Mrs Clark's statements at the deposition is that if one sticks to her time frame, she would have had to have heard the news of the assassination being broadcast over the "walkie talkie" sometime between 5:00 and 5:15 PM, an hour or so before it actually occurred.

Since prior to testifying at the trial, Mrs Clark asked for and was given a copy of her deposition to review, she could have become aware of this one-hour discrepancy. Her initial story would have had the assassination taking place around 5:15 PM rather than 6:01 PM. This clearly would not do, so, in her testimony at trial, she changed the time.

She extended her husband's arrival to about one hour after she came in at 4:15 PM, and she lengthened the nap to a full 45 or 50 minutes. She could not, however, change the time when she said she awakened Lieutenant Clark because that was determined by the known time of the assassination, and when it came over the air – between 6:05 PM and 6:10 PM. Thus, she could not alter the time when she left the house for the cleaners, which must have been between 6:10 PM and 6:20 PM depending upon her state of readiness.

Given the time it would have taken her to drive to the cleaners – 15 to 20 minutes – she would have arrived at the earliest around 6:30 PM to pick up Lieutenant Clark's uniforms. When speaking with Jim Douglas, she confirmed that she did arrive at the cleaners around 6:30 PM. After the trial, I had an opportunity to speak with D.V. Manning, a long-time friend of Mr Dent, the owner of the cleaning establishment, who eventually bought the business from his old friend. Mr Manning said that the cleaners usually closed no later than 6:00 PM. Then, I spoke with staff who were on duty on April 4 only to learn that in fact they went home at 4:00 PM that day.

Next I spoke with Mr Dent's daughter, Ms Tillie Folk, who remembered her father calling right after the assassination and telling them not to go anywhere because of the riots that were certain to occur. This call was, of course, shortly after 6:00 PM. She said that her father usually had dinner with the family at 6:30 PM. That night was no exception. Since the shop was about 15 to 20 minutes from his house, Mr Dent was sitting down having dinner by 6:30 PM. According to Mrs Clark's story, she would have arrived at the cleaners sometime between 6:20 and 6:30. Dent Cleaners would have been closed when she arrived, and she would not have been able to get the clean uniforms for her husband. Mrs Clark's story is untenable.

Eventually I located and spoke with Tom Dent, Ms Folk's brother, who was also in Memphis on the day of the assassination. Tom Dent, who lives and teaches school on the island of Guam, put the last nail in the coffin of Mrs Clark's alibi for her husband. In two lengthy telephone conversations, March 31 and April 21 2000, Mr Dent confirmed that in fact, he was working in the store on the day of the assassination. He said that earlier in the day his father was in and out, but that afternoon, he was in the dry cleaning section in the back of the shop. Tom Dent said that he knew Lieutenant Earl Clark, and in fact the MPD officer was himself in the shop during the afternoon of April 4, for about 20 minutes. Tom Dent said that Earl Clark came in sometime between 4:30 and 5:00 PM and went into the back to have a word with his father. He said that his father, who was a hunter, sometimes provided bullets to Clark and other officers. Apparently, the elder Mr Dent knew a man who loaded bullets for them. The inventory included 30.06 cartridges. He said hello to Clark as the officer entered and went in the back to see his father. Clark was definitely not there to pick up his dry cleaning. He remembers him leaving sometime after 5:00 PM, and believes he drove off in a white private car. He was wearing a gray uniform shirt and trousers.

Tom Dent said that he left the shop at 5:50 PM that evening and went home. He said it was his father's practice to lock the doors every evening at 6:00 PM. He went on serving anyone in the store but let no one else in. That evening, he said, his father followed him home – it was about a 15 to 20 minute drive – and arrived around 6:40 PM.

Why would Rebecca Clark and presumably her husband Earl have had to concoct the false alibi story if Earl Clark was not deeply involved in the assassination of Martin King? If Judge Swearingen had remained on the bench, we would have sought a hearing on the charge of perjury. With him in retirement, this seemed futile, though we resolved to depose Mrs Clark one more time.

This deposition took place in Memphis on April 27 2002. The day before, I attended Mrs King's 75th birthday celebration which took place on board the Henry C. Grady paddlewheel boat on the lake in Stone Mountain Natural Park, and then went on to Memphis that evening. I thoroughly enjoyed spending several hours with the entire family and was especially pleased to meet Martin's fiancée Andrea. I also appreciated spending time with Bernice, the youngest daughter. I had not had the opportunity before, never wanting to intrude on her privacy since I knew how deeply she had been affected by the loss of her father when she was three years old. Bernice, a preacher and a lawyer, is without peer when it comes to preaching. Her passion, clarity, and power ever remind me of her father. We agreed to keep in touch.

In Memphis I impulsively drove to the Ridgeway Inn where the television trial jury was housed and where Wayne Chastain and I would frequently go to respond to our thirst. I sat at our usual table and thought of the past and the long struggle for some time and then I left to begin to prepare for Mrs Clark's deposition.

The deposition began around 10.00 AM in Daniel Dillinger and Dominsky's newly merged offices at 100 North Main Street. Brian Dominsky was the court reporter and the deposition was videographed. I led Mrs Clark through the story. She had told us that her blood pressure had climbed to horrific levels after she received my subpoena. She also said that she had spoken with US Assistant Attorney Barry Kowalski, calling him at the Department of Justice after she received the subpoena. I explained to her that we were obligated to schedule this deposition because of new information. She stuck to her story except that she denied having told Reverend Jim Douglas that the police walkie talkie was the size of a television remote control. She described it as being larger and square. Somehow she had become aware that instruments of the current remote control size were not available in 1968.

When confronted with the affidavit of Thomas Dent, the son of the owner of the dry cleaners where she stated she had gone on the afternoon of April 4, she seemed disbelieving. I informed her, as noted above, that Mr Dent, whom I located on the island of Guam where he is married and teaches school, categorically stated that he was working in the dry cleaners on the day of the assassination and that he had not seen her at any time. He said he never recalled her picking up her husband's dry cleaning but that Lieutenant Clark – whom he knew – always came in himself.

Mr Dent also confirmed that his father always closed the shop promptly at 6:00 PM and that they ate together every evening around 6:30. On the evening of April 4 1968 he recalled that his father got home between 6:30 and 6:40. It was a 20-minute drive and Mr Dent stated that he left about 10 minutes before closing.

Thus it was clearly apparent that Mrs Clark's story would not hold up. Even if Mr Dent was wrong about seeing her husband in the shop around 5:00 PM, she could not have reached the cleaners while it was open. She admitted that the drive from her home to the cleaners was about 15 to 20 minutes. Mrs Clark had no explanation for the discrepancy. She simply stonewalled, saying her husband would have no reason to send her if the store was closed.

She appeared to be entirely unbelievable. Aware of this, she repeated the offer she made to Jim Douglas that she was willing to take a lie-detector test, if we would make the results public. She also named a number of policemen who were close to her husband including one who handled snakes. It occurred to us at this point that there is very good reason as to why lie-detector tests are not admissable in court. Technology now has likely developed to the point where, with state-of-the-art government-provided technical, chemical, or hypnotic assistance, she would likely be able to defeat the purpose of such a test. Her request that the results be made public were in line with such a tactic.

Our position in respect of a perjury prosecution remained unchanged. Little could be gained and the judge might well refer the matter to the Shelby County district attorney and we knew what disposition would result.

We believe that the purpose had been served. Mrs Clark had been confronted with the truth and the alibi she provided for her husband had been shown to be a tissue of lies. She was genuinely surprised when I told her that although I believed that Lieutenant Clark was deeply involved in the assassination, new information received in 2001 was leading me to conclude that he had not pulled the trigger.

Tom Dent's recollection that Earl Clark was wearing a gray uniform late in the afternoon of April 4, indeed within an hour and a half of the killing, conflicts with Jowers's statement that he remembers seeing him in a white shirt and blue trouser uniform in late morning. It should also be noted that Jowers had contended that the man who gave him the still-smoking rifle – who he thought was Clark but was not absolutely certain – was also wearing a white shirt.

This could very well mean that someone other than Clark handed over the gun to Jowers, and Clark went down over the wall. Once again, I reflected on the possibility that the shooter could have been the fifth and only unnamed person attending the planning sessions at Jim's Grill.

One woman told me about a friend of hers who was in the army in 1968, based just outside of Washington, and whose military responsibility concerned logistics, troop transportation, and movements. The inform-ant, who provided her full name and details, told me that her friend revealed to her that on the morning of April 4 1968 his unit was ordered to be ready to transport considerable numbers of soldiers into the capital that evening. When Dr King was killed, they were in fact at the ready and moved quickly into Washington in anticipation of turbulence. After-ward, of course, the friend realized that on the morning of April 4 the army was aware of the fact that Dr King was going to be assassinated and had decided to order preparedness for the inevitable riots. I asked the lady to ask her friend if he would talk with me. He refused. He had no wish to disrupt his present job or to court any possible notoriety.

What we now know

So, with the trial, and the information received in the aftermath of the trial, I believe it useful to summarize what we now know.

Martin King stayed around the motel all day. There were various sessions with the Invaders and others without them. Martin went down to his brother A. D.'s room, 201, at one point in the late afternoon, and they called and spoke to their mother. He went back up to his room between 5:40 PM and 5:45 PM to prepare for the meal at Reverend Kyles's house. At one point he asked Ralph to call Mrs Kyles to enquire what they would be eating. Around 5:45 or 5:50 PM, Andy Young would emerge from his room and put his coat on as Bevel and Orange were tussling, Jesse Jackson was out of his room, 305, and down in the parking area, for a time standing near the swimming pool, occasionally glancing at his watch. Reverend Kyles was going around from room to room for a while, even for some reason entering 307, which had been abandoned by Dorothy Cotton, Martin's assistant, about an hour and a half earlier. Eventually, after having a quick word with Martin at the door of room 306, he would walk to the north end of the balcony and wait.

Elsewhere at the motel, *New York Times* reporter Caldwell was in his room, 215, at the lower level; Dorothy Cotton had gone to the airport earlier in the afternoon, leaving her room, 307. The Invaders milled about but some were talking in their two rooms, 315 and 316. As the afternoon drew to a close, the Justice Department's Community Relations Specialist James Laue was about. An NBC reporter, Jean Smith, also decided to leave earlier that afternoon, and another unknown black guest with a considerable amount of luggage was preparing to leave. He would put in a call to Yellow Cab and ask for a driver to take him to the airport.

Frank Liberto remained at his Scott Street market produce warehouse during the afternoon. Late in the afternoon, between 4:45 PM and 5:00 PM, he would take two telephone calls, one right after another, apparently from Earl Clark who may have made them from the rear of Dent Cleaners. These were the phone calls overheard by John McFerren as he completed his shopping for the day at LL& L, Liberto's warehouse.

We now know that it was not possible that Earl Clark went home that afternoon for any extended period, if at all, despite the desperate and perhaps understandable attempts of his former wife to shield herself and her family from the stigma surrounding the possibility of her husband's involvement in the assassination. We now know what he actually did on the afternoon of April 4.

It is likely that he left a rifle up in room 5-B of the rooming house with Raul. The rooming house registration book has disappeared, making it impossible to see if there were any other rooms let out during that week. When, at the television trial, I questioned the MPD officer (Glyn King) who inspected it shortly after the assassination about why he had not taken it into evidence, he simply said he did not know. Clark and/or the fifth person who in all likelihood was also an MPD sharpshooter descended the back staircase and one of them was fleetingly seen going down the stairs by Grace Walden Stephens who was lying on her bed looking through the opening in the door. Clark and his colleague probably entered the brush behind the rooming house no later than 5:45 PM, making their way very far forward to a previously chosen spot on the north side of the lot, some feet back from the wall. They were eventually joined by Loyd Jowers shortly after getting settled. They knelt on the ground still soggy from the previous night's downpour and watched and waited.

James was out of the rooming house most of the afternoon having been told by Raul that he expected some gun dealers to come late in the afternoon, and he wanted to see them by himself. After returning with the binoculars, James left, went outside, and ate a hamburger. He walked around for a while and then went to the Chisca Hotel for some ice cream. He came back in around 5:00 PM, or a little earlier, and Raul told him to go to a movie but to leave the car since he would need it later. James went downstairs, walked around and sat in the car for a while and eventually decided to have the flat spare tire repaired just in case Raul had any problem. (That morning, he had changed the right rear tire, which was getting flat, putting on the spare.) Raul remained in the rooming house, monitoring events. He may have intended to drive James's Mustang away himself before the shooting, ditch it somewhere, leaving the car registered to Eric Galt to be found by the police thus completing the circumstantial evidentiary case against James Earl Ray. It would eventually emerge that, as Harvey Lowmeyer, James had purchased a rifle (not the murder weapon), which would be thrown down near the scene. As John Willard he rented room 5-B in the rooming house and later bought a pair of binoculars. Finally, the car, a white Mustang, seen leaving the scene soon after the shooting, when found would be registered in the name of Eric S. Galt, the identity used for the last nine months by escaped prisoner James Earl Ray, whose print on the thrown-down rifle would reveal his true identity.

In the end, the process was somewhat delayed, and Raul probably had to leave on foot since James drove off himself to try and get the spare tire repaired, in the process almost hitting Ray Hendrix and William Reed as they walked from Jim's Grill to the Clark Hotel, as he turned right on to Vance Avenue in search of a service station.

An unnoticed MPD traffic car pulled up and stopped at the intersection with Mulberry, having been directed into position either by Raul or Clark, once Clark and the fifth man were set and the time appeared near.

Everything was in readiness. All eyes were now on the Lorraine Motel, where shortly after 5:40 PM, Martin King had returned to his room and began to get ready to go to dinner, chatting all the time with his friend David.

A few doors away, between 5:45 PM and 5:50 PM, a housekeeper knocked on the door of one of the Invaders' rooms and advised them that SCLC was no longer going to pay their bills, and they would have to leave. In response to the question about who actually gave this order, she said it had been Reverend Jackson. Charles Cabbage looked over her shoulder and saw Jesse Jackson standing by the swimming pool, glancing at his watch.

Annoyed, but puzzled more than anything else, the group quickly packed up their things, including their weapons, and in disgust began to move out. Surely, their bill for that night had to have been paid. The daily checkout time did not go beyond noon, and here it was nearly 6:00 PM. So, if the bill was already paid, why were they being summarily evicted? It made no sense but if, for some reason, SCLC had decided on the spur of the moment that they didn't want their help, then that would be their loss.

As the Invaders were moving out heading toward the south stairway, Reverend Kyles approached room 306 and knocked on the door. Dr King opened it. Kyles pressed him to leave, saying that they were running late. Martin would have told him that they were almost ready. He closed the door, and Kyles walked away back near the position where he had been standing. He put his hands on the railing and waited. About this time,

Raul left the rooming house, going down the front stairs and out on to South Main Street. He must have been furious when he discovered that James's Mustang was gone, but he probably began to walk north toward the city centre.

A couple of minutes later, Dr King came out on the balcony by himself leaving the door to the room somewhat open since Ralph Abernathy had delayed for a moment saying that he had forgotten to put on aftershave lotion. Martin stood alone at the railing in front of the room waiting for his friend David and began to chat with the people down in the parking lot. Chauffeur Solomon Jones got the engine running, Bevel and Orange ended their horseplay, Marrell McCollough moved toward the north stairway. Andy Young had by now put on his coat (as he did so he was being observed by the sniper team on the roof of the Illinois Central railroad building) and Yellow Cab no. 58 driven by Buddy pulled into the driveway at just about or a little before 6:00 PM to pick up his passenger who was impatiently waiting off to the side and who immediately brought his luggage over to the rear of the cab so that it could be put into the trunk. At this moment, Ernestine Campbell, the owner of the Trumpet Hotel, had begun to drive home, proceeding west on Butler toward Mulberry with her windows closed. As she passed the motel driveway opening on Butler, she glanced to the right, and through the passenger side window, she saw Dr King standing on the balcony. When she reached Mulberry, she stopped briefly and turned right heading north.

As cabbie Buddy was helping to load the luggage, he stopped to look at the bushes across the road because some movement or something caught his eye. His passenger immediately re-directed his attention to Dr King standing on the balcony. The shooter took careful aim from a low position slightly above his target, with Jowers kneeling not far away off to the side and just behind him. It was a head shot he was looking for, and for him it was a piece of cake. He had the full target less than 200 feet away. As he squeezed the trigger, Martin King must have moved slightly. The shot rang out, striking Dr King in the lower face and jaw proceeding downward nicking the spine, and coming to rest just under the skin beneath the left shoulder blade.

The shooter handed the gun to Jowers, who raced back in through the rear door of his cafe. He was inside within 20 seconds after the shot, being confronted inside the door by Betty Spates. He would placate her, eject the shell, throw it into the toilet where it refused to flush.

He then wrapped the weapon in a tablecloth, put it under his apron and slipped into the cafe behind the counter. He accomplished this within a minute after the shot was fired. The customers were still talking, drinking and playing shuffleboard. He quickly and discreetly placed the rifle on the shelf under the counter and went over to taxi driver Harold Parker, and asked if he had heard the noise. Then, he went back behind the counter, where he remained until sheriff's deputy Vernon Dollahite burst open the door and ordered him to lock the place up and keep everyone inside. Jowers then rushed from behind the counter to lock the door.

Clark, meanwhile, had raced down over the wall to the ground and raced north on Mulberry to the intersection at Huling where he entered the MPD traffic car, which began to move west, picking him up on the north end corner, and driving away at a fast clip.

The shooter also instantly ran in the other direction, entered the alleyway between the buildings and eventually went down into the cellars. Immediately after the shot, Marrell McCollough raced up the stairs, running past Reverend Kyles to reach the prone body of Dr King to check him for life signs. As others began to gather, he responded to a question and said that the shot came from the building across the street. Jesse Jackson also began to climb up the north stairway, hesitating on the first step to take out or put something into a bag he was carrying. (The reason for, or purpose of, the bag, as well as where it came from, has never been clear.) As this was happening, Ernestine Campbell had stopped in front of the driveway and observed him. The Reverend Jackson looked up and was startled when he saw her and then turned to climb the stairs. Ernestine waited for a short while and then began to pull away glancing at the side view mirror, in which she saw tail lights and the back of Buddy's yellow cab.

Buddy had meanwhile called his dispatcher and described what he had seen including the man coming down over the wall running to the MPD traffic car.

Under some pressure from his passenger to get to the airport, he drove away out through the Butler Street exit. At the airport, after dropping off his passenger, he told fellow cab driver Louie Ward what he had seen. He then repeated the story to MPD officers who showed up to interview him. He was also interviewed that evening at the Yellow Cab company by officers and was to give a statement in the morning. He never made it. Louie Ward was told sometime later that his body was thrown out of a car on Route 55. Though it was rumored that the body was found the next morning, no record of the death exists.

Right after the shot, Earl Caldwell rushed outside and saw a figure in the bushes. Solomon Jones turned and also saw a person come down over the wall running away. He jumped inside his limousine, backed it up, and tried to give chase, driving back and forth trying to get out of the parking lot. Caldwell saw Jones trying to get out, and being blocked.

Memphis *Press Scimitar* reporter Wayne Chastain was on the scene within minutes and was one of a group gathered at the end of the driveway who heard Solomon tell about seeing a man come down from the wall after the shot.

The army photographers (elsewhere referred to as Reynolds and Norton) were operating two cameras that afternoon. At the time of the shot, one was trained on the balcony and the other spanned the parking lot up into the bushes and caught the shooter as he was lowering his rifle and Jowers running back toward the rooming house. They finished those shots and left the same way they came up, down the iron ladder on the north side of the fire station. The films were developed and handed to Colonel Downie. Realizing what they had, however, a set was quietly kept by Norton. The team on the roof of the Illinois central railroad building (elsewhere referred to as Warren and Murphy) were shocked at what they heard and saw. Initially, they believed that the other team must have jumped the gun and fired. They broke radio silence and asked for instructions. There was a period of silence, and then they were ordered to disengage. They packed up, went down from the roof the same way they came up, by the stairs, then headed west across the railroad trails to the river where they took a boat upstream to an appointed spot. They sank the boat and got into a car that was waiting to take them back to Camp Shelby.

MPD policemen saturated the area in force within minutes of the shooting. They advanced, wearing white uniform shirts and blue trousers.

It can be presumed that all of the other units of the task force wrapped up their activity after the shooting, and withdrew from the area. There continued to be a military intelligence, FBI, and MPD presence at the hospital and in the city as turbulence was expected.

Then, within about eight minutes after the shot, police barricades were set across the Butler and Huling intersections with Mulberry. At various times throughout the day, Bell South Telephone repairman Hasel Huckaby noticed a man hanging around Huling. He apparently had gone into the building adjoining the rooming house, and was seen by Olivia Catling running out of the alleyway on to Huling, jumping into a Chevrolet car, and driving away at high speed. She noticed that he turned left on Mulberry and went north, passing right in front of her and her children standing on the corner. He also passed directly in front of the unconcerned MPD officers manning the barricade. Soon after, a fireman standing on the sidewalk next to the wall, who may have been walking along Mulberry at the time of the shooting, yelled to a police officer nearby that the shot came from the bushes.

James Earl Ray first heard the sirens as he waited to be helped at the service station. Feeling uneasy and impatient as it became obvious that he was not going to be waited on anytime soon he began to drive back to South Main Street, where he intended to leave the car for Raul. As he reached the area, he found it swarming with police and was diverted away. He didn't need any encouragement to leave. He was an escaped convict and being around police made him nervous. He headed south through Mississippi toward Atlanta. On the way, he heard on his car or some other radio when he stopped, that Dr King had been shot and they were looking for a white man in a white Mustang.

Inspector N. E. Zachary raced from headquarters to the crime area and took control of the bundle which, with other evidence, was turned over to the FBI for prompt transportation to their laboratory. The FBI moved in quickly and in force and effectively began to monitor the investigation. Dr Martin Luther King Jr was rushed to St Joseph's Hospital where he was pronounced dead within the hour.

10

A VISION UNTO DEATH AND A
TRUTH BEYOND THE GRAVE

In order to fully comprehend the significance of the life, thought, and work of Martin Luther King Jr and the profound enormity of his loss, it is vital to consider his vision of the human condition – not only its vast potential, but the gradual dehumanization which he saw as the consequence of the dominance of western materialism. He was convinced that the values of love and caring, which had forever underpinned humane civil societies, were in decline in his native land. The dominion of materialism had virtually excluded spirituality or cleverly diverted an unconscious yearning for a spiritual connection into an insatiable quest for money, which sometimes went hand in hand with burgeoning, fashionable religious enterprises offering banal pseudo-spiritual comfort and fulfillment.

He believed this way was the slippery slope to personal and cultural self-destruction. He knew it was far easier to understand how this process could be reversed than to inspire a people to action in order to bring about necessary change. The promise of survival as a people was not enough; the values of materialism by the 1960s were all but inextricably linked to one's identity and sense of worth.

Consequently, what was required, King believed, was a fundamental change in how we viewed ourselves and our world, nothing less than an alteration of our perception of reality. To understand how difficult a task this was, I remind the reader of expert witness Bill Schapp's trial testimony on the effects of long-term neurological imprinting.

Martin King began to address these struggles with his opposition to the Vietnam War. He was in the process of expanding his efforts to transform the dominant values and belief systems, well in place by the 1960s, with the Poor People's Campaign. This campaign was to have been the first nationwide effort for people – with the most needy of them in the vanguard – to take back responsibility for their lives and begin to reweave the fabric of their families and communities so that they could once again be caring places for human beings and all other life. Considering where American society was headed in 1967, the campaign was a revolutionary undertaking comparable to that transforming change ushered in by Copernicus in the sixteenth century. When he published *Revolution of the Celestial Spheres* in 1543, it caused an historic confrontation between science and the church as to what was the more valid source of knowledge – the processes and results of scientific observation and experimentation, or divine revelation.

For thousands of years, the Judaic–Christian tradition and legacy personified God as a being living in a totally separate realm whose special attention was focused on earth and its inhabitants. The earth was believed to be the center of the universe with the sun, the planets, the stars, and the moon revolving around it. God's will was revealed to earth's inhabitants through his prophets or, in Christianity, his son Jesus. The Ptolemeic perception of the world and the universe remained the foundation of all scientific, moral and political thought and authority until only the last four hundred years.[60] The Copernican revolution, which postulated the thesis that the earth was only one of the planets revolving around the sun and that the sun itself was one of countless living stars in the universe led to a confrontation with the prevailing perception that divine revelation, not science, was the most valid source of knowledge about life and how it should be lived. The intellectual and moral authority of the church was weakened and gradually eclipsed by the elevation of materialism. Matter emerged as primary with physical measurement and only things suitable for scientific study deemed capable of providing explanations to issues, problems, or events. Scientific enquiry and reason were the fonts of all knowledge. The idea of a spiritual meaning in the universe was inevitably discarded and, along with it, non-material values, aesthetics, feelings, and other aspects of human experience.

This change reached its ultimate voice through the seventeenth-century philosopher Thomas Hobbes who maintained that absolutely nothing exists outside of matter. In tandem with the demise of spirituality and the elevation of materialism, the succeeding four hundred years of human history would witness the competition between the European materialists (often with their house religions in the forefront) and the traditional spiritualistic cultures of indigenous people in various areas of the world. The result would be the slaughter and subjugation of primitive peoples, the virtual wholesale elimination of many of their cultures, and the establishment of the religion of materialism, Christianity.

Europe's decimation of the world's tribal peoples sprawled across five continents over these five centuries, put the Europeans in possession of most of the world's material resources, and caused the deaths of hundreds of millions and the complete extinction of distinct tribal peoples. Continuing still, it constitutes the most persistent act of human destructiveness in the history of our species and the planet.

In the North American theater of this conquest, the European immigrant descendants carried the materialistic torch forward against the native Americans. Through genocidal actions, lies, broken agreements, and incarceration on reservations, tribe after tribe was subjugated in much the same fashion as was visited upon their brothers in Tasmania, Mexico, Africa, and elsewhere.

During these four hundred years, when not openly supportive of the conquest of materialism, organized religion continued to attempt to minister to a vastly less significant spiritual life whilst the increasingly mainstream secular society embraced the physical world as the primary reality and materialism as the dominant value. These values ultimately led to economic growth, and the indulgence of our physical appetites became the primary purpose of human activity. This was the antithesis of traditional eastern thought and perception – and of the early Christian church – which perceived spiritual energy as the foundation of all matter and the primary source of knowledge.

Riding the Copernican wave over the last four hundred years, economists have gradually attempted to elevate their craft to the level of pure science, focusing on the behavior of markets involving prices and flows of money which are easily measured. All values are reduced to market values and market prices. Air, water, and essentials of life provided freely by nature are valueless unless scarcity sets in. Gold, diamonds, and other precious metals, and stones which are relatively useless in sustaining life, are valued highly. The value of a human life is determined by calculating a person's lifetime earning potential. Thus, it has been said that economists know the price of everything and the value of nothing.

The state of the world that Martin King and his colleagues inherited was an increasingly dehumanized society which defined the success of human beings in terms of the amount of money they made. Life energy was devoted to and traded for the acquisition of money. The amount one had determined one's feeling of self-worth.

The seemingly insatiable quest for money and material consumption which he confronted then, and which has grown in exponential proportions today, is a consequence of a society that is incomplete and dysfunctional, which denies and coopts the spiritual side of life by allowing monetary values to become the primary foundation of cultural values and relationships.

Martin knew, as did Gandhi, that people who experience an abundance of love in their lives rarely seek comfort and meaning in compulsive, personal acquisitions. For those deprived of love, no amount of material acquisition, consumption, and indulgence can ever be enough. A world starved of love, in which human caring and the spiritual dimension are de-emphasized, will eventually become one of material scarcity, massive inequality, overly stressed environmental systems and developing social disintegration.

Any place we know? Arnold Toynbee noted that civilizations in decline were characterized by a tendency toward standardization and uniformity, in contrast to the stimulation of diversity which occurs during a growth period. As the growth of corporate power parallels the increasing dominance of materialism, the movement for community control and localization becomes the natural reaction to the process of societal dehumanization that Martin King sought to reverse. With his passing and in his absence, it would be hard to imagine a world plunging more rapidly than our own toward a globalized economy, dominated by transnational corporations committed only to profit and mass production.

Martin King did not confront globalization or a globalized economy in 1968, but he saw the foundation stones which were even then corrupting and coopting the diversity of rich local cultures, ever seeking to force localities to become dependent on global corporate entities and institutions. Underlying the Poor People's Campaign was the goal of empowering people in their communities to create a better life in balance with nature, becoming part of the wider world as zones of accountability and responsibility, which they manage themselves. He would have instinctively known that the more globalized the economy, the greater will be the dependence of local entities, and the power of central institutions.

Non nobis solum nati sumas

For him the concerns were not new. Post-Copernican materialism manifested itself in the twentieth century most visibly in the acquisition of money (Veblen's "conspicuous consumption") and the dehumanization of human beings by assessing their worth in terms of the amount of money they earn and the things they acquire. Complementing this ethos was the growth of central institutions and centralized governmental control.

In a commencement address at Lincoln University in Pennsylvania on 6 June 1961, Martin King said:

> Through our scientific genius, we have made of this world a neighborhood; now through our moral and spiritual development, we must make of it a brotherhood. In a real sense, we must all learn to live together as brothers or we will all perish together as fools. We must come to see that no individual can live alone. We must all live together; we must all be concerned about each other.

He would often take to quoting John Donne, the English poet who, railing against the natural impulses of materialism and the elevation of things over people, warned his contemporaries that "No man is an island, no man stands alone . . . Each man's death diminishes me, because I am involved with mankind . . ."[61]

Coming face to face with native American poverty in 1961 also had a profoundly depressing impact upon King. Even then, six years before he opposed the war in Vietnam, which he saw as a young materialistic civilization fighting an ancient culture, he felt a kinship and involvement with the starving indigenous people of his own land.

In twentieth-century America he saw a materially advanced technological civilization running away from, and behaving contrary to, its underlying Judaic–Christian heritage and culture. He said we had put guided missiles in the hands of misguided men and, like Thoreau, he believed we had developed improved means to reach an unimproved end.

He was right, of course. In the post-Second World War world, realpolitik, the political brother of materialism, ruled the day. The entire German intelligence apparatus under Hitler was assimilated into the American intelligence establishment and set the tone for much of the United State's Cold War anti-Soviet policies. War criminal Nobusuke Kishi, the former minister of munitions in Tojo's war cabinet, was put in as Japan's prime minister in 1957, and the CIA financed and firmly planted one-party rule in Japan which legitimated Japan's role as a satellite of the United States. Rather than liberating colonized peoples around the world, as promised, in national mass movements of liberation in Indochina, Malaya, and Indonesia against the French, British, and Dutch, the Americans turned up on the side of European imperialism.

In South Korea, a brutal dictatorial government was set up and defended by the US government. From 1961 to 1993, the Americans supported the regimes of three army generals. During the 1980s, two senior CIA officials were sent as successive ambassadors. Only the actions of the Korean people themselves through demonstrations and street confrontations in 1987 finally brought democracy to the fore. The eventual prosecution and conviction on grounds of sedition, state terrorism, and corruption of two surviving dictators received only minimal coverage in the United States media. The post-war legacy that caused Martin King to accuse his government of cultural betrayal included the following legacy of American dictatorial support:

1. Chiang Kai-shek and his son Chiang Ching-kuo in Taiwan. (Taiwan started to democratize only in the 1980s after the Carter administration had broken relations with it.)
2. Ferdinand Marcos in the Philippines (brought down by Corazon

Aquino and her People Power movement after Presidents Ronald Reagan and George Bush had hailed him as a democrat).

3. Ngo Dinh Diem (assassinated on American orders), General Nguyen Khanh, General Nguyen Cao Ky, and General Nguyen Van Thieu in Vietnam.

4. General Lon Nol in Cambodia (and eventually Pol Pot and the Khmer Rouge).

5. Marshal Pibul Songgram, Sarit Thanarat, Praphas Charusathien, and Thanom Kittikachorn in Thailand.[62]

6. General Suharto in Indonesia.[63]

This legacy in East Asia was mirrored in our own hemisphere where dictators and oligarchs fronting for American corporations were put in power and maintained often by the most brutal state terroristic acts including the use of death and torture squads in the Dominican Republic, Guatemala, El Salvador, Panama, Haiti, Chile, Bolivia, Argentina and Uruguay. It is not necessary to detail here these extensive covert operations, most of which have been hidden from the people who pay for them, the American citizens. Suffice it to say that the post-1945 worldwide satellite system of states which it has constructed and sustained on authoritarian foundations is remarkably similar to that of the "evil empire" – the old Soviet Union. If some critics, like historian Paul Kennedy, are correct, the effects of "imperial overstretch" could ultimately bring upon America the same fate as befell the USSR.

In 1968, the consequences of these post-war policies and covert operations were only gradually becoming apparent. The economic effects of facilitating the development of client states like Japan would slowly hollow out America's industrial and manufacturing base, but in a development much more sinister to the nation's democratic institutions, post-war America began to breed a military establishment which would gradually grow beyond civilian control. By the year 2000, the pre-1960 warning of President Dwight Eisenhower about the power of the military-industrial complex was all too real. Martin King saw it as violating Americans' cultural heritage by making us the greatest purveyors of violence on the planet. In fact, in our lifetimes, the American military establishment has virtually become an autonomous system. It is today an entirely mercenary – voluntary – force increasingly separate from all but the transnational corporate interests it protects.

The Pentagon sets its own agenda in collaboration with its transnational corporate masters. Gone is the older notion that the military is only one of several means that a democratic government uses to implement its policies. As their size and prominence grow, the armed forces of any empire tend to overshadow and displace other instruments of foreign policy. Militarism rules abroad and sets the tone at home.

But there is a cost, not only to democracy but to the existence of the empire itself. The Soviet experience is instructive. The collapse of the USSR occurred because the collective costs of the Cold War finally overwhelmed its productive capacities. The arms race with the United States, an unwinnable war in Afghanistan and the cost burden of their Eastern European satellite states proved to be unsustainable. In Martin King's last year the demands of the Vietnam War made it impossible for the military to put down a serious domestic insurrection. Thirty-two years later, having spent $5.5 trillion in developing a nuclear arsenal, the military and its corporate beneficiaries, in a post-Cold War period of peace, are relentlessly pressing for the construction of a Star Wars defense umbrella even to the absurd point of jeopardizing our nuclear disarmament treaty arrangements.

For the last two years, the defense budget has risen drastically with substantial funds earmarked for new weapons development and purchase. In 2000, the Pentagon spent $310 billion which was more than the world's next ten largest militaries combined. The first billion-dollar cost overrun occurred in 1969 on the Air Force's C-5A plane. Billion-dollar overruns are now commonplace.[64] How can this be in a time of peace? Special interest control once again is evident in the fact that defense contractors are amongst the largest political contributors. This is despite the fact that Russia has cut its military budget to $65 billion and reduced its army from 5 million to 1 million.

This enormous US public expenditure is carried out, incredibly, without the Pentagon being able to pass a basic audit which is required of every corporation. The books are in such a mess that no one is able to trace the expenditure of billions of dollars.

This overall Pentagon scenario further illustrates the virtual autonomy of the military in contemporary American society. Health and welfare programs receive ten percent of the discretionary budgetary funds, education receives six percent while the defense budget consumes fifty percent of the total. There is no rational justification for this state of affairs other than the fact that it is driven by the greed of the defense contract conglomerates. In Martin King's time, Vietnam made guns and butter impossible. Now in peacetime only corporate greed prevents the people from receiving basic essential services.

Such greed and hubris may well be the final straw which causes the American empire to unravel and the entire system to full apart. The growth of militarism, as Martin King prophesied, may finally cause the end of democracy in America, with the unraveling ultimately resulting from an economic collapse spurred on by the exploitative hegemony called globalization by which America seeks to impose its model on the major economies of the world – a model in which unbridled, non-value-producing speculators thrive and consumerism is a sacred activity. Indeed in late 2002 we began to see all credibility and legitimacy stripped away from the American system of capitalism. The legacy and fruits of greed and the corruption of major corporate executives are obvious in the demise, disgrace, and fall of pillar after pillar of the corporate structure. The fates of Enron, Tyco, and WorldCom are there for all to see and unfortunately feel as masses of middle-class Americans see their savings and pensions disappearing.

Though he could not have predicted the details of the demise of democracy and the ultimate alienation of America from its cultural and spiritual roots, as well as the consequences of its Cold War policies upon the nation and its system of government, Martin King instinctively knew that the only alternative to disaster was to promote the perception of the oneness of humankind over the public policies of the nation.

Early on, Martin King, like his mentor Mohandâs Gandhi, developed a world view, turning the global neighbourhood made possible by technological advances in transportation and communications into a brotherhood. This theme ran throughout his speeches over the last eight years of his life. [65]

He knew that if the torch of brotherhood were taken up, its bearers would face hatred like they had never known. So, he urged his followers not to hate those who hated them, for hate, he said, was too great a burden to bear.

Whilst disagreeing with Algerian psychiatrist Frantz Fanon's acceptance of violence as necessary in the context where Fanon lived and worked (articulated in his seminal work *The Wretched of The Earth*) King agreed that the challenge was not to turn new, emerging societies into mirror reflections of Europe or the United States, not even ideal reflections. Neither was it desirable to imitate institutions which had been derived from those models. Rather, he argued, new concepts must be advanced and a new man brought forward – one who embraced the brotherhood of all.

In order for this to occur, he said, these courageous pioneers would have to suffer being called social misfits or as he put it "maladjusted." He said that concerning certain values and practices of the existing social order, and in particular the growth of militarism, he was proud to be maladjusted and he called upon all people to become maladjusted. He said he refused to adjust to a socio-economic order which deprived the many of necessities and allowed luxuries for the few. He refused to adjust to the madness of militarism and the self-perpetuating use of violence in the development of the American empire. He refused to adjust to an economic system in which people had become objects – things used in pursuit of riches by others and disposed of when no longer needed. Long before globalization was in mode he knew that a global system, dreamed of by corporate imperialists, would harmonize standards across the globe down to the lowest comment element. Social responsibility would be regarded as inefficient in a global free market, and demands for a living wage would be a targeted source of inefficiency and purged wherever possible.

As to the conventional thinking and practices on these issues, he was indeed proud to be maladjusted. He spoke a truth unto death echoing the wisdom and experience of the ancients, that we exist not for ourselves alone.

Disciple and master

Firm in his belief in a social order which put more value on the happiness of human beings than on the acquisition of riches, King gradually
embraced a combination of the Christian doctrine of love with Gandhi's
method of non-violence as a potent weapon for oppressed people seeking
freedom.

Martin King may never have known or appreciated that his actual
degree of his kinship with Gandhi went far beyond "method." Gandhi
admitted that he transformed his life and thought after reading the critical
analysis of Victorian political economy (the economy of a state and its
citizens) by John Ruskin. Ruskin, primarily remembered as the father of
art criticism and the leading art theorist of his age, was an outstanding
man of letters, painter, and draughtsman, whose social commentary
shocked and angered the nineteenth-century British establishment, which
also included many of his personal admirers.

Ruskin contended that criminals should be regarded by their society as
any other manufactured product. They are products, which we turn out.
We will need fewer prisons, he said, if we seek a system that will develop
honest men rather than one which regards criminality as inevitable and
thus focuses on punishing its criminal products.

Anticipating our contemporary environmentalists, Ruskin despised a
world, which he saw emerging, where the deification of money – the
physical symbols of the wealth of the day – eclipses the intrinsic value of
joyful human labour. "As the art of life is learned, it will be found at last
that all lovely things are also necessary; a wild flower by the wayside,
tended corn, wild birds and creatures of the forest, as well as the tended
cattle; because man doth not live by bread only."[66] He saw the timeless
beauty of all things on earth surrounding humanity and establishing for
all time an endless, lasting chain of brotherhood, linking one generation
to another in a way that man's ephemeral riches could never sustain.

Ruskin was appealing to activist prophets of the oppressed like Gandhi
and King because he never knew from around which corner genius would
come, not to put money in someone's pocket but to enhance the quality
of life in his or her time and place. As a much younger man, I remember

being impressed by an engraved quotation of Ruskin's on a public building: "A man never stood so tall as when he stooped to help a child."

This, I thought, from a specialist in pre-Raphaelite art. He led me to T. E. Lawrence. Ruskin led Gandhi to a vision of justice denied him by his British legal training. Indirectly, then, Ruskin, a link in the long chain of prophets and visionaries, had his impact on Martin King.

As though anticipating the depth of feeling of seers like Gandhi and King when coming face to face with the misery of the poor, Ruskin asked: How is it possible to desire luxury and wealth if the accompanying suffering is clearly seen existing side by side with such affluence? Only, he said, could the most ignorant and cruel man sit at such a feast of plenty, and even then, a blindfold would likely be in place.

In our times, however, it is possible to live in a world of luxury and never have to see the misery of the poor, who are not really amongst us. In Dickensian London, the poor were highly visible, yet in contemporary America, who amongst the middle, upper-middle, and upper classes journey to the urban ghettos or the rural south to see how the most impoverished of our people live? How many of us know about the existence of masses of rural poor who live in dirt floor shacks with no indoor plumbing and electricity?

In our cities, the cardbox houses tend to be consigned to particular areas. The wealthiest amongst us move quickly by, prevented from observing our less fortunate fellow citizens by the dark, tinted windows. The numbers of poor people grow. Their isolation mounts. Even though they increasingly surround us in the great cities of the world, they are unseen, and are often deliberately overlooked.

Ruskin was sensitive to the problem of those who do not see. As one apart from the fray, however, his insights were invaluable to Gandhi and through him to King. He could lecture men of action, "As the art of life is learned, it will be found at last . . . this true felicity of the human race must be by individual, not public effort."[67] So also he inspired the pre-Gandhian genius of T. E. Lawrence who suffered pain, lived, and triumphed on behalf of justice and freedom for another ancient colonial people.[68]

Gandhi saw Ruskin as the product of a realm which tended to afford reverence and a special place in history for those whose words and deeds epitomized the conscience of the nation at the time. Had not the moral power of Thomas à Becket caused Henry II to walk on his knees from Canterbury city limits to Becket's tomb in the cathedral? Had Thomas More in death not sealed Henry VIII's moral bankruptcy for all ages of Englishmen? Did not T. E. Lawrence's bold public repudiation of the king's honours inspire future legions in support of the anti-imperialist ethic of the right of people everywhere to self-determination?

In such circumstances, the English were predictable and Gandhi knew it. He understood that there was no way that the political descendants of Becket, More, Bacon, and Coke, and the cultural heirs of Shakespeare, Wordsworth, Byron, Blake, Ruskin, and Lawrence, would long tolerate the slaughter of unarmed Indians who themselves laid claim to their lush 5,000-year-old Indus Valley civilization which they sought to reclaim armed only with their moral integrity and a willingness to be beaten, tortured, arrested, and die. Gandhi reasoned that at some point, the word would go out from the government of the day – enough, no more. He was right. One slaughter too many occurred and it made even the walls of Sandhurst bleed.

Lady Mountbatten's quiet, love-inspired efforts also reflected the engagement of upper-class conscience and at the end of the Second World War, it was also clear that the Empire was no longer economically feasible. The objective factors and subjective conditions came together. India prevailed. The second largest mass of humanity on the planet was freed from the harness of European colonialism.

Gandhi personified the struggle of these masses to reclaim their historical and cultural legacy. He was produced by times which were ready to receive his message. Even his assassination was derived from the seeds of his own successful strategy and commitment to the right of self-determination of peoples. His integrity and moral essence would not allow him to turn his back on the aspirations of his Islamic brothers for their own home. He was no more inclined to preside as a neo-colonialist ruler over the developing Islamic independence movement than he had been to accept British colonial rule. The Hindu religious fanatics who had followed him in the anti-colonialist struggle turned against him. His commitment provided India with an opportunity to regain its soul. It cost the Mahatma his physical life.

Similarly, Martin King initially led the struggle of black Americans to gain control of their souls against powerful local state and regional forces. These European-descended neo-colonialist ruling forces also employed a brutality which knew no limits. In post-war America, times were also ripe for unprecedented changes, and Martin King's non-violent movement appealed to that section of the northern population which had historically supported the Bill of Rights, the anti-slavery campaigns, the underground railroad, the suffragette movement, the New Deal and the anti-fascist movement. So long as they did not move next door, blacks had a right to demand their civil rights.

When unarmed innocents courageously confronted dogs and billy clubs, Martin King knew that the northern liberal conscience would kick into high gear as the British conscience had done when Gandhi's unarmed followers were mowed down. Martin was correct. His friends in the north tipped the balance and the timing was right. He would win that battle – but it was a regional victory.

Had he closely examined the circumstances surrounding the post-First World War slaughter of veterans in the nation's capital by their own soldiers under Douglas MacArthur's orders, protecting the economic interests of his masters, it would have given him pause. He would then have understood how Gandhian tactics whilst working in the faraway south with the support of the northern conscience would meet formidable resistance when used against those dominant economic interests who long ago decided that they would selectively export their moral concern to causes which, and shores where, their own material interests were not adversely affected. Northern jobs, housing, and education were excluded from the morality call-up of this ruling segment of the American population.

Martin King's transfer of energy and resources to oppose the war was a move beyond the traditional civil rights struggle and few of his colleagues cared to link up the denial of civil liberties and existence of dehumanising poverty at home with the daily atrocities being committed on an ancient people by a new colonialist crusade 10,000 miles away. Not only would they reject the relationship but most, ignoring the moral dimension, would trade off some progress on the home front rights issues for providing support of the war effort.

He refused, and thus alienated most of his own as had Gandhi on the Muslim state issue. Amongst those offended by his commitment to end the war were powerful economic, military, and political leaders – including the president – who, so they thought, had bought his allegiance by facilitating the passage of civil rights legislation. They and the powerful corporate interests in the shadows felt betrayed.

As with Gandhi's anti-colonialist rebellion, the struggle against segregation in the 1950s and 1960s was an idea whose time had come. The emergence of a leader in both struggles who personified the hopes and dreams of his people and who articulated the moral imperative provided the necessary subjective component.

So too with the war, when Dr King came out formally in opposition, popular support of the military adventure was lacking. The people reacted to the lies they were told. The body bags were increasing, and all for what? On the subjective side of the equation, no leader had emerged by 1967, who could articulate the tragedy of the powerful few benefiting from the wasting of resources of many. No one had emerged who could bring together the disparate groups in opposition to the continued degradation of the cultural life of his native land.

Martin filled that void. To the chagrin of the powerful economic interests and their steward government, his leadership against the increasingly unpopular Vietnam adventure had public approval and support. The vehicle for the expression of this growing anti-war movement, non-violent action, and civil disobedience which included draft resistance and flight, draft-card burnings, peaceful demonstrations, sit-ins and teach-ins had an impact across the country. It all began to unravel, however, as indignation and anger took a more violent turn.

The Pentagon demonstration involving some 200,000 largely middle-class Americans coming on the heels of the 1967 urban riots was regarded as a preview of what would happen in the nation's capital with the Poor People's Campaign.

Objectively, the nation's poor were in bad and worsening condition. They were suffering at home so that their own young could be cannon fodder 10,000 miles away. Martin King agonized over the problem of the Vietnam War. Whenever he expressed concern for the people of Vietnam and the American soldiers sent over to kill them, he was attacked by fellow civil rights leaders, members of Congress, and brother clergymen for not concentrating on civil rights.

At one point during this time of inner turmoil, his path became clear. Recalling that moment, he later wrote:

> As I went through this period one night I picked up an article entitled "The Children of Vietnam," and I read it. And after reading that article, I said to myself, "Never again will I be silent on an issue that is destroying the soul of our nation and destroying thousands and thousands of little children in Vietnam." I came to the conclusion that there is an existential moment in your life when you must decide to speak for yourself; nobody else can speak for you.[69]

I was the author of that article which appeared in the January 1967 issue of *Ramparts* magazine. We would meet soon after and his resolve would harden.

With the steady deterioration of the quality of life in urban America, city after city erupted in violence for the next six months of 1967. Military intelligence was derived from those urban riots that Martin King had singular popularity amongst the urban poor and that he had every intention of mobilizing the largest gathering of American poor ever assembled in the nation's capital. It was to be a peaceful encampment to remind the Congress that these legions of poor people existed, that they had faces and voices, families, rights, and hopes which were unfulfilled, and they were not going to go away.

Like Gandhi's ragged forces confronting the might of the British Empire, Martin King's equally unkempt wretched of America were scheduled to come to the seat of power and demand the unthinkable – the reallocation of resources and priorities in the richest country on earth so that no child would go to bed hungry, health care and education would be available to all, and basic food, shelter, and clothing would become a right of every person. Such was the concept of brotherhood. The Indian rebellion against the rule of the British Empire was, of course, indirectly a struggle against the commercial interests and wealth sustained by the British government, but the goal was separation and independence from the political control and decisions of Whitehall. The point was that the empire had seen its day. The end was inevitable. The Congress Party and the nationalist movement hastened its end.

In the American south, continued segregation of the races was also on a tight time line. The Supreme Court decision in *Brown v. Board of Education* overturning *Plessey v. Ferguson*'s doctrine of separate but equal education for blacks and whites spelled the end of the day for the segregation of the races. Martin King and his followers accelerated this inevitable process. They moved forward the hour hand of the death-knell clock.

From the moment that he formally opposed the war, followed by his commitment to the Poor People's Campaign, Martin King began a fateful struggle against another type of colonial domination and another colonialist master. This enemy would emerge as the most powerful domineering force ever to span the globe. During the last year of his life, he became locked in a deadly struggle with the behemoth of transnational corporate colonialism and the awesome power of its steward state, the United States of America.

Whilst the earlier forms of oppression confronted by Gandhi and King were in decline, when King turned his attention to economic injustice, it was another matter. He had come to realize that the fundamental, underlying injustice in American life was the exclusion of the poor of all races and cultures from the opportunity to attain even the bare minimum of the necessities of life. Martin King, then, entered a new and different arena. He was involved no longer in fighting regional, social injustice but rather in attempting to confront the core issue of economic injustice in American society, which went hand in hand with waging a costly war and the growth of militarism. This new struggle brought him into direct conflict with the federal government and its numerous agency surrogates whose mission it was to serve and protect American corporate interests at home and abroad. The new post-war corporate colonialism was very far from being a spent force in 1968. If his opposition to the war was unacceptable to the corporate beneficiaries, the Poor People's Campaign was intolerable. Not only could it turn into a revolution which could only be stopped, if at all, by the massacre of Americans but, in the very least, millions of Americans would unavoidably be required to see for themselves the previously unseen massive number of their impoverished fellow citizens.

As the graphic photographic depictions of the effects of the war in

Vietnam had turned mainstream middle-class Americans against the war, the daily reminder of the effects of poverty upon millions of Americans might cause an outcry for action, which would not be satisfied by an illusory war on poverty. The only acceptable response would be the concrete provision of training programs and services designed to begin to alleviate the large, and growing, gap between the rich and the poor.

This movement then was really more akin to a class revolution than an anti-colonialist struggle, but it had elements of both. The irony is that the man who unleashed this wind of change, the leader destined to ultimately ride the enveloping whirlwind, was never a political or ideological revolutionary. More a classic liberal than a radical movement leader, Martin King never lost hope that the system could be compelled to live up to its stated ideals and respond to the genuine needs of its poorest citizens. He was hardly a revolutionary up to the time of his death, but this is not to say that he – like any of us – was not subject to the process of radicalization.

Had he lived and been confronted with the abject failure of liberal democracy to alleviate the suffering and deprivation of its teeming masses, his formidable conscience might well have required him to advocate root and branch recontruction of the government of his native land, as, in fact, was urged by Mr Jefferson as the responsibility of each new generation.

11

THE STATE'S CASE: THE HOW AND THE WHY OF THE ASSASSINATION

Throughout the entire history of this case, the state's case has never changed. Despite the range of new information, witnesses and other evidence which emerged in the course of my investigation – now spanning a quarter of a century – the official version of how Martin King was assassinated remained as it was from the outset. A line of writers endorsed, virtually without deviation, the official government position, that James Earl Ray was the lone assassin, although a credible motive was never put forward.

At this point I believe it may be useful to look closely at the state's case as well as its articulation by a number of writers over the years. The most recent is Gerald Posner, whose book on the Kennedy assassination was highly criticized for its support of the official position. After the Jowers trial and even though he never attended the proceedings (at one point, he had stated that he was going to "monitor" them), Mr Posner was, after the twelve-hour window of factual coverage, instantly available on network television and on op ed pages in newspapers across the country. Without any actual knowledge of the evidence which the jury heard during the nearly month-long trial, he criticized the jury, the judge, and Jowers's defense counsel. He was sadly unaware of the various motions that Jowers's defense counsel Garrison made in an effort to have the proceedings dismissed or to obtain a directed verdict, and he also knew nothing about the laidback but very thoughtful style of Judge Swearingen. Had Posner appeared in Memphis, Attorney Garrison was determined to serve him with a subpoena and put him on the stand so that he could attempt to make his case – the government's case – against James Earl Ray as the lone gunman. He elected not to be tested under oath.

As noted earlier, except for one lengthy letter published by the *Washington Post* and a 200-word letter published by the *New York Times*, there was no opportunity for me to give our side of the story in print. Colleagues attempted to have articles published in various mainline papers and magazines, but there was no interest. In television, the King family and I appeared on a CBS morning program for about two minutes, and there was a Court TV panel program, in which clips of Mr Posner were regularly inserted. The mainstream media is still virgin territory in relation to the revised history of why and how Martin King was assassinated.

Mr Posner is only the latest in a list of writers who have publicized the government's position. That list includes William Bradford Huie, Gerold Frank, and George McMillan in the late 1960s and 1970s. David Garrow wrote an historical work dealing with Dr King's civil rights activity, and then, having done no investigative work on the assassination, emerged in the late 1970s and 1980s as a defender of the government's position having little knowledge of the actual evidence in the case.[70] Though Professor Garrow's primary work *Bearing the Cross* came out in 1986, it followed his earlier civil rights writings on Dr King in 1978, 1981, and 1983. Incredibly, but predictably, he emerged in the late 1970s and 1980s as the principal writer/spokesperson for the official assassination story in response, I suppose, to Mark Lane's *Code Name Zorro* which was published in 1978 and which was the result of Lane's on-the-ground work. Garrow, on the other hand, devotes about four pages in his 624-page work to Dr King's last trip to Memphis. He covers the assassination in less than two pages of narrative largely derived from other secondary sources. Some expert. In contrast Howard Weissberg's book *Frame Up* had to be self-published even though it came out of a serious on-the-ground investigation and raised a number of inconsistencies and weaknesses in the state's case in 1969.

Professor Phil Melanson's three books on various assassination issues

Martin Luther King on the balcony of the Lorraine Motel on Wednesday April 3 1968, the day before his execution (Associated Press).

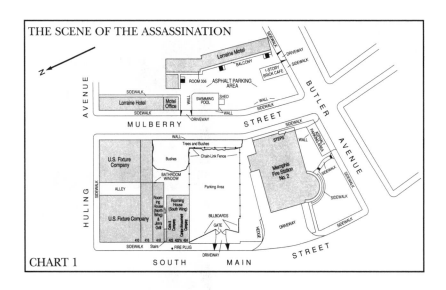

THE SCENE OF THE ASSASSINATION

CHART 1

Jim's Grill, the rooming house, and the entrance to Canipe's (just visible at no. 424), on South Main Street.

The view from the balcony of the Lorraine Motel across the street to the bushes, the wall, and the windows of the rooming house (top, photograph by Ernest C. Withers); an MPD officer standing guard over the bundle dropped in Canipe's doorway (above left, photograph by Sam Melhorne, *Commercial Appeal*); a staged photograph of an MPD cruiser pulled up to the sidewalk, taken after the hedge had been cut down the morning after the shooting (Memphis Police Department Evidence Files).

Major General William P. Yarborough and J. Edgar Hoover flanked by aides (Yarborough Collection, Boston University).

Frank Holloman, director of Memphis Police and Fire Departments in 1967–68, photographed c. 1968; he had previously been in charge of J. Edgar Hoover's Washington office (Memphis State University Collection).

The real Eric St Vincent Galt as shown in a 1967 photograph from his Top Secret NSA file; James Earl Ray had been given his identity from July 1967 to the day of the shooting.

The television trial of James Earl Ray, 1993; James participated from prison by monitor.

The spread of six photographs used to identify Raul (top left); Yolanda King and Dexter King in court with William Pepper (top right); Loyd Jowers passing in front of Coretta Scott King during the 1999 trial.

Clockwise from top left: John McFerren who just over an hour before the killing heard Memphis produce dealer Frank C. Liberto talking on the telephone and ordering someone to "Shoot the son of a bitch when he comes on the balcony"; Carthel Weeden, who was in charge of fire station no. 2 in 1968, testifying in the 1999 trial to putting two army officers in civilian clothing on the roof of the fire station; Ambassador Andrew Young testifying to damning admissions by Loyd Jowers; LaVada Addison Whitlock, who owned the restaurant that Frank Liberto frequented, testifying in 1999 that Mr Liberto had told her that he had arranged for the killing of Martin Luther King; Louie Ward, the driver who had heard the story of the fleeing shooter from a fellow taxi driver who then fell, or was pushed, from a speeding car on the Memphis–Arkansas bridge.

William Pepper briefing Coretta Scott King before the 1999 trial (top); William Pepper with Jackie Smith in front of the Lorraine Motel, where she has been camping since the motel became a museum and she was kicked out.

between 1989 and 1991 were largely ignored. Although Garrow is still trotted out from time to time, Gerald Posner replaced him as the primary spokesperson and publicist for the government's position with his book *Killing the Dream*, which was published in 1998. In arriving at his conclusion that James Earl Ray acted knowingly and alone, Posner relied heavily upon FBI documents, and the previous work of authors Huie, Frank, and McMillan. He also referred warmly to Shelby County District Attorney General Gibbons' office, expressing gratitude for their hospitality and cooperation. He said that their office ". . . at times seemed like a second home ... It is hard to overestimate the assistance they provided . . ."[71] He noted that Chief Investigator Mark Glankler (who under oath at the Jowers trial admitted that his investigation team had interviewed only two of twenty-five material witnesses heard by the jury) ". . . shared the inside story of his own extensive work, and without his cooperation, it would have been impossible to resolve many of the recent issues raised by the Ray defense team . . .". I wonder which issues those were and how they were resolved. Posner also obtained the assistance of former judges James Beasley and Robert Dwyer who ". . . were generous in taking time to reconstruct the behind the scenes details of the original investigation."[72] Judges Beasley and Dwyer, of course, ran away from testifying at the trial, using the state attorney general to file a motion to quash their subpoenas. Denied by the trial judge, their motions were upheld by the Criminal Court of Appeals. This meant, of course, that they would not have to be cross-examined about their representations to the guilty plea jury, an experience they must have dreaded.

In conducting his work Posner ignores or dismisses Professor Melanson's work on the case and very clearly has tied himself without exception to the state and the prosecution side. He never interviewed James Earl Ray, nor did he ever submit a formal request to me for an interview. His view of James is based upon suspect – as even he admits – inmates, who were possibly informants, and on law enforcement personnel and government writers like Huie, Frank, and McMillan. When Ralph Abernathy and I met James for the first time in 1978, we found a completely different person to the one we had imagined. Our preconceptions had been formed by the very same sources upon whom Posner relied.

James was neither a racist nor a violent person. Easily led, yes. Petty criminal, yes. Aggressive and violent, no. Capable of killing, no. Ralph and I agreed on this point, as did the attending Boston psychiatrist Dr Howard Berens. Posner's view of James, developed in a long pseudo-psychological narrative which occupies a substantial portion of his book, is simply wrong. The author has no qualifications or expertise to put forward a psychological evaluation. Further, any attempt to offer such an evaluation without ever having interviewed the subject is not only unscholarly but unfair. But then, in his investigation of the case, neither did he interview Glenda Grabow, John McFerren, Captain Emmett Douglas, Nathan Whitlock, LaVada Addison, Earl Caldwell, Maynard Stiles, Louie Ward, Carthel Weeden, Steve Tompkins, Charles Hurley, Steve Cupples, Floyd Newsom, Norvell Wallace, Barbara Reis, Loyd Jowers, James McCraw, Bill Hamblin, J. J. Isabel, James Milner, Leon Cohen, Jack Terrell, and Jim Smith (and a score of others who have material pieces of information). It is difficult to understand how one conducts a serious independent investigation without even speaking to such important witnesses.[73]

The Memphis jury found that a conspiracy existed which involved Loyd Jowers, agents of the Governments of the City of Memphis, and the State of Tennessee, and the Federal Government of the United States, and that James Earl Ray was an unknowing patsy. In this context, it should be instructive to see how the state and Posner deal with the range of evidence that there was indeed a conspiracy. Posner did gain interviews with Raul and the Alpha 184 team leader, obviously because with these individuals, his previous work on the Kennedy assassination, in which he concluded that JFK was murdered by a lone gunman, thus rationalizing the government's official version, made them comfortable.

I attempted to interview Raul well before we initiated litigation against him. I told him that I simply wanted to discuss the allegations and the information I had. If he was not who he was alleged to be, I would certainly have ended any consideration of him. He refused.

As for the team leader, I would have loved to interview him, but staff could find no trace of him and assumed he was dead. They didn't pick up on his prison record and re-location to Costa Rica. ABC, with the army's help, did locate him, but the network and their correspondent Forest Sawyer were not interested in a fair, probing interview.

Why?

From the beginning, the state and its publicists have had a problem ascribing a motive to James Earl Ray. Huie suggested that the assassination was an effort by a nobody to become somebody, that James wanted recognition and fame and believed that the assassination would give it to him. (Remember, Huie also did not ever interview James face to face.) To anyone who has known James, this is absurd. He was basically a quiet and diffident person who preferred to go unnoticed and be left alone. Whatever self-image problems he had, there was never any indication that he thought they could be solved by harming someone else. Even when he lost a job and participated in the occasional stick-up, he always kept the firing pin chamber of his pistol empty. He did this so that in his clumsiness he would not shoot himself in the foot or discharge his weapon against someone else.

Gerold Frank implied that money and racism were intertwined as motives, but he relied chiefly upon an inmate who had a long reputation of being a heavy drug user and government informant.[74]

Posner ultimately agrees with the HSCA conclusion that James's motive had to be money. In this instance, the money specifically was a bounty on Dr King's life offered by two Missouri racists John Kauffmann and John Sutherland who, according to Russell G. Byers, offered him $50,000 to kill King. Byers said he turned the offer down and mentioned it to a FBI informant, who passed it on in 1973. The FBI, however, ignored the information. Because Byers had a brother-in-law in the Jefferson City Penitentiary whom he visited, and James Earl Ray was in the same penitentiary and knew the relative in passing, the HSCA and Posner, on a leap of faith, without any direct evidence claimed that James heard about the offer and decided to take it up. Posner also refers to another inmate statement reported by, guess who – the FBI.

All of this flies in the face of the undisputed facts, that: 1) James Earl Ray never met Kauffman or Sutherland or even heard of them or their offer, and there is absolutely no proof to the contrary; and 2) James's goal was to get out of the United States and go to a foreign country and at the first opportunity. With money in his pocket from his job at the Indian

Trails restaurant in Winnetka, Illinois, he headed for Canada and the port city of Montreal looking for a way to travel out of North America. This was clearly his intention until in the Neptune bar he met Raul, who turned him around.

How Posner and his cohorts could distort this course of conduct and tie James to a bounty without any direct evidence boggles the mind, unless we realize that they are doing the best they can to bolster the state's patently untenable claim that James Earl Ray had a motive. The simple truth is there was no motive. James Earl Ray had no reason or other inducement to kill Martin Luther King Jr.

How? – according to the state and its publicists

In light of the pieces of credible new evidence, which had been uncovered particularly since 1992, and other evidence which had long been available though ignored, dismissed, or suppressed, those individuals and agencies continuing to advocate the lone gunman, no conspiracy case have had an increasingly difficult time. Why they continue to try is another matter, and I will suggest an answer in a later chapter.

In order to understand the scope of the effort to continue to breathe life into the fictional account of the assassination, I believe it will be useful to analyze the key issues one by one.

The key issues

The Lorraine Motel

On March 29 1968, the FBI issued from Headquarters with J. E. Hoover's initialled approval a COINTELPRO (Counter Intelligence Program) memorandum directed at Dr King and designed to influence him to stay at the Lorraine Motel when he returned to Memphis on April 3. The memorandum went from G. C. Moore, Chief of the Racial Intelligence Section, to William C. Sullivan, Assistant Director in charge of the Domestic Intelligence Division. It recommended placement of a news item with the Bureau's friendly sources, which in part would read as follows:

The fine Hotel Lorraine in Memphis is owned and patronized exclusively by Negroes but King didn't go there after his hasty exit [from] the demonstration of March 28. Instead, King decided the plush Holiday Inn Motel, white-owned, operated, and almost exclusively white patronised, was the place to "cool it." There will be no boycott of white merchants for King, only for his followers.[75]

The HSCA, and the various government publicists, dismissed the significance of this memorandum, which, however, did find its way into print. While Gerold Frank ignores the issue, Huie also claims that King always stayed at the Lorraine. Posner makes the mistake of relying on Billy Kyles for the assurance that Dr King always stayed at the Lorraine, and so for him the memorandum and any press release would be irrelevant. At one point, however, he explicitly misrepresents my work. He writes in an anecdotal note that:

> James Earl Ray's latest attorney, William Pepper, contends in his book *Orders to Kill* that "a team of federal agents conducted electronic surveillance on Dr King in his suite at the Holiday Inn Rivermont Hotel on the evening of March 18." Pepper cites a source "Who must remain nameless." The problem, however, is that King actually spent the night of March 18 at his regular motel, the black-inn Lorraine.[76]

Nameless source, indeed. I wish this could be attributed solely to sloppy research or shoddy scholarship, but that would be difficult. In *Orders to Kill*, I described my conversation with Jim Smith on this issue:

> Since there was considerable confusion about where Dr King stayed in his previous trips to Memphis, I asked Jim Smith what he knew. He knew that on at least one occasion – the evening of March 18, 1968 – Dr King stayed at the Rivermont. Smith knew this because he was assisting a surveillance monitoring team. The unit operated with the collaboration of the hotel and placed microphones throughout the suite. The conversations in Dr King's penthouse suite were monitored from a van parked across the street from the hotel. Since Smith hadn't placed the devices he didn't know exactly where they were. Another source – who must remain nameless – described the layout to me. Every room in Dr King's suite was bugged, even the bathroom. My source said they had microphones in the elevators, under the table where he ate his breakfast, in the conference room next to his suite, and in all the rooms

of his entourage. Even the balcony was covered by a parabolic mike mounted on top of the van. That mike was designed to pick up conversations without including a lot of extraneous noise because it used microwaves that allowed it to zero in on conversations.[77]

The "nameless" source only revealed the details of the location of the microphones, which I was able to precisely describe. The question of Dr King staying at the Rivermont was indeed confirmed by Jim Smith, who testified to this at both the television trial and the wrongful death action brought by the King family. Posner has never interviewed him.

Posner is wrong. King stayed at the Rivermont on March 18 and March 28 and on other occasions as well. In fact, on March 18, Dr King met community people at the Lorraine during the day before his speech, but he slept at the Rivermont. On March 28, he and Abernathy actually had reservations at the Peabody Hotel but were led to the Rivermont by the MPD after the break-up of the march. In fact, until the night of April 3, he never stayed overnight at the Lorraine. First of all, Martin King had not visited Memphis many times. He had, however, on occasion (as on March 18) arranged for a room there (I understand it was room 307) to have meetings during the day with community people who were not comfortable going to see him in the white-owned hotels where he stayed overnight. Reverend Jim Lawson told me that at this time the white-owned hotels were beginning to be desegregated, and black leaders believed that they had an obligation to become guests and establish a presence in what had formerly been white lodging bastions.

Captain Jerry Williams, who also testified at the television trial and the civil action and who formed the unit of black detectives who provided 24-hour protection for Martin King whenever he visited Memphis, except for the last visit when the unit was not formed, confirmed that on no occasion did Dr King stay overnight at the Lorraine. Williams insists that usually he stayed at the Holiday Inn or the Admiral Benbow, and the bodyguard unit would stay with them on a 24-hour detail. This unit of black detectives was accepted by Dr King. If, of course, Dr King regularly, or even ever previously stayed overnight at the Lorraine, there would have been no reason for the FBI to attempt to embarrass him into staying there on his last visit. He might, in fact, have been expected to do so.

Posner also contends that Lorraine owner Walter Bailey said that his records showed that King had stayed more than thirteen times and 306 was always his room. There is an indication that Bailey made this statement on July 10 1968.[78]

There is also the status of Walter Bailey himself. He was very close to the local police since he was running a "hot sheet" operation with prostitutes using the facilities on a regular basis. At one point after the assassination, he told his driver William Ross – who told me about the conversation in 1992 – that Dr King had to die because he was taking on forces, including government, which he couldn't overcome. Between April 5 and July 10, Bailey may well have come into line and was prepared to cooperate fully and publicly with the official story.

The faulty recollection on this issue of Ralph Abernathy, and I have long hoped that is all it is, has always been worrying. Not only has he said that they always stayed at the Lorraine but that they stayed in room 306. On the last visit, he said someone else had been put in room 306, and they had to wait for a day, stay in another room that first night and move in the next day.[79]

This is so clearly wrong that it is indeed troubling. The Lorraine register shows Dr King and Reverend Abernathy in room 306 on April 3, as does the MPD surveillance report by Willie B. Richmond. It also shows room 306 empty on April 2. No one had to be moved out. Members of the Invaders also recall that King and Abernathy were in room 306 from the beginning, as do other visitors, including Reverend James Lawson.

In another instance, when testifying before the HSCA in August 1978, Abernathy stated that on the final afternoon, when Martin was visiting with his brother A. D. in room 201, Martin called and asked Ralph to join them, and he did in fact join them though he couldn't remember the names of the other people present.[80] In his autobiography, published 11 years later in 1989, he does not mention anything about changing rooms; neither does he say that he went down to A. D.'s room. In fact, he recalls that he remained in their room.[81]

Perhaps Ralph was simply demonstrating a faulty memory. This is more believable in respect of the minor issue as to whether or not he went down to A. D. King's room at around 4:00 PM on April 4. In respect of where they stayed in Memphis, however, on various visits and the issue of a room change, Ralph's errors are more difficult to understand.

What is clear, I believe, from the weight of the evidence overlooked or ignored by the proponents of the official story, is that Martin King never stayed overnight at the Lorraine until his last visit. He occasionally took day rooms for meetings, but at night he stayed elsewhere.

The room – 306 or 202?

Not only was Dr King's stay at the Lorraine on April 3 and 4 his first overnight lodging at the motel but, in fact, he was not supposed to be in the exposed balcony room 306. Retired New York City police detective Leon Cohen had moved to Memphis and started a second career as a private investigator. He came to befriend Walter Bailey. As noted earlier, Cohen testified at the civil trial that on the morning of April 5, right after the shooting, he discussed what had happened with Bailey who was quite upset, not least because his wife raced to her room after the shot, locked the door, and suffered a cerebral haemorrhage. She was also taken to St Joseph's Hospital, and died some days later.

Cohen said that Bailey told him that the assassination did not have to have occurred. He said he had scheduled Dr King to stay in a more secluded room, 202, but that he received a call some time before the visit from SCLC in Atlanta. The caller insisted that Dr King be moved to the balcony room 306. Bailey said he argued against it for security reasons, but the caller was adamant and so he then arranged for Dr King and Dr Abernathy to share the double-bedded room.

Independently, some time afterward, Wayne Chastain spoke to Bailey and was also told about the room switch, though on this occasion Bailey distanced himself from responsibility saying that his wife was visited by an SCLC advance man who insisted on the change.

When I interviewed Olivia Hayes in late 1992, she confirmed that Dr King was to be in room 202 but was somehow moved up to room 306.

Thus, there are three separate independent accounts of the room change. Abernathy's testimony about someone else being in that room and their having to wait a day is clearly wrong, and had Posner spoken to

Leon Cohen, Olivia Hayes, or King's local attorney Lucius Burch, or asked Wayne Chastain or Attorney David Caywood (because he did talk to them) about the issue of the room, he would have obtained a very different picture.

Security

The official position has been that there was a police security detail assigned to King on his last visit. Indeed, Inspector Don Smith – who was not chief of detectives as claimed by Posner[82] – did designate a group of white detectives (Lieutenant George Davis, Lieutenant William Schultz, and Detective Ronald Howell) to meet the King party at the airport on April 3 instead of the usual unit of black detectives. This group of white officers were joined at the Lorraine Motel by Inspector J. S. Gagliano and Lieutenants Hamby and Tucker.

This team had never previously been assigned to guard Dr King and would not have been suitable. The detail was removed on the afternoon of April 3 following a request from Smith to Huston, chief of detectives, ostensibly because the King party was not cooperating. As SCLC officials, Jim Lawson and Hosea Williams told me that, while the white security force was not trusted, there was no overt lack of cooperation. MPD detective Jerry Williams testified at both the television trial and the civil action, and I included his story in *Orders to Kill*. Posner was, and if not should have been, aware of the role of the unit of black detectives on earlier visits as well as the failure to put them in place this time. In any event, he does not mention them or their absence, which occurred only on Dr King's last visit.

In respect of the removal of the TACT 10 unit from the vicinity of the Lorraine, the official position has always been that they were removed at the request of an unnamed member of Dr King's party. Posner repeats this position.[83] Had he heard the testimony of Professor Phillip Melanson in the civil action or read either Melanson's or my writing on this issue, he would have learned that Inspector Sam Evans told both of us on separate occasions that it was Reverend Kyles – whom he said he knew very well – who requested the pullback. Neither Melanson nor I believed Evans. Kyles, first of all, was not a member of the King party. He had no connection to or position in SCLC. He was a local preacher with no authority to request anything on behalf of the King group. But, if Posner had been aware of Sam Evans's claim, then he could have asked Kyles about it. In the past, Kyles has denied making any such request and doubtless he would have done so on this occasion. In this instance, he would have been telling the truth.

The removal of Detective Redditt and the two black firemen

The fact that the removal of Detective Ed Redditt was based on a bogus threat on his life is acknowledged by Posner,[84] but he does not probe deeply enough to understand the status of Philip Manual, the federal official who provided information about the threat. Manual's involvement with the 902nd Military Intelligence Group, whose Colonel John W. Downie, I believe, had coordinating responsibility for the military task force in Memphis on the day, is at least an interesting coincidence. The fact that the threat was bogus and that Redditt was taken away from the scene is more sinister. At an earlier time, Ed Redditt did some harm to his credibility because he appeared to describe his role as that of a security officer rather than a surveillance operative, a member of a two-man intelligence team. He was, however, primarily a community relations officer, who had been seconded to the intelligence detail, and, at the end of the day, because of his ties to the community, he was not trusted. That is why he was removed about an hour, or a little more than an hour, before the killing and physically transported by Lieutenant Arkin to Central Headquarters (where he said he had never seen so much army brass) and then taken home. Posner attempts to diminish Redditt's removal by stating that ". . . a black police officer replaced Redditt . . .[85] One wonders where that came from. It is patently wrong. No black police officer replaced Redditt. Willie B. Richmond, the other officer – who is black – simply continued the surveillance by himself.

Floyd Newsom and Norvell Wallace received orders to report to other fire stations late the evening before the assassination. They told me over 15 years ago that they never had received a satisfactory explanation for their transfer. They continued to maintain this position at the television trial and in the more recent civil action. In its 1979 report, the HSCA concluded that this removal was the result of a request by Detective Ed Redditt.[86] This, then, has become the official explanation, and Posner cites it in his work.[87] It has made no sense to Newsom or Wallace or even to Redditt, who made no such request and who himself was considered so untrustworthy that he was removed from the station on the afternoon of the killing. As is often the case, it is only when one goes to the relevant volume covering the hearings that it is possible to get an understanding of what took place. The HSCA Report conclusion is not substantiated by Redditt's actual testimony in open session or the references to his testimony in executive session.[88]

What is clear was that the request to remove Redditt, Newsom, and Wallace originated with the MPD. The police wanted both black firemen out of there, as well as one of their own detectives whose ties to the community were too close. Richmond could stay because he was a regular, trained intelligence officer who would perform as expected.

Neither Newsom nor Wallace was interviewed by Posner or mentioned in his book. Curiously, also absent from his index is Frank Holloman, the former FBI administrator who had been an FBI agent for a quarter of a century and who ran J. Edgar Hoover's office for the last years of his tenure. The Director of Police and Fire personally confronted Redditt in the room with "brass" and told him he had no choice but to go home under guard.

The departure of the Invaders

The sudden departure of the Invaders at 5:50 PM has been left out of the official report and ignored by the proponents of the official story. Nowhere is it mentioned in the writings, including Posner's book. The order given to this group to leave the motel between 5:45 PM and 5:50 PM within 11 minutes of the assassination is more than an insignificant coincidence. Here I am speculating, but either their forced departure (which made no sense at all in terms of saving on the room charges bill or checkout time) was designed to get them out of the way like the transfers of the black firemen and the removal of the black detective, because they were black youths and clearly a security risk, or the reason is more sinister. It is conceivable that the sudden order to leave could have prompted a violent reaction, which could have enveloped the entire motel in turbulence, resulting in a riot, allowing anything to happen with both civilian and army snipers in place.

The fact that the order appears to have been given by Jesse Jackson is also curious. Reverend James Orange recently confirmed again that Reverend Jackson had nothing to do with the Invaders and would have had no reason to give such an instruction.[89] In my opinion either Jackson did not give the orders and the attribution is wrong, or he is implicated in the conspiracy.

The Kyles factor

Though the issue of whether or not the Reverend Kyles was in the room with Dr King and Reverend Abernathy during the last hour of Martin's life is a peripheral one, it is significant to the extent that it relates to Billy Kyles's credibility. It also has some interest because if he was not in the room when he says he was, then, as Willie B. Richmond's report indicates, he did knock on the door at 5:50 PM in an effort to hurry Dr King out on to the balcony. Of course, if he was in the room with Dr King then he could not have called King out on the balcony minutes before he was shot.

The official history of the events of that afternoon has, in respect of this issue, been largely created by Reverend Kyles, whose version has been spread far and wide. In my last conversation with Ralph Abernathy, he vehemently insisted that at no time was Kyles in the room with them on that afternoon. (Remember that Martin was down in his brother's room until just after 5:30 PM when he rushed upstairs to get ready.) In addition, as Martin went on to the balcony, Abernathy wrote:

> As I was putting cologne on my face, I heard him talking to Jesse, who was down below in the courtyard. I was pleased to hear the conversation and the warmth in Martin's voice. Relations between them had been cool for the past few days, ever since the exchange after the Saturday meeting. Now Martin was clearly going out of his way to assure Jesse that everything was all right.
>
> "Jesse," he called out, "I want you to go to dinner with us tonight."
>
> Then I heard Billy Kyles' voice, coming from the opposite end of the balcony.

"Jesse took care of that even before we had a chance to invite you," he yelled. "But tell Jesse not to invite too many other people.[90]

As we have seen, one has to question Ralph's memory, but, at least, in his last conversation with me and in his autobiography some years later, he puts Kyles outside of the room and even at the other (north) end of the balcony as King leaves the room.

When one reads the surveillance report of Willie B. Richmond, he explicitly notes Kyles knocking on the door of room 306 at 5:50 PM, Martin opening the door, having a brief word and then going back inside, and Kyles walking north along the balcony stopping some distance down to lean on the railing. I interviewed Richmond in 1992, and he also testified in 1999 at the civil trial. His story has always remained consistent. When Reverend Kyles testified for the defense in the civil trial, he stated that Richmond had become an alcoholic, and he believed that he committed suicide or at least that he was now dead. The jury having heard Richmond's straightforward testimony smiled as co-counsel Akines informed Reverend Kyles that his dead man had earlier sat in the very chair he occupied and testified.

Since Posner relies on Kyles as a source for various pieces of information, one wonders why he would not have reviewed Richmond's surveillance report, and read Abernathy's account of events. This should have caused him to reject anything the man said.

Charlie Stephens

Charles Quitman Stephens was, of course, the state's chief, indeed only eyewitness. The evidence is now overwhelming that he was dead drunk at the time of the killing and saw nothing. Previously, however, he was given credibility by writers sympathetic to the State. Gerold Frank took his account at face value.[91] Posner sets the official account out and then in a note, writes

> There has been much controversy over the years as to whether Charlie Stephens had been drinking that day, especially since he later developed into the state's key eyewitness against Ray. Even if sober, his testimony was not that compelling, as the best he could say for the prosecution

was that the man leaving the scene of the crime looked like the 5B tenant by build, hair, and clothes. However, the author spoke to ex-Memphis homicide detective Roy Davis. "I took the written statement from Stephens at the police station within a couple of hours of the shooting. He was not real drunk, but he was not sober even then. I distinctly remember that he said he could not identify the man. I would not like to rely on him as my only witness.[92]

The presence of army photographers on the roof of the fire station

This, like the involvement of the military itself, is an issue that was not raised before 1995. Proving it is fraught with difficulty because of the ability of the military to close ranks and order silence whenever under attack.

We do know, however, with certainty that on the morning of April 4 1968, Carthel Weeden was approached by two army officers in civilian clothing who showed him credentials and asked to be taken up to the roof of the fire station so that they could photograph everything that went on that day. He took them up there and left them unpacking their camera gear near the northeast corner of the roof. Their presence was long rumored, but as set out earlier, it was not until I met Weeden that I was able to get the details.

Even though I wrote about it in 1995, Posner ignored this event. All he had to do was interview the captain of the fire station, which he should have done because of the position he held over a facility that is so significant to this case.

The two Mustangs

The official position from the outset has been that there were never two Mustangs, only one, which belonged to James Earl Ray. The confusion arose, the state said, because James actually moved his Mustang when it was parked up front of Jim's Grill at the time he went to buy binoculars at the York Arms Company further along South Main Street. Then, according to the official explanation, when he returned he found his parking place taken by another car and he had to park in a spot just south of Canipe's Amusement Company, which was at the southern end of the rooming house.

Posner adopts this story in its entirety and contends that James gave different versions of where he parked his car even saying on one occasion that he parked it six blocks away and on another a mile away and on another two miles away.[93] He cites no source for this contention but uses it to discredit James and take attention away from the real issue of the two Mustangs. James did initially park the Mustang a considerable distance from Jim's Grill and then walked all the way until he located the cafe. Then, he went and picked up the car and drove down to the grill and parked right in front. He has always said this, but he has never been certain as to how far away he was when he first parked the car.

Posner blithely associates Frances Thompson – a Seabrook employee across the street from Canipe's – observing a Mustang – the second Mustang – pulling up and parking south of Canipe's with James returning from purchasing the binoculars. He also mentions Peggy Hurley leaving work at 4:45 PM and noting that a man is still sitting in the Mustang, which is parked in front of her husband's car.[94] As usual, he has not interviewed either Peggy or her husband, who picked her up. If he had, as I did in 1992 and as Charles Hurley testified in the television trial and in the more recent civil case, he would have learned that the official story does not hold up. Charles pulled up behind the Mustang parked south of Canipe's and parked and waited for Peggy. Whilst waiting, he noticed that the car had Arkansas license plates. James's Mustang had Alabama plates. Back in 1972, Gerold Frank, at least, acknowledged the state's problem and tried to explain it away. He said that Hurley had been mistaken because both Arkansas and Alabama had red and white plates. True, except that Arkansas plate numbers begin with three letters (Charles Hurley even remembered two of the three letters) and Alabama plates have numbers. James's Mustang Alabama plate number was 1–38993. The other thing that Frank did not inform his readers of was that whilst Arkansas and Alabama plates were both red and white, Arkansas plates had a white background with red letters whilst Alabama plates had a very noticeable red background with white letters.

In fact, James set off for the York Arms Company not once but twice, having not gone far enough the first time, returning to get further directions from Raul. His Mustang remained parked in front of the grill. All Huie, Frank, McMillan, or Posner had to do was examine the fact pattern set out above or perhaps interview Steve Cupples or any one of a number of the Tayloe Paper Company employees who came to Jim's Grill after work – after 5:00 PM – on April 4 and noticed James's Mustang parked in front of the cafe. For example, Cupples told me that he vividly recalled the Mustang in front of the bar, because he said "I got dust on my new blue suit squeezing between its rear bumper and the front bumper of the car that was parked tightly behind it." He said he was certain that the Mustang was there between 5:15 PM and 5:20 PM and that its back bumper was "virtually even" with the north entrance door to the rooming house which was adjacent to the grill. Cupples said he had been visited by the FBI on four occasions. An FBI form 302 statement he gave was readily accessible to Posner or any researcher. This evidence would have left no doubt as to the truth about the existence of the two Mustangs.

The alibi

The state has long maintained that James Earl Ray had no credible alibi for where he was at the time Dr King was killed. He does, but James did not help himself in the establishment of his alibi. He told me that as he began to distrust William Bradford Huie, who was providing his first lawyers Art Hanes Sr and Jr with funds derived from a contract he had with *Look* magazine, he made up at least one story: After the shooting, Raul ran from the rooming house and threw himself into the Mustang pulling a sheet over him and telling James to drive away. This was nonsense designed to lead Huie on. James had gradually come to believe that Huie was working with the FBI because he said "He learned that agents from various field offices were interviewing witnesses whose names he had given to the writer." Unfortunately, making up stories seems to be a Ray brothers' idea of having fun. Jerry Ray has done more than his share. At one time, Jerry, who eventually came to totally distrust writer George McMillan, would tell him the most outrageous stories in exchange for money. Anyway, James, who made up fewer stories than

Jerry or John, nevertheless hurt his own credibility by spinning such a tale.

Others, too, have harmed him in this respect. Renfro Hays, the Hanes's initial investigator, has probably done more damage to the search for truth and justice in this case than just about anyone. He convinced one Dean Cowden to falsely provide a statement that he saw James at a Texaco gas station about six blocks from the rooming house about five minutes after the assassination. Jowers's attorney at the time, Mark Lane, believed the story and ran with it only to have Cowden admit it was completely untrue in testimony before the HSCA on August 18 1978.

For a while, we searched for an Esso gas station attendant named Willie Green. I became doubtful about the Green story after I was finally able to view an NBC interview of Green by Earl Wells. It was true that Green identified a photograph of James, just as he had done for *Press Scimitar* photographer/reporter Ed Reid, but his account of James's actions, including the use of a public telephone, just did not match James's recollection. As a result, I came to doubt the accuracy of that witness.

James's alibi, however, has nothing to do with those accounts. Posner notes that: "There are no witnesses to support Ray's ever changing story of being at a service station at the time of the assassination. Rather, after Ray returned to the South Main Street rooming house after buying the binoculars, there is no evidence he left before King was murdered."[95] He is wrong.

The alibi evidence has been held in the FBI and the Shelby County district attorney's files for 32 years. Certainly exculpatory, it was withheld from the defense from the very beginning and has been missed or ignored by writers on both sides of the case.

In 1992, in preparation for the television trial, whilst reviewing documents in the attorney general's file, I came across a statement of two witnesses made both to the FBI and the MPD. At the time, I was astounded that no mention had ever been made of them by the defense. Then I realized that they had never been made available to any of James's lawyers. These statements were made by Ray Alvis Hendrix, a member of the Corps of Engineers working on a barge on the river; and William Zenie Reed, a photographic supplies salesman. The two men had been drinking together in Jim's Grill on the afternoon of April 4. Hendrix and Reed were staying at the nearby Clark's Hotel on Second Avenue. They left the bar sometime between 5:30 PM and 5:45 PM. Hendrix realized that he left his jacket in the bar and went back in to retrieve it. Meanwhile, Reed, waiting outside, examined a Mustang parked in front of Jim's Grill. Since he was considering buying a car and was interested in the model, he gave it a fairly close look. When Hendrix emerged, the two men walked north on South Main, reaching Vance Avenue a couple of blocks away. They were about to cross the street when a white Mustang, also going north on South Main, caught up with them and made a right turn onto Vance. If they hadn't stopped, they could have been struck, though the car wasn't moving very fast. Reed observed that it was being driven by a dark-haired man. Just a short time later, after they reached their hotel, they heard sirens. Reed stated that while he couldn't be certain, the car turning on to Vance seemed to be the same car that he had been inspecting. Hendrix recalled that Reed had commented to that effect.

The statements of Reed and Hendrix appear to corroborate Ray's story that he had parked his Mustang in front of the grill, then driven it away prior to the shooting to see about having a tire repaired.

I put the evidence forward at the television trial and the civil action and also wrote about it in *Orders to Kill*, during the time of Posner's research and publication. In addition, as noted above, I had of course come upon the statements back in 1992, in, of all places, Posner's "second home."

Raul

The state has always vehemently contended that the man James Earl Ray always insisted was his "handler" or "controller" does not exist, or if he does exist, he is one of James's brothers, probably Jerry.

In the most recent discussion of Raul, Gerald Posner, at first, takes issue with how James spelled his name and alleges that we had changed it to match the spelling of the man, who we have located and believe to be the person who instructed and set up James. He notes that James previously spelled the man's name "Raoul." The truth is that James never knew how to spell the man's name. He was guessing from the sound of the name. In fact, at first, he did not spell it "Raoul." If one reviews the 20,000 words, with very few exceptions, he spells the man's name "Roual." In his book, the editors realizing that there were two ways of spelling that name – Raoul and Raul – spelled it Raoul. Early on, we also adopted that spelling because we did not have any indication of the other spelling.

Posner reviews the Herman/Billings exhibition of the photo spread and the investigation of the attorney general's office which was proceeding at the same time with an interview of Raul at his home in suburban New York. They concluded that this man could not have been the right person. They found that following his immigration from Portugal, he had obtained a job with an auto maker, rarely ever travelled, and had never been to Tennessee or Texas. He also said he had no family member named Amaro. When the district attorney's investigators ran his fingerprints against all unmatched prints in the King file and found no matches, they closed the file on Raul. Posner was granted an interview with Raul and, in addition, said that he had access to all of the work records, interviews with colleagues and a review of pension contribution documentation obtained by the district attorney's office which maintains copies of those records. It was extraordinarily unprofessional for the district attorney general's office to share whatever information they have with a book writer and not be willing to discuss it with counsel actively involved in post-conviction relief litigation on the other side. In my view, this indicates that what they were really interested in doing was conducting a public relations exercise on this issue and that they were not really interested in putting forward information or documentation which could be checked and in all likelihood would not stand up to scrutiny. Hence, they willingly shared it with an advocate of their position.

Posner attempts to discredit Glenda Grabow and questions her stability. He makes an issue of the fact that at first she knew the man not as Raul but as "Dago," a nickname. He focuses on her allegations about the Kennedy assassination and her having seen him with Jack Ruby. Posner states that there is no evidence that Ruby was ever in Houston. He obviously never spoke with some of the Carousel ladies who would have informed him to the contrary.

He claims that April Ferguson and Gene Stanley (a Knoxville attorney who represented Randy Rosenson, a peripheral figure in the case) who Herman and Saltman allegedly said had identified Raul, backed away when he spoke with them. As for Sid Carthew, he questions his reliability based upon his association with right-wing politics in England.

Posner closes his analysis by quoting Kenny Herman saying that the Oliver Stone movie will be the last word. He quotes Herman as saying ". . . in Hollywood, they aren't interested in the facts, they are just looking for the best story."

I have no way of knowing whether or not Herman was quoted correctly but unfortunately, James's defense has suffered from the thoughtless words and deeds of people who had the responsibility to aid his quest for a trial and indeed were paid to represent his interests. Though Herman and Billings insist Posner took statements out of context and distorted and misrepresented what they said, in my view, if only a portion of what he reports is correct, their conduct was stupid at best and reprehensible at worst. All of Posner's claims here distract from the real issue – whether or not the man in suburban New York (it was on my motion that the file was sealed) is indeed the person who controlled James.

At this point in time, we have the benefit of additional information that further convinces us that the Raul we identified is that right person. I know nothing about whether or not April Ferguson or Gene Stanley identified the spread of photographs. Jack Saltman insisted that April did so in his presence without hesitation.

As to Glenda Grabow, in fact, the story she told to Saltman was the same in every detail that she told me under oath. Her husband Roy and her brother Royce – independently – have confirmed her story. Royce, though young, vividly remembers the face of Raul or "Dago" as they first knew him. Glenda and Roy gave me the original of their telephone bill during the period when she called Raul on his home telephone before he knew that we were looking at him. The bill shows that they talked for six minutes on April 20 1996.[96]

Posner notes that James also identified the photograph of Raul and incorrectly states that this was the first positive identification James ever made. He seeks to discredit the identification by contending that James, at various times, did say that one or another person resembled Raul. So he did, but he never made a positive identification until, in fact, 1978, when he received the very photograph that is contained in the spread. His recognition of Raul at that time was even reported on a limited basis in the press.[97]

The effect of Posner's failure to tell his readers about the earlier identification aids his efforts to discredit James's 1994 re-identification.

In the interim, Loyd Jowers positively identified the photograph of Raul as the man who brought him the murder weapon.

Posner did not – perhaps was unable to because of his publication schedule – mention the documents which former FBI agent Donald Wilson found in James's car, on which Raul's name clearly appears. So, then, from the white Mustang itself come pieces of paper not only with an indication that Raul exists but also confirming Glenda Grabow's credibility, since just before Raul's name is the Dallas telephone number of the Vegas Club owned by Jack Ruby.

At one point after publication, Posner commented that he was suspicious of the documents because Wilson came to me. In fact, Don Wilson went to the King family who he wished to help. They referred him to me.

For whatever reason, Posner does not discuss British television producer Jack Saltman's earlier telephone conversation with Raul around the time of his daughter's wedding during which Raul admitted that he had a relative named Amaro in Houston, and also he ignores a subsequent tape-recorded conversation with Raul's daughter at the door of their home, though he mentions the visit.[98]

Thus, he has failed to mention what the jury at the civil trial heard quite clearly: namely that Raul's daughter, looking at the photograph shown to her by Saltman (without the spread), commented that "Anyone can get that picture of my father."[99]

There it is. His own daughter confirmed the identification of her father by James Earl Ray, in addition to identifications by Loyd Jowers, Glenda Grabow, Royce Wilburn, Sid Carthew, Beverly Oliver, Chari Angel, and Madeleine Brown. Is anything else really needed? If it is, then Portuguese journalist Barbara Reis's testimony under subpoena surely completes the picture.

The reader may recall that she told the jury that she interviewed a significant member of Raul's family in Portuguese, and the person told her that the one comforting part of this whole siege was the fact that the government was giving them so much help. She said that on at least three occasions, government agents had come to their house to advise them and to monitor their telephone calls.[100] Imagine that degree of care and consideraton by the government for just a little old retired autoworker.

Finally, Posner refers to work record documentation. I obtained, under subpoena, Raul's work history and was told that it was the same report given to the US attorney general's team. I was told that there were no other records available. Whether this is true or not, I do not know. The records I received indicated that at various times he did, in fact, take considerable time off in blocks of days. Even with the cover provided, I believe that it is quite possible that he could indeed have come and gone from the gunrunning activities based in Houston.

The military involvement

The most sensitive aspects of my investigation on the case dealt with the involvement of the military. Ever since the condemnation of the military for its extensive domestic surveillance of civilian political activity by the Senate Judiciary Subcommittee on Constitutional Rights (the Ervin Committee), in 1972, the army has been extraordinarily sensitive about any additional information coming to light about its intelligence activities or other covert domestic operations.

The focus of the Ervin Committee was the period of the 1960s; the targets of army surveillance were social change organizations such as SCLC, and their leaders. Dr King was high on the list of leaders to be targeted. The Ervin Committee found that at the height of the activity army surveillance was both "massive and unrestrained." The army engaged over 1,500 plainclothes agents to collect information which was placed in data centers around the country. No individual organization or activity which expressed "dissident views" was immune from surveillance, and no information once obtained was too irrelevant to be placed on one or another army computer. The army attempted to justify this activity saying it was necessary in order to be able to deploy troops and conduct operations in the cities of America when required.

The very forces and individuals who criticize and dismiss our work as being that of "conspiracy buffs" themselves advanced the conspiracy theory in the 1960s that all of the turbulence and disorders was being caused by a defined group of political activists determined to overthrow the government. The Ervin Committee found that this ". . . conspiracy theory was one of the underpinnings of the Army surveillance program."[101] The committee also met with little co-operation from the army and the Pentagon and it expressed skepticism about undertakings it was given.

The Ervin Committee concluded in its 1972 report ". . . that military surveillance was both unauthorized and in violation of the first amendment." The most significant upsurge of this activity was noted to have occurred between September 1961 and March 1968, precisely the period leading up to the assassination of Dr King. Such was the concern for the Poor People's Campaign planned for the spring of 1968 that it was ordered to be infiltrated by the 109th, 111th and 116th Military Intelligence Groups.[102]

At one point, the Ervin Committee focused briefly on the 902nd Military Intelligence Group and noted that it has been under the control of the ACSI at the time – General William P. Yarborough – and that unlike all of the other MIGs, which were assigned to regional areas, it had world-wide jurisdiction to carry out a variety of sensitive counter-intelligence tasks. It also was involved in the covert penetration of civilian organizations within the United States. So much for subsequent denials about 902nd activity inside the United States.

It has not been widely known that in 1967 and 1968 the army's participation in the Justice Department's civil disturbance structure was significant and extensive. The army had by far the greatest resources to bring to the task force. At the time, the FBI had only 40 black agents out of a total of 6,300 agents. Military intelligence was far better able to readily produce black agents of suitable ages to infiltrate black organizations. One such agent in Memphis was Marrell McCollough, who was reactivated in June 1967 and, through assignment to the MPD, infiltrated the Invaders. The SCLC was itself infiltrated under this program.[103]

The collection of photographs and the development of "mug books" (the reader may recall that Warren described their use to Steve Tompkins) was combined with the army wanting to know where surveillance targets would be staying in various cities, as well as details concerning housing facilities, offices, bases of operations, churches, and private homes. The committee noted, "Why such information was sought has never been explained."[104] It was noted that the special instructions to agents did not emphasize obtaining information that might have been useful to troops trying to clear the streets or enforce curfews – but rather upon identifying individuals and organizations and personal activities. Agents often operated as press photographers and newsmen with bogus credentials.

During civil disturbance alert situations such as those that existed in Memphis in March and April 1968, special "hot lines" were installed between the police departments and the "intelligence emergency operations centers (IEOCs) of the local military intelligence offices. At the same time, the army autovan telephone system linked each IEOC with Fort Holabird, the Pentagon, the local army command and any special task force, as I believe was present in Memphis on April 4. The Ervin Committee noted that the intelligence command published a "blacklist" in the fourth of the six volumes of "mug books." It contained photographs and profiles of more than 1,000 individuals and linked each to one or more organizations or groups. Political beliefs were profiled as well as personal information. No purpose was ever disclosed for the use of these "mug books," which appear to have been a giant rogues' gallery. When their existence was revealed in 1970, the army quickly ordered them destroyed. No explanation has ever been given as to why they were compiled.[105]

The numbers of files on individuals ran well into the millions (8,000,000 were on file at Fort Holabird alone) and over 770 organizations were included for surveillance, with many targeted for infiltration. The ACSI in 1968, General Yarborough, was almost prosecuted along with others but was spared this ordeal as the army promised to be good in the future.

The Ervin Committee is likely only to have scratched the surface with its report, regularly acknowledging the failure of the army to explain various tactics, interests, and practices; 23 years later, in 1995, the military would close ranks and seek to deny any information which pointed to even more sinister activity being afoot in 1968.

In commenting on the revelations contained in the military chapter in my *Orders to Kill*, Posner early on states that in preparation for the mock trial, I hired Tompkins as a consultant. This is patently incorrect. I approached Steve four months after the trial, and it would be some time before he agreed to help. Posner relies on official records to contend that the 20th SFG was never federalized, and therefore that no members of the unit were ever in the places Warren told Steve they were in 1967. I have no doubt that there would be no official records of small sniper units carrying "mug books" being in those places.

Posner quotes Daniel Ellsberg's statement that the copy of the cablegram or "orders" given to Steve were not authentic. That may or may not be true, but it never made sense to me that a "grunt" like Warren would have the ability or interest to fabricate such a cablegram. I also did not believe that Steven Tompkins would give me the cablegram if he believed it was not authentic. There would be no point.

The 20th SFG sources and Posner maintain that the unit was in none of the places I mentioned, including Camp Shelby. This is indeed strange since Jack Terrell (I call him "Carson" in *Orders to Kill*) – who Posner pointedly ignores – told me of the regular annual sessions that his best friend J. D. Hill attended at Camp Shelby in fulfillment of his annual 20th SFG training obligation. Posner notes that no Robert Worley (the Alpha 184 team leaders' executive officer) or J. D. Hill was found on the rosters. He or they must have been looking at the Alabama rosters. On the rosters I obtained Worley is listed in a Louisiana unit and J. D. Hill was listed in Mississippi. As for the contention that the Alpha 184 did not exist at the time, Steve has always insisted not only that it did exist then but that it has continued to exist, but as a highly secret unit. The army and Posner also contend that J. D. Hill was not on active duty with the unit on April 4 1968. Their records show that he left the unit on May 7 1966 and did not return until May 7 1968, after the assassination. I cannot comment on these official records. I can only confirm that Jack Terrell (who I – and others, including ABC who has used him as a consultant and a source in the past – find highly credible) has always stated what J. D. Hill told him about his involvement with the unit, or one of the units, assigned to the Memphis operation. Finally, at one point, in a footnote, Posner admits that his 20th SFG source Rudy Gresham told him that he had found Worley who also officially was not on duty in 1968. He reportedly died in a car accident.

Posner then covers the ABC *Turning Point* program, on which they produced the officer I had named as the team leader although I had been informed by my investigators that he was dead. Posner, again in a footnote, states that he had left the country after having "trouble with the law in Birmingham."[106]

He writes that the soldier killed a man in a bar brawl and was held responsible for criminally negligent homicide. That may have been an earlier case, which was dismissed because no witnesses showed up. In the criminally negligent homicide case, he actually shot a man allegedly coming at him with a knife outside of the bar. It is true that my investigators could not find him and, in light of the feedback from Warren that he believed a "clean-up" operation was underway, we believed him to be dead, and we were wrong. Steve, having the under-standable desire to protect the deep cover source I called Warren, gave me the wrong name. On the one hand, I wish he had simply told me that he could not give me the soldier's real name; on the other hand, I understand he had to protect the identity of his source. Posner raises the possibility that Warren and Murphy may be fictitious characters. They are not. As is noted in my working papers, some of which were introduced into evidence at the civil trial, Warren's degree of detail leaves no doubt that he was there. He even knew what Andy Young was doing just before the shot. When Steve met with the man we believed was the colonel who led the 902nd MIG – John Downie – the man told him that he was legally dead and had been given a new identity. It increasingly appears that the man who Tompkins met was a disinformation agent and not Colonel Downie after all. Posner contended that I claimed to meet regularly with the colonel.[107] I have made no such claim. To the contrary, I have always made it clear that Steve not I met with Downie or "Gardner" as I called him. In his criticism of my contentions about the military, Posner neglects to even mention the relationship of the 902nd MIG with Eric S. Galt, the warehouse manager with top secret clearance at the Union Carbide company in Canada. As discussed earlier, around the very time that James assumed the identity of Eric S. Galt (August

1967), the real Eric S. Galt was meeting with officers of the 902nd in furtherance of a particular project. This may well indicate the involvement of the military at a much earlier time than previously realized but amongst other aspects of this complicated scenario it is never mentioned in Posner's chapter entitled "Military Hoax."

As for J. D. Hill's involvement with a sniper unit in Memphis, ABC interviewed Terrell for three hours and did not use a second of the interview, though Terrell had been a valued credible source in the past. They appeared to have relied on an "official" record shared with them by the army. There is no indication that Posner tried to interview Terrell. He never referred to Hill's story which basically corroborated that of Warren and Murphy. Posner quotes former Yarborough aide Gresham as stating that he obtained the team leader's Birmingham fire department work records which purportedly showed that he did not work on April 4 but was "on call." On the day of the assassination, Posner asserts that the person alleged to be the team leader was working with a house painting crew on a job in Birmingham.[108]

In a deposition, this alleged person maintained that he was helping someone build a house.[109] What he didn't realize was that his former superior officer General Cobb said that he saw him around the fire station three or four times on April 4.[110] They have a problem.

Posner did not know about Captain Carthel Weeden's confirmation that he put the Psy Ops soldiers referred to as "Reynolds and Norton" on the roof of the fire station so that they could photograph the events of April 4 1968. He didn't know it because like the previous official investigators, he never interviewed the captain.

Perhaps most critical is the refusal of Posner and other defenders of the military to even address the joint venture gunrunning relationship of elements of the military with the Marcello organization. Warren's credibility surged when he described how he would drive weapons stolen from Camp Shelby – that military base where the 20th SFG never trained – to barges on Carlos Marcello's property. He said someone named "Zip" or "Zippy" was running the operation for Marcello and they were given the number of a man named Joe Coppola in case they had any trouble on the road with their truck. As noted elsewhere, when I checked I learned that Zip was Zippy Chimento, a confidant and associate of Marcello. Joe

Coppola was nothing less than the Commissioner of the Louisiana state highway patrol. A 20th SFG officer in the Baton Rouge network was the liaison in Louisiana, and the weapons went around the Gulf into Houston where they were offloaded and prepared for shipment to Latin and South American purchasers. Those were the shipments that Glenda Grabow described on the odd occasion when she drove on to the docks with Raul to pick up a shipment. The public actually caught a glimpse of this relationship when the army's provost Marshal General Carl C. Turner took the fall and went to prison for the weapons thefts that hit most arsenals, bases, and camps in the south and southeast. It was when I discovered this relationship that it became impossible not to include the backup military task force in my original work on the assassination.

At the end of the day, the army task force was not called upon to act. Warren had insisted, so Steve told me, that they would only be ordered to fire in the event of a riot. It never made sense to me until I learned that the Invaders were heavily armed when they were summarily and in a most provocative way ordered to leave the Lorraine.

The obvious difficulty with the evidence is that a number of the sources do not want to be identified and come forward and that someone – here Steve Tompkins – had to be in between. The direct corroborative recollections of Jack Terrell, however, made a difference as did the revelations that, in fact, it was confirmed that there were two Psy Ops soldiers on the roof who filmed the events of April 4 1968, including the assassination.

On the other side, there is the alliance between Gerald Posner and the military. There is, on his part, overwhelming reliance on "official" documents: even the most politically unsophisticated now understand that the government can produce any records or documents required to give credibility to its version of events.

Finally, Posner somehow associates my examination of the involvement of the military with an alleged neglect of the struggle to obtain a trial for James. Unlike Posner's fleeting interest in the case, by the time he published, I had been investigating the case for 20 years. After I became convinced that James was an unknowing patsy, I agreed to represent him. I realized that the only way James would get a trial would be for us to solve the case. When I became aware of the gunrunning relationship between the Marcello organization and the army, I believed it impossible to exclude the military involvement, even though my first publisher promised lucrative rewards if I would do so.

The full extent of the military's involvement may never be known. It is likely that we have only seen the tip of the iceberg in this respect but given the nature of the beast, which is driven by secrecy and unswerving loyalty, we may not get very far beneath the surface.

After *Orders to Kill* was published, I received a call from Colonel Dan Marvin, a former Green Beret, who said that when he was at Fort Bragg, he was approached and asked to carry out an assassination of an American citizen with sensitive materials in the United States. He refused, saying that he had never signed on for that work inside the US. Marvin said he was a sniper and had no hesitation in plying his trade on foreign soil, but he drew the line when asked to kill Americans in the US. He knows another professional was approached and that the target died of an unexplained heart attack not long after. Colonel Marvin told me that when he read *Orders to Kill*, he was astounded that the role of the army was finally coming out. He picked up the phone and called General Yarborough, long since retired, in order to congratulate him. He thought Yarborough was my source and was surprised when the general vehemently denied helping me. Marvin said he was referred to Rudy Gresham and he told his story to Gresham who counseled silence and loyalty whilst Marvin was talking about truth and the Constitution.

The assassination, the rifle

The state has never been able to confront the fact that it could not prove that the weapon purchased by James, and found in the bundle in front of Canipe's, was the murder weapon. The fact is that the ballistics tests conducted by the FBI on the morning after the killing could not establish that that weapon, to the exclusion of all others, was the one from which the bullet was fired that killed Dr King. Posner and others supporting the government line, however, totally ignore the results of the accuracy test that the FBI completed. Its report clearly indicated that the rifle failed the test which meant that the scope had not been sighted in. To shoot a target using that scope would have meant that the shot would have gone some three and one half inches to the side and four inches below.

The other part of the state's scenario related to the rifle in evidence is the allegation that James dropped it in Canipe's doorway when he was fleeing after having seen a police car pulled up to the sidewalk in the fire station driveway. Posner sets out this scene in a drawing.[111]

The problems with this longstanding fiction are many. There was in fact a large hedge in between the fire station driveway and the parking lot next to it which would have blocked James's view of any car parked in that spot.

Posner in his drawing of the scene depicting the state's scenario does show the hedge, but in such a way that it appears somehow to have shrunk and become thinner, closer to the sidewalk.[112] In *Orders to Kill* I published a photograph of the officer standing over the bundle at the time. Over his left shoulder, the full hedge is clearly depicted.

Because this was a problem for the state's case, the hedge was cut down the next day by the same crew who cut down the bushes at the rear of the rooming house. I obtained a photograph taken of the hedge after it was cut, clearly showing it still lying in place. I also wrote about Douglas's statement. Posner clearly knew about all of this evidence. He appears to have ignored it because it contradicts the state's and his own version of events.

The alteration of the crime scene – the cutting down of the bushes

The state has long maintained that the bushes behind the rooming house were not cut down on the morning after the killing. To admit otherwise would, of course, be to admit that the MPD had drastically altered the area of the crime which is unthinkable in an objective investigation.

The HSCA, according to Posner, searched the records of the city public works department and found no record that a clean-up took place but could not rule it out. Posner notes that Kay Black, the reporter from the Memphis *Press Scimitar*, first raised the issue shortly after the murder.

He then goes in to announce that he has solved the mystery and that the work was done in early August, four months after the assassination. He said that if any work was done after the killing, it was only minor and aimed at removing some "overgrowth" to assist the police.[113]

Neither the HSCA or Posner interviewed Maynard Stiles, the public works administrator who ordered the extensive clean-up pursuant to the 7:00 AM request of Inspector Sam Evans on April 5. Kay Black told me of this event back in 1978 when she said former mayor William Ingram called her in the morning and told her to get over to the rooming house where they were changing the crime scene with a massive effort.[114]

The bundle of evidence

The state's case, memorialized by each of the publicists from the beginning, is that the bundle containing the rifle was dropped in Canipe's doorway at about 6:03 PM, some two minutes after the shooting, after which the person who dropped it drove away in the white Mustang parked just south of the store.

In fact, Judge Arthur Hanes told me and testified at the civil trial that Canipe told him that the bundle was dropped before the shot, and he was prepared to testify for the defense at trial. We also now know that the second Mustang had Arkansas plates and that James was seen driving away considerably earlier. It therefore appears clear that someone else took James's belongings and dropped them to set him up and went off in the second white Mustang, so it would appear that he fled the scene of the crime. The set-up story put out by the state and embraced by the chain of publicists like Posner falls apart with the revelation that there was a second Mustang, that an MPD car was not visible from the sidewalk near Canipe's, and that the bundle was actually dropped before the shooting.[115]

The admission of Loyd Jowers

The new Jowers evidence has given the state's official story and its publicists a terrible jolt. Whilst they contend that they didn't believe him and insist that he has made it up for money, the fact is that no investigator from the attorney general's office has ever tried to interview him and, of course, he has never been interviewed by Posner.

Unfortunately, the details of Loyd Jowers's involvement in the assassination were, early on, muddied by others trying to capitalize on his story. Though Jowers himself has not benefited in any way and in fact has lost everything including his wife, the fact that there were others on the fringes trying to make money out of the revelations has allowed the significance of his account to be clouded.

It is also true that Jowers told a different story for many years. He certainly never wanted to be implicated in the assassination. When I met him in 1978, he was presenting himself as just an innocent bystander, who, however, was willing to identify a mysterious stranger who was in the grill that afternoon.

Betty Spates, Jowers's waitress, first surfaced in 1969 after telling a local bailbondsman that she believed her "boss man" Jowers had killed Dr King and that James was innocent. Posner states that she recanted to two investigators who noted her admission in a memorandum. Posner says she said that some "supporters of Dr King" offered her $5,000 to make the story up. I have known Betty Spates for ten years. Posner has never even interviewed her. She has been very susceptible to official pressure and intimidation because there have often been during this period charges pending against one or another of her sons by the very attorney general's office which has wanted her story about seeing Jowers running from the bushes with a rifle to go away.

Posner attempts to discredit Jowers by saying that he named Frank Holt as the assassin he hired. In fact, Jowers never said that. Herman and company came up with Holt after Jowers associate Willie Akins (who met Jowers after the assassination) said that Jowers wanted him to kill Spates and Holt because they could put him in the bushes at the time of the killing. Posner did not interview Akins. I traveled to Houston where he is incarcerated in order to do so. He said that he couldn't do it because he became personally involved with Betty, and Holt just went away. Akins also told me that in the early 1970s, Jowers did tell him about his involvement in the assassination, usually talking about it after drinking.[116]

Posner next attacks John McFerren whose story about Frank Liberto's involvement is supportive of Jowers's allegations about Liberto setting the assassination in motion. It is true that after John overheard Liberto on the telephone, he became suspicious of everyone and did make claims which had him imagining that he saw James around Liberto's, but then he was unable to identify him from a photograph. He also imagined hearing his name mentioned in one of the calls, but when we went over what he did actually hear and see and what he originally stated and told the official investigators – not what he may have extrapolated at some point down the road after he heard that the assassin was someone named James Earl Ray – John McFerren's story has not changed for 32 years.[117] Posner points to paranoia. Yes, John is nervous because he has been beaten up, shot, an attempt to poison him has occurred and he has been denied gas and oil deliveries and continually threatened ever since he came forward. He testified at the civil trial and repeated his story under oath. Posner claims that Attorney David Caywood, who was with John briefly on the evening that he was interviewed by the FBI and the MPD at the Peabody Hotel, told him that he does not remember hearing John say "on the balcony."[118] When I spoke more recently with David Caywood, he told me that first of all, he was not in the room when John was being interrogated and that he did not recall saying that, but what he could remember was that when the FBI agents came out of the room after interviewing him in teams, for hours, they said they believed he was being truthful because whilst they gave him an opportunity to expand upon his story he wouldn't take it, saying that he didn't know. He recounted the same details over and over again.

Posner next attempts to undermine Jowers's story by claiming that taxi driver McCraw lied about going to pick up Charlie Stephens, finding him dead drunk and noticing the bathroom empty just before he left – minutes before the shooting. McCraw testified under oath. Posner says that the taxi company records did show McCraw working on the afternoon but had no record of him being given a call to the rooming house. The attorney general – and Posner – find no more reason to believe him about his statement concerning Jowers showing him the murder weapon on the day after the killing.

Posner notes that King had not decided to return to Memphis until March 30 and yet Jowers said Liberto approached him earlier. In fact,

Jowers has maintained that Liberto approached him before Dr King returned for the march on March 28. His commitment was given in his speech on March 18. It was between March 18 and March 28 that Liberto approached Jowers. Posner overlooks the promise of a second visit.

He cites Jowers's call to Mark Glankler. Jowers, when intoxicated one evening and besieged by members of his family, called to try and get the attorney general's people to leave the family alone. In desperation, he said Ray's gun was the murder weapon. He told me and his lawyer that this was a ploy to try and get them to lay off the family.

Posner insisted that the most effective refutation of Jowers's claim that he ran back inside the restaurant with the murder weapon is the fact that, in his initial statement, he said he was in the grill and heard the shot and asked a patron, Harold Parker (now deceased), if he heard the noise. Then, a few minutes later a deputy sheriff stopped by the restaurant and ordered it shut down. On April 15 1968, Parker, unaware of Jowers's statement, confirmed that account.[119]

In fact, Jowers went into the kitchen with the murder weapon within twenty seconds after the shooting. Having broken it down, he was in the main part of the cafe within a minute or so. He promptly went up to Parker and asked if he heard the noise and thus called attention to his presence in the cafe. About two minutes or so after he entered the cafe from the kitchen, Deputy Sheriff Dollahite appeared at the door. Posner has overlooked the actual timing of the events. Jowers was in the grill very quickly after the shooting.

Posner also overlooks LaVada Addison Whitlock's unassailable account, under oath, of Frank Liberto's admission to her of his involvement. He attempts to attack her son Nathan's credibility concerning Nathan's separate confirming conversation with Liberto, and he does so without ever interviewing Nathan. Neither, of course, does he interview Mrs Addison in his search for the truth about Jowers's story and Liberto's involvement.

He also has never interviewed Bill Hamblin, McCraw's roommate who over a 15-year period told about Jowers giving him the gun to get rid of. Neither did he speak to James Milner and J. J. Isabel about Jowers's admissions to them going back twenty or more years.

The style of publicists for the government's case is to utilize the tactic of discrediting the work of people who oppose their views. So, for example, allegations by Ken Herman that I paid $14,000 for a photograph or $25,000 for information on the military, which are totally untrue and baseless, are repeated without my ever being interviewed. I was approached by Gerald Posner at one point and told him that his past work did precede him, and I believed he was not to be trusted. However, I said that I would answer his questions, but that we must memorialize everything. All questions and responses must be in writing. I never heard from him again.

The overwhelming number of his cited sources are government (FBI, HSCA, or Attorney General's Report) documents and records, as well as the writings of other, largely discredited former publicists of the government's line, Huie, Frank, and McMillan – writers with a similar purpose and goal. Even then, his selective use of available materials is evident. Though he likes to pretend that he is revealing the attorney general's file for the first time, in actual fact under Tennessee's sunshine law, it has been open to the public for years and in 1992, I and my staff spent days pouring over the file. It was there that we found the long-suppressed Reed and Hendrix statements and photographs of the bushes razed to the ground. Posner must have seen these materials, but like most witnesses and evidence contrary to his official view of the case, he elected not to recognize them.

At the end of the day, Judge Arthur Hanes appears to best sum up Gerald Posner's approach to this investigation. Remember, Hanes said when Posner called him, he invited him to come down and he would show him the evidence that proved that James Earl Ray was not guilty of the murder of Martin Luther King Jr – that he was innocent of the crime. Judge Hanes said that he never heard from Posner again. Neither did the scores of witnesses who the jury heard when they rendered their verdict that a conspiracy existed involving Loyd Jowers, of course, but, with greater liability, agents of the governments of the City of Memphis, the State of Tennessee, and the government of the United States of America.

12

THE UNITED STATES ATTORNEY GENERAL'S REPORT

Following the King family's meeting with President Clinton and their request for the appointment of an independent "truth and reconciliation" commission, the president decided to instruct the attorney general to conduct a limited investigation of the new evidence contained in the allegations of Loyd Jowers and Donald Wilson. Then, on 26 August 1998, the attorney general directed the Civil Rights Division with the assistance of the Criminal Division to conduct the investigation.

The investigative team consisted of four attorneys from the Department of Justice (DOJ) and three investigators. The attorneys were Barry Kowalski, Lisa J. Stark, and Seth Rosenthal from the Civil Rights Division and Attorney Jerry Massie from the Criminal Division. The investigators were Inspector Yvonne Bonner from the United States Marshals' Service, Special Agent Brad Farnsworth, from the Bureau of Alcohol, Tobacco, and Firearms, and Inspector R. Nolan Carwell from the United States Postal Service.

Methodology

The DOJ task force purportedly reviewed ". . . tens of thousands of pages of federal, state, and local documents . . .," along with hundreds of pieces of evidence, hundreds of witness statements and the work products of private investigations.[120]

In respect of official records, they claim to have examined ". . . documents and evidence from the original 1968 criminal investigation conducted by the FBI, state and local law enforcement, and the state prosecutor's office; the 1976 and 1977 investigation by a Department of Justice task force (DOJ task force); and the 1977 to 1979 investigation by the House Select Committee on Assassinations (HSCA); and the 1993 to 1998 investigation by the Shelby County, Tennessee district attorney general's office. The 14 published volumes of testimony and evidence and relevant records had been sealed at the National Archives since 1979. The FBI, the Central Intelligence Agency (CIA), and the Department of Defense also furnished relevant, and in some cases classified, records not available to previous investigations."[121]

The final investigative report was completed some 22 months after the charge, in June 2000. It states that the task force conducted its own original inquiry of the Jowers and Wilson allegations and interviewed more than 200 witnesses, with interviews being conducted, where possible, in person, but otherwise by telephone.

In addition, the DOJ task force arranged for scientific testing and analysis to be done on the two documents obtained from Don Wilson. A cryptologist was brought in to look at one of the documents which contained ". . . a list of numbers and words, . . ." in order to ascertain whether or not a code was being used.[122] Handwriting samples from relevant subjects were also compared with the writing on the Wilson documents.

The report stated that the task force also consulted with "experts" at the Ford Motor Company in order to evaluate photographs taken at the time of the recovery of the Mustang in order to determine whether or not the passenger side door was locked or open as Don Wilson claimed (Wilson claimed it was locked but ajar, not open).

I believe it useful and necessary to look at the report, section by section, in order to attempt to understand why the attorney general's team ultimately dismissed all of the new evidence and came up with the same conclusion that has been the official story for 32 years – i.e. that the assassin was lone gunman James Earl Ray.

Loyd Jowers

The report emphasizes that for a period of some 25 years after the assassination, Jowers did not claim to have had any involvement in the assassination. This, of course, is true. Jowers was never interested in putting himself in the frame. He was most fearful of going to jail. When he did come forward in 1993, it was because he had learned that we had received information directly incriminating him, from Betty Spates, James McCraw, and Bobbi Balfour.

In a desperate effort to head off what he believed would be a criminal indictment by any grand jury which heard the evidence, he asked his lawyer to seek immunity from prosecution. This request, and the proffer which accompanied it, was greeted with silence by the Shelby County district attorney general who had requested it in the first place. The report also notes that immunity for Jowers was not out of the question but that a "proffer" would be necessary. Indicating that it had been too limited, the report dismisses the fact that the proffer had previously been submitted and was there for review. In that proffer, however, Jowers, through his lawyer, undertook to admit his involvement, even having received the murder weapon from the actual assassin, breaking it down, and concealing it. It appears to me now, as it did in 1993, that the submission should have been sufficient for the prosecutor to take it forward and at least attempt to interview Jowers. For the district attorney general to not even respond to the request and simply ignore it, was regrettable. For the US attorney general's team to dismiss it out of hand is, in my view, an inappropriate response by investigators who were purportedly seeking the truth.

The report inaccurately states that: "In his only statement under oath since his 1993 revelation, Jowers did not confess. Specifically, in a November 1994 sworn deposition in *Ray v. Jowers*, approximately a year after his initial appearance on *Prime Time Live*, Jowers refused to adopt his televised confession."[123] This is not so. Whilst at various times during that lengthy deposition Jowers, ever fearful of prosecution, did contend that he was not involved, when I finally pressed him on the truthfulness of his statements on the ABC program he confirmed that they were true by agreeing that the transcript of his statements on the program could be admitted.[124] Thus, the entirety of Jowers's admissions about his involvement in the assassination of Martin King became a part of the record of his testimony under oath in the deposition taken on November 2 1994.[125]

As to the identity of the assassin, the report dismisses Jowers's later consistent identification of Memphis Police Department Lieutenant Earl Clark as being involved. It alleges that earlier he made references to local black man Frank Holt and Raul as possible assassins – these names were certainly mooted at one time or another – but it is not clear to what extent Jowers initiated their introduction. (The investigators rely on a hearsay statement of Gerald Posner, in which he states that Lewis Garrison told him at one point that Raul was the shooter. Garrison denies that he said any such thing, and in any event, it was not Jowers speaking.) The report cites the discredited ABC polygraph examination of Jowers, without revealing that testimony at the trial revealed the entire exercise was organized to set Jowers up and the fact that the polygrapher was later fined for misconduct.[126] For quite a period of time and certainly during the interviews he gave with Ambassador Young, Dexter King, and myself, Jowers always contended that it was Clark who gave him the rifle. When and as he told the story, there was no motive for him to lie.[127]

When Jowers consented to be interviewed by Sam Donaldson on the *Prime Time Live* program in 1993, he was clearly trying to bring the story forward whilst, to the extent possible, distancing himself from direct involvement. Hence, he talked about being involved in the financial arrangements and locating a shooter. He was, however, always consistent about the fact that Liberto sent $100,000 along to him.[128]

As to how much Jowers knew, I believe there is little doubt that he was aware of what was going on. There were, after all, meetings held around him and in his presence in Jim's Grill. These sessions involved MPD officers, two of whom he knew quite well. Though he has tried to distance himself from having knowledge about the assassination and thereby ease his discomfort in front of the King family, I believe it is simply not credible that he did not know that the assassination of Martin King was being planned. He did indicate, at an early stage, that he was first told by someone other than Liberto that he was going to be approached to play a role in the killing. He named the person, who seemed to have some inside knowledge, but since then, he has wished to keep the man's name quiet. We deposed this person and, not unexpectedly, he denied having any prior knowledge.

The report makes much of the fact that Jowers did not precisely know Raul's name. Hard of hearing, even then, he consistently stated that he thought the name sounded like "Royal." The report neglects to mention, however, that he unhesitatingly picked Raul out in the photo spread as the man who visited him and gave him the murder weapon.[129]

In respect of the MPD involvement, Jowers, at least in our experience, has been consistent. He has consistently said that Liberto told him that the police would be nowhere around. He has also consistently named his former friend Inspector John Barger, undercover officer Marrell Mc-Collough, and Lieutenant Earl Clark as participating in the planning sessions. Another officer was present as well but Jowers maintained that he did not know his name. I have increasingly found that to be curious.

The report continually refers to the discredited ABC polygraph interview as a source for Jowers's inconsistencies. I am not able to comment on that session, because as noted earlier, ABC has steadfastly refused to allow any access to its materials and its FBI polygrapher has been sanctioned and fined by the Tennessee regulatory authorities for misconduct in conducting the examination. I can state, however, that Jowers's attorney, Garrison, present throughout, categorically denies that during that interview Jowers recanted his statements about the MPD involvement and the roles of the officers involved. Conducting an analysis of the existing evidence for any indication of corroboration of MPD involvement, the report concludes that there was none.

The Justice Department team found it implausible that Jowers would have been told to be at his back door at 6:00 PM due to the fact that this would have required someone in Dr King's group to arrange to have him in position at that time. The report concludes that Dr King's appearance on the balcony just before 6:00 PM was "coincidental."[130]

The report states that the DOJ investigation uncovered no corroborating evidence to support Jowers's contention that he received the murder weapon from the shooter (who was dressed in blue trousers and a white tee shirt) immediately after it was fired. I have long believed that Jowers was not at the back door but actually out in the brush area with, or near to, the shooter, and that he took the rifle from him at that point and ran back inside with it just as Betty Spates originally maintained.

The report cites the absence of footprints (ignoring those in the alleyway) as an indication that neither Jowers or anyone else was out there. First, no one, including the DOJ team, really knows anything about that area, because it was totally compromised the next morning by the massive MPD supervised clean-up. Secondly, the brush cover, even wet, was certainly heavy enough to prevent any footprints from being left behind.[131]

I recall that Betty Spates always insisted that the knees of Jowers's trousers were wet as though he had been kneeling in the wet brush. The report notes that Spates's accounts vary, as indeed they do (I have come to believe, for a variety of reasons related to her own security and that of her children). Her presence in the grill is questioned. It is true that she was not working that day. She said that she came across to the grill very close to 6:00 PM and went into the kitchen to look for Jowers. Jowers himself denied that Spates was present, because her account directly involved him in the killing rather than being on the periphery as he preferred. Needless to say, if Jowers was out in the bushes with, or near to, the shooter, this would confirm Betty Spates's story.

The DOJ investigators chose to disbelieve the Jowers/Spates story of how the rifle was taken into the grill and placed under the counter. In fact, the discreet manner in which, he and Betty said, he carried the weapon and concealed it, is highly plausible. The report proceeds to find no plausible evidence that the fatal shot was fired from the bushes behind Jim's Grill.

In cavalier fashion, the report also dismisses the eyewitness accounts of Solomon Jones, Reverend James Orange, and *New York Times* reporter Earl Caldwell. It rejects out of hand Jones's comments overheard by then reporter Wayne Chastain and others that he saw a man come down from the wall. Since Jones was an MPD informant, I believe that his initial, spontaneous comments were likely to be truthful and accurate, but it is also probable that over time, he could have been induced to say almost anything that the MPD wanted to have on the record. It is his subsequent comments that the report chooses to find credible, not his earlier spontaneous declarations. Also dismissed out of hand is Reverend Orange's observation of a puff of smoke rising from the bushes right after the shot, ". . . because there were no footprints in the muddy area . . ."[132] What muddy area? Once again, the bushes and ground cover were very thick, and, in any event, the entire area was sanitized during the next light of day. Incredibly, the report states that even if Orange's observation was accurate it ". . . does not suggest that presence of an assassin at that location."[133]

As for Earl Caldwell, the report concludes that if he saw anyone in the bushes, it was most likely to have been a policeman. Gerald Frank's interview with Caldwell is cited as an example of an account given by the reporter close to the event, in which he did not mention seeing a figure crouching in the bushes. The report does not, however, disclose Frank's relationship with the FBI. The report says that Caldwell acknowledged not writing about his observations in his *Times* report (he always said that the paper had a policy prohibiting reporters from becoming a part of the story being covered). He set out his observations in a manuscript completed some years after the fact in the 1970s. He may also have mentioned his observations in the *Times* talk piece following the assassination. The DOJ report contradicts itself by stating on the one hand that there is no such reference made and then by stating, ". . . In the *"Times Talk"* article, his testimony at the mock trial and his interview with our investigation, he recalled Solomon Jones driving Dr King's car back and forth in front of his room, *immediately after he saw the figure in the brush. In fact, he related that Jones' erratic driving distracted him from watching that figure.*"[134]

In any event, the report goes to considerable lengths to attempt to justify its position of denying the validity of the independent observations of Jones, Orange, and Caldwell, once again citing the MPD reports about the absence of footprints.

In discussing the various sightings of a man coming down over the wall after the shooting, it summarily dismisses Wayne Chastain's account of Jones's comments soon after the event, and discredits Louie Ward's story about what he was told by a fellow cab driver who he knew by the nickname of "Buddy" but whose full name he thought was Paul Butler. The report disbelieves Louie's account and goes on to state that no witnesses or photograph revealed the presence of a taxicab around the motel immediately after the assassination.[135] The DOJ investigators

obviously did not interview Ernestine Campbell, the owner of the Trumpet Motel who observed the yellow taxi cab in the driveway of the
Lorraine through her passenger side view mirror as she pulled away from
a stopped position in front of the driveway shortly after the shooting.
Ernestine told me this story during the civil trial but was too frightened
to testify. She has, since then, again confirmed the observation to me.

Olivia Catling's story of seeing a man running – the report said "walk"
– from a driveway and get into a car on Huling and speed away in front
of a police barricade was disputed as an ". . . implausible route for the
assassin . . ."[136] No one ever suggested that the person was the "assassin,"
just someone who may have had some role to play in the conspiracy. In
fact, such a person was observed earlier in the afternoon of April 4 by a
Southern Bell Telephone repairman – Hasel Huckaby, who had parked
his truck on Huling whilst working on lines at Fred Galt's warehouse.
Olivia Catling was confirming in 1999 what he told me in 1992. At that
time, he made it clear that the man, though pretending to be drunk,
appeared too well dressed to be a local wino. He suspected that he was a
law enforcement officer, possibly an FBI agent.

The building at the end of the alleyway, from which Catling saw the
man emerge, adjoined the rooming house. A number of photographs
taken at the time show a window in that building, which is right next to
the bathroom window, propped open with a stick. We do not know the
role if any of this person. Neither do we really know how many people
may have been out in the bushes, but it is disappointing that the DOJ
task force seemed to be interested in denying any fact or occurrence
which indicates a scenario different from the official story.

Another example of this is the report's conclusion in a footnote[137] that
there is no evidence that an alleged second Mustang on South Main had
anything to do with the assassination. This seems to ignore Charles
Hurley's very credible account of a second Mustang with Arkansas plates
parked just south of Canipe's store about an hour and a quarter before
the killing. Sitting in the car was a man wearing a windbreaker – James
was dressed in a suit on that day. This is the precise location from which
the Mustang pulled away after the bundle was dropped in Canipe's
doorway. James's Mustang had been parked further north in front of the
door to Jim's Grill and had been noticed in that spot by a number of

witnesses who observed it between 4:00 PM and 5:45 PM. It is clear that the bundle dropper drove off in the Mustang with Arkansas plates some while after James drove off in his Mustang with Alabama plates having been seen by witnesses William Reed and Ray Hendrix as they exited Jim's Grill between 5:30 PM and 5:45 PM. Reed and Hendrix gave from 302 statements to the FBI and the MPD and, though long ignored, they should certainly have been accessible to the DOJ task force. To ignore this kind of evidence, in my view, is to clearly reveal an orientation to defend the status quo in the case at all costs.

The location of the shooter – the rooming house

The report supports the official view that the assassin fired from the second-floor bathroom window and not from the brush area behind Jim's Grill.

James's plea bargain, discussed earlier, is, of course, used against him, as are the statements of two rooming house residents, both of whom had drinking problems and one of whom – Anschutz – could not identify the person he allegedly saw leaving James's room. In fact, the state's chief witness, Charlie Stephens, was dead drunk at the time of the shooting and could not identify anyone. This was confirmed not only by then reporter Chastain, but also by MPD Lieutenant Tommy Smith who interviewed Stephens shortly after the killing. No mention is made of Stephens's condition in the report.

The DOJ investigators also disbelieve taxi driver James McCraw's statement that when he arrived to pick up his fare, Charlie Stephens, he found him too drunk to carry. At the time McGraw left the building – about 5 to 10 minutes before the shooting – he consistently said, the bathroom was empty.

In considering the evidence rifle, the DOJ report, like all of the other official investigators, turns the usual forensic processes upside down. Instead of stating the clear truth that the death slug could not be matched to the alleged murder weapon, the report focuses on the fact that the rifle could not be conclusively excluded. Exclusion of a weapon is far more difficult than matching it to a death slug. The fact is that if the death slug cannot be matched with the weapon, there is no murder weapon in evidence. The opinion of Judge Joe Brown, who presided over the hearings on the rifle and concluded that it was not the murder weapon, was also dismissed by the report. Most significant in Judge Brown's opinion was an FBI report of an examination conducted on the morning after the killing which showed that the rifle had not been sighted in and would not have been fired accurately. Incredibly, the report states that the sight was ". . . only an insignificant three inches off to the right and less than an inch low when test fired at 205 feet . . ." First, three inches off to the right is certainly not an "insignificant" deviation. Second, the FBI examination report stated that the sight was causing the rifle to fire not less than an inch low but rather "four" inches below the target, making the DOJ's submission clearly false.

The report also dismisses and misrepresents Judge Arthur Hanes's recollection that Guy Canipe told him that the bundle containing the rifle and certain of James's belongings was dropped in front of his shop about 10 minutes before the shot. The report calls Judge Hanes's statement a "current recollection"[138] when, in fact, Art Hanes has carried this memory with him for 32 years.

In their haste to dismiss Judge Hanes's evidence, the DOJ task force tripped over itself.[139] The report cites Canipe's 1969 statement that the police arrived some 10 minutes after the bundle was dropped. Since Canipe did not actually hear the shot, his frame of reference was the dropping of the bundle.

The TACT 10 lead officer on that day was Sheriff Department officer Lieutenant Judson "Bud" Ghormley. From the outset, Ghormley maintained that he arrived at Canipe's and discovered the bundle two or three minutes after the shot. His "soft bones" deterred him from jumping down from the wall and so he ran straight up South Main from the fire station.

Ghormley so testified at the October 1974 evidentiary hearing for James. At the same hearing, former public defender Hugh Stanton Jr testified that an investigative document identified Guy Canipe as having said that a man dropped the bundle 15 minutes before the sheriff appeared. So, there it is.

Ghormley arrives at Canipe's door and discovers the bundle/rifle two or three minutes after the shooting. Canipe confirms that the police arrived either 10 minutes after the bundle was dropped (statement to defense counsel in 1969) or 15 minutes after it was dropped (1969 Public Defender's Investigative Report).

The DOJ report adopts Canipe's statement that 10 minutes lapsed between the dropping of the bundle and the police arrival. If it took the first officer Ghormley two to three minutes to arrive, this means that the bundle/rifle was dropped at least seven or eight minutes before the shot was fired.

The logic is irrefutable and is derived from the very sources available to the MPD and the FBI in 1968 as well as to the DOJ task force in 1999 to 2000. The rifle purchased by James Earl Ray had been planted – thrown down – nearly 10 minutes before Martin King was shot, by a person who was long gone by the time Sheriff Bud Ghormley arrived on the scene. It is no wonder that as he ran north on the Main Street sidewalk from the fire station toward the rooming house, he didn't see a car speeding away. It had been gone for at least five to seven minutes.

In the face of what appears to be clear evidence that the rifle was planted and in the absence of any scientific evidence linking the evidence rifle to the murder, the DOJ remarkably concludes that the rifle in evidence is the murder weapon and the fatal shot was fired from the bathroom window by James Earl Ray, who somehow drove off before the shooting in the second Mustang with Arkansas plates, which was parked just south of Canipe's.

The location of the murder weapon

The report rejects Jowers's claim that after receiving the rifle, he wrapped it in a cloth and carried it from the kitchen into the grill, where he placed it under the counter. The report states that none of the patrons observed Jowers with the rifle or hiding it. The report states that such an account is "illogical" and such an action "improbable."[140]

The investigators also rejected taxi driver James McCraw's story that Jowers showed him the rifle. They attempt to discredit McCraw by noting that he has continually expanded his story over the years. Witnesses, often fearful of becoming overly involved, at a time close to an event will frequently hold back pieces of information only to let them out at a later time when somewhat of a relationship has been developed with an investigator.

McCraw had been consistent in respect of Charlie Stephens being too drunk to carry, and the bathroom being empty within minutes of the killing on April 4, but this account is similarly dismissed by the DOJ investigators. He also had consistently told about hearing Lieutenant Earl Clark threaten to kill Dr King when he returned to town. Betty Spates, prior to Jowers's confirmation, corroborated McCraw's 1992 allegation that Jowers concealed the weapon under his counter. The DOJ investigators did not bother to reconstruct the interior of the grill. If they had, they would have seen that it took only a few quick steps to go behind the counter from the kitchen door.

Jowers's – and ultimately McCraw's – efforts to keep some distance between themselves and direct, culpable involvement, resulted in Jowers varying his accounts about what he did with the real murder weapon. The last thing he would admit was being responsible for having it thrown into the river. Hence, one time he said he gave it to Raul and another it was to an employee of Frank Liberto. Similarly, the now deceased McCraw never admitted to us that he actually took the murder weapon and disposed of it. To do so would have made him directly involved in the assassination. His long-term friend William Hamblin said McCraw would only discuss this action when he was intoxicated and then the account he gave was always identical. In light of all the facts, this version seems to me to be the most credible, and it was set out under oath by Hamblin. The DOJ disagreed.

The Liberto involvement

The report discussed Jowers's allegations concerning Liberto as well as John McFerren's account of overhearing Frank Liberto telling someone on the telephone to "shoot the son of a bitch when he comes on the balcony" or words to that effect. The DOJ investigators found that McFerren's other earlier, and mistaken, allegations about James Earl Ray render his specific allegation against Liberto as incredible. The report quotes Memphis attorney David Caywood, who was with McFerren on the evening of April 8 when he was officially interviewed, as saying that he did not remember McFerren saying that he heard Liberto use the words "on the balcony." As noted earlier, when I subsequently spoke with Caywood, he not only did not make this assertion, but he insisted that when he spoke to the rotating interrogators – he was not actually present in the room during the questioning but sat outside – they unanimously indicated that McFerren's story was consistent and apparently truthful. John McFerren, then, and now, has never had a reason to lie about what he heard; neither did the report put forward any explanation as to why he might lie. It is true that John, having heard about the arrest and guilty plea of James Earl Ray came to believe wrongly that James's name "Ray" was mentioned in the conversation between LL & L partner Jim Latch and Liberto as Latch turned the phone over to Liberto, but this was some eight years after the event and the reference was never a part of his original account.[141]

But other accounts of Liberto's involvement surfaced, and of course these, as well, had to be explained away and rejected for the official story to remain intact. In particular are the story of Liberto's admissions of involvement made independently to Nathan Whitlock and his mother LaVada Whitlock Addison.

Nathan Whitlock was portrayed in the report as a paranoid, profiteering individual whose account of his conversation with Liberto was not deemed credible. It is true that Nathan, a struggling taxi driver, has sought payment for photographs that he has retained, but should he not do so? Why should he be expected to simply turn over such material to commercial entities which will use them for their own profit-making purposes? I suggest that this in no way detracts from the accuracy or credibility of his account of Liberto's incriminating remarks made to him directly some ten years after the killing and which, in any event, were initially made to his mother LaVada.

Unable, on any grounds, to discredit Mrs Addison, the DOJ investigators characterize the comments made by Liberto to her to be a ". . . false macho boast."[142] They regard her not wanting to hear what Liberto was saying as her categorical disbelief, which it certainly was not. Mrs Addison quite simply and understandably did not want to get involved. She did not want to hear what he had to say. It was too unsettling. Far from a "macho boast," her description of Liberto's comments when something about the case came on the television in the cafe indicated that he spoke quite softly, even reflectively, though decisively.

The report even goes so far as to deny the existence of any Liberto family involvement with Carlos Marcello. This was certainly not the impression I obtained from Art Baldwin, the Memphis topless club owner who detailed Liberto's relationship with the Memphis godfather and the Marcello organization. Whitlock's recollection of Liberto telling him about pushing a cart as a youngster through the New Orleans streets with Carlos Marcello is compatible with this relationship.

The report calls the sources of Liberto's alleged mafia ties to be "unreliable." If this is the case, then the MPD task force, on which S.O. Blackburn served, to keep Liberto under surveillance due to such connections and illegal activity, must also be "unreliable." If the DOJ investigators had interviewed Blackburn, he would have connected Jowers to Liberto through Jowers's ownership of the Tremont cafe on Calhoun, which was used as a gambling room then by Jowers and Liberto.[143]

Finally, the DOJ totally ignored the extensive research in Memphis, completed by *Time* magazine stringer William Sartor immediately after the assassination, in which he established Liberto's ties to the Marcello organization. My entire file on Sartor's work is in the King Library and Archives with the rest of my papers on the case. The DOJ task force spent several days going over this material.

The report finds no credible evidence to sustain Jowers's contention that he received $100,000 from Liberto in the bottom of a produce box by way of an M. E. Carter Produce Company delivery, with the funds originating in New Orleans.

Jack Saltman insists that in his first interview with Jowers, prior to the *Prime Time Live* program filming, Jowers claimed he kept $90,000 of the money, passing on $10,000 to someone else – ostensibly the triggerman. Jowers's attorney Garrison questions whether that conversation even took place. Jack's degree of detail is impressive. In fact, Jowers did – as Saltman contends he admitted – acquire the Veterans Cab Company within the year after the shooting. He obviously had to get the money from somewhere: Saltman insisted Jowers told him that was what he did with the King money. Despite this sequence of events, the report states, "...the financial records we reviewed did not reveal any significant improvement in Jowers's life style at any time after the assassination. Nor did any witness we interviewed, including family members, detect that Jowers received a substantial windfall. Accordingly, there is no evidence to corroborate Jowers's claims (apparently now abandoned, in any event) that he received $90,000 for his role in the assassination."[144]

It is true that Jowers's later accounts, particularly in his sessions with Dexter King, claimed that he simply handed the money over to Raul. Whilst the report also contends that there was no independent corroboration for him receiving the money, in fact, both Betty Spates and her sister Alda Mae Washington recalled (also confirmed by Saltman interviews with them at the time) seeing a large amount of money rolled up and hidden in the disused kitchen stove in the grill.

Alda Mae eventually retracted her story saying that she only began working at the grill several months after the killing, but this was not her position, nor that of Betty, closer to the time of Jowers's admissions in 1993.

In light of all of this information, it clear that the DOJ investigators have selectively decided who and what to believe so that denials are applied to the Jowers/Liberto relationship and involvement, Liberto's Mafia associations, and the other incriminating admissions by Liberto. The basically unsubstantiated official story is incredibly endorsed here as elsewhere.

The involvement of the Memphis Police Department (MPD)

The report next turns to a consideration of the involvement of the MPD, which, of course, is another element of Jowers's story. The DOJ investigators considered the following events:

1. The alleged removal of officers to facilitate the assassination.
2. The alleged meeting of MPD officers at Jim's Grill.
3. The alleged participation of MPD Lieutenant Earl Clark.

In discussing the "removal" of the security detail, the report avoids discussing the major issues: that is, why the security unit of black detectives, previously formed by black officers like Jerry Williams, for Dr King's visits, was not in place during his last visit. Instead, a team of white MPD officers, never used before, was ordered to form a "security" detail which, itself, was withdrawn late on the afternoon of the first day – April 3. The report quotes Reverend Kyles as saying that Dr King's group did not want police protection. If the DOJ investigators had interviewed the Reverend James Lawson on this issue, they would have learned that this was not the case. Lawson would have told them that the group of black detectives had previously been accepted as a local security force, and that no decision had been taken by either SCLC or the local strike support group – whose meetings were rarely attended by Reverend Kyles (Kyles had no position whatsoever with SCLC) – to reject the assistance of Jerry Williams and the usual black detectives. Captain Williams has consistently said that he never received a satisfactory explanation as to why he was not allowed to put his usual team in place, but instead a group of white officers, an unlikely security force, was formed. The report further confuses this issue by linking hostility directed toward Ed Redditt at the airport, with an alleged rejection of the usual MPD security detail. Redditt had been identified as a surveillance officer, so it is understandable that there was hostility toward him. There had never been that reaction to Jerry Williams and his discrete team which watched over Dr King, 24 hours a day, during his previous visit. At no time did Jerry Williams, or his team, face a lack of cooperation or experience frustration as they provided security. Jim Lawson remembers being impressed with their sincerity when they advised him on a previous occasion that, so long as they were on the job, no harm would come to Dr King.

On his last visit to Memphis they were not on the job, and the DOJ report ignores their absence and does not even raise the question as to why they were removed.

The removal of the TACT 10 unit from a base at the Lorraine Motel to the periphery of the fire station is discussed in two different sections of the report. It acknowledges Inspector William Crumby's statement that TACT commander Sam Evans requested permission to withdraw the unit from the area of the Lorraine, ostensibly at the request of a member of the King group (who Evans identified on separate occasions to Professor Melanson and to me as Reverend Kyles). The report denies that Evans ever requested such permission and accepts Kyles's denial that he ever put forward such a request for the King group, on whose behalf, in any event, he had no authority.

The report even attempts to muddle the fact that the TACT 10 pullback ever occurred, claiming that a number of TACT unit cars were in the area at the time of the shooting. Indeed, they were in the area, on the periphery at the fire station, where they had been moved from the Lorraine on Sam Evans's order.

In discussing the removal of Ed Redditt, following the report of what turned out to be a bogus threat by Philip Manual, who is described as being a staff member of the McClellan Senate Subcommittee on Investigations, the report concludes that there was nothing sinister about Redditt's removal since the threat was, at the time, believed to be real. In any event, the report notes that the other African-American detective on the fire station surveillance detail, Willie B. Richmond, was left in place, which would not have been the case if the removal was designated to facilitate the assassination.

The report ignores the fact that whilst Richmond was a reliable member of the MPD's intelligence division, Redditt was seconded on to the surveillance detail from his primary position which was in community relations. In his main police work, he was quite close to and sympathetic with the community and thus, unlike Richmond, he could very well be unreliable in the face of an assassination attempt on Dr King. To avoid the risk of that possibility, it made eminent good sense to get him away from the area of the crime scene.[145]

As to Jowers's allegations that MPD officers met in Jim's Grill to plan the assassination, the DOJ investigators concluded that Jowers's accounts were so vague about the meetings as to render the allegations useless. It is true that in his effort to distance himself from having any prior knowledge about the killing, Jowers did not admit participating in the meetings. This position made it difficult for him to acknowledge that he knew that the meetings were planning sessions for the assassination. What the report fails to do, however, is to consider his contention that it was only later, after the killing, that he realized what purpose was served by those sessions. The report also ignores the total context and time in which the MPD officers came to meet in Jim's Grill. It is important to remember that initially Jowers had been told when his help was being solicited by Liberto that the MPD were in on the killing and that no policemen would be around the scene of the crime at the time of the crime.

Even if Jowers, a former policeman, did not participate in the meetings attended by two of his friends – Barger and Clark – which itself is very unlikely, with the background he had he could certainly have reasonably surmised that these meetings of the several MPD officers were about the assassination about which Liberto had spoken to him.

The report puts a considerable amount of trust and belief in the self-serving denials of the officers (those still living) as to their having participated in such meetings. What, indeed, would we expect them to say? Marrell McCollough, described in the report as the "Undercover officer," allegedly passed a lie detector test along with some others and issued a sworn affidavit and unequivocally stated that he had ". . . never met Jowers."[146]

The lie detector test aside, since we have no access to it and we know that they can be controlled by learned techniques and a skillful examiner, one has to wonder why McCollough in a telephone conversation from CIA Headquarters admitted to Sam Donaldson's (the TV newscaster) producer Ira Rosen that he did in fact know Loyd Jowers. The report ignores this conversation.

The report notes that each of the people – still living – named by Jowers consented to be interviewed and two of them gave statements under oath, whilst Jowers refused to speak with the DOJ investigators even though an opportunity to obtain immunity was offered. As noted earlier, the report ignores the fact that there had been, since 1993, a proffer from Jowers with the Shelby County district attorney general, and that it had never been taken up. If the DOJ task force really wanted to hear from Jowers, all it had to do was obtain an actual offer of immunity from the state with any reasonable conditions attached to it. Jowers's attorney Lewis Garrison says all they received were vague and essentially worthless references concerning the possibility of immunity being granted. Jowers comes under further criticism in the report because he did not make his allegations under oath in *King v. Jowers* et al. This is disingenuous at best. After the first week, Jowers became too ill to even leave his bed and attend the trial. In fact, Attorney Garrison filed a motion for a mistrial based upon his client's inability to assist in his own defense. Though strongly argued the motion was denied, but, the fact remained that neither side could require Jowers's testimony, and it was not the defendant's fault.

The report also quickly dismisses Jowers's tenuous allegation that MPD Lieutenant Earl Clark was the assassin. The report states that: "We found no credible evidence to sustain Jowers' various assertions concerning the Lieutenant . . ."[147]

The DOJ task force interviewed Rebecca Clark, his first wife, who he divorced in 1975.[148]

In a footnote, the report noted that "police witnesses we interviewed claim that the Memphis Police had portable radios (walkie-talkies) in 1968, not withstanding a contrary, unsubstantiated assertion by the lawyer questioning the ex-wife at the trial."[149] It is simply incredible that the DOJ task force investigators did not ask or would not have asked the ex-wife to describe the radio she said was sitting on her dining room table. It gets worse.

On the facts of her statement to the DOJ task force, if she woke Lieutenant Clark up "immediately" after hearing about the assassination and that was about 45 minutes after his arrival, that meant that he could have entered the home around 5:15 to 5:30 PM. On its face, this recollection indicates that he arrived home well over an hour after she did – hardly "a short while later." At the very least, this discrepancy should have caused the DOJ investigators to enquire further, if, that is, they were interested in learning the truth about whether or not Lieutenant Clark was involved as Jowers alleged.

That the DOJ task force with all of their access and resources did not look any further at this important issue is a further indication of the biased way in which the entire investigation was conducted. If they had checked further, they would have established beyond any doubt that the ex-wife lied about her and her husband's movements on the afternoon of the killing. The sworn statement of Thomas Dent leaves little doubt that Lieutenant Clark was not at home that afternoon. Even if Clark had been home and sent his wife to pick up his uniform as she stated, the store would have been closed before she even left home. Nothing better demonstrates the pre-determined farcical nature of this investigation than how the alibi of Lieutenant Earl Clark was examined.

The balance of the report on Jowers attacks his credibility and says he was not serious about obtaining immunity. (A considerable dispute did develop between Attorney Garrison and his client Jowers, on one hand, and the DOJ task force.) I still believe that the immunity envelope was not pushed as far as it might have been across the table to the DOJ side, but, as an opposing counsel, there was only so much I could do. A pecuniary motive was ascribed to Jowers who is accused in the report of hoping to create a sensational, marketable account of the assassination which could earn him a lot of money. This is ironic because as a result of his disclosures, Jowers lost everything and died a poor man.[150]

The report speculates about why all of this "false" information was generated and impugns the motives of the individuals, many of whom I came to know and respect. In an effort to discredit some of the statements, the report bandies about the word "hearsay" without informing non-legally trained readers that there are many exceptions to the exclusion of hearsay evidence and which, in fact, make the statements credible and admissible.[151]

No, I'm afraid that the report's speculations, shoddy analysis of Jowers's motivations, and those of others – some who knew him and some who did not – and its shockingly inadequate investigation of critical accounts, which were accepted without question, add to a dismally one-sided, unjustified conclusion concerning the involvement of Loyd Jowers in the assassination of Martin Luther King Jr.

The allegations of Donald Wilson

The report states that the DOJ task force investigators met with Don Wilson on September 16 1998 and contends that, at that meeting, Don told them that he had obtained five documents from James's Mustang on April 11 1968. Two were business cards and two were pieces of paper with handwritten notations on them. The fifth piece of paper had the telephone number of the FBI's Atlanta field office written on it.

The report summarily reviewed the history of the events leading up to the DOJ investigators ultimately acquiring two of the documents.

Don's contact with the King Center and myself, following the HBO/ Thames Television mock trial, and the King family's public call for a trial for James, was followed by the meeting with Fulton County, Georgia district attorney Paul Howard. Don publicly stated his desire to turn the documents over to Attorney General Reno, and though this was never accomplished, he finally met on September 16 1998 with the DOJ task force.

The report states that he refused to display the original documents when he learned that on orders from Washington, the task force had posted a United States marshal at his bank and obtained a search warrant for his bank safe deposit box. The next morning he turned over two of the documents he allegedly took from James's car.

The report omits some critical details about this history. First, Don Wilson, from the outset, wanted to meet with Attorney General Reno and turn the evidence over to her. He tried to contact her over a period of three or four days after the meeting with district attorney Howard in Atlanta. When he called, he was passed around to different people. He never did obtain a response from her, but the FBI issued press statements and releases that the documents and his allegations were a complete fabrication. They said that their records indicated that he was not one of the officers who examined the car – he was not even there; in other words, he was a liar.

So, as Don Wilson persisted in trying to get a meeting with the attorney general, the FBI continued to attack him in the media. She ignored him, and they called him a liar. He withdrew his offer to cooperate. Then, in September 1998, he received a cordial letter from Barry Kowalski the DOJ task force leader, which stated that he, Wilson, was critical to the DOJ investigation. Wilson asked Kowalski how it was that the DOJ thought he was critical and yet the FBI was publicly calling him a liar and labeling the documents as fabrications. Kowalski's response was that "We can't control the FBI," to which Wilson responded "The Attorney General is the boss of the FBI." Kowalski changed the subject and said they wanted to do an honest above-board investigation. Wilson agreed to be interviewed.

Don said he felt comfortable at the meeting and that they said "all the right things." He decided to turn over the original documents and took task force representatives along to his bank, where he is on the board. He obtained a conference room, where he intended to effect the turnover, but as they were about to begin a secretary motioned him to come over. He excused himself for a minute and went over to talk with her. She told him they had seen a man watching the bank for some time, and they were afraid he was going to rob it and called the police.

The police arrived. They surrounded the car and ordered him out – they had his hands on top of the roof then. He identified himself as working for Mr Kowalski of the Justice Department. They had Don and the bank under surveillance.

Don went back to the conference room and asked them point blank, "Does the federal marshal in the parking lot out front work for you?"

This was very embarrassing. Kowalski and his group were unresponsive and looked at each other. Don said, "The police were here a little while ago. He said that he works for you. What is he doing here? These people at the bank are frightened."

Then Kowalski said, "This was decided in Washington. We don't know you. We don't know if we can trust you."

Don said, "I don't understand what you're talking about. I'm here to help you as a witness. Am I the target of an investigation? Why am I under surveillance?"

They wouldn't answer the question.

Don then told them, "Mr Kowalski, I was prepared to give you the original documents. I will give you copies today. I'm going to withhold the originals because I feel this relationship is rapidly going downhill. I don't believe that this is an honest, fair, objective investigation. I feel I'm the target."

Don said that, for a while, they did continue the interview but from that point, the questions were about Dexter King, Oliver Stone, and myself – not about the evidence in the investigation.[152] As they parted, Kowalski said to let him know by Friday. Then, later that afternoon Don said Kowalski called and a series of threats began.

According to Wilson, he said, "I'm going to put you in jail. We've got a search warrant that the US Attorney General authorized, and a federal judge signed it." Don said he called several times that evening and then, Thursday morning after Don left for work, he said that Kowalski called again and very badly verbally abused his wife, telling her that her husband was a liar. She called Don crying and upset. He said he called Kowalski who threatened to send someone out to the school. He then also placed people in the bank's conference room. At one point, when Don complained about the harassment, he was told that "the federal government has absolutely no regard for your feelings or your family's feelings at all."

I was in eastern Europe when this was going on, and I spoke with Barry Kowalski by phone to question him about the treatment of the Wilsons. His response was that he only did what was necessary to secure these vital documents and that if they had not taken the action they did, Don Wilson would not have turned over the originals to the government or to me. Having come to know Don, I believe, without question, that he always wanted to do the right thing. He even seemed willing to separate the DOJ from the FBI attacks on him, until, however, he became aware that they had him under surveillance as though he was a suspected criminal rather than a cooperating provider of vital materials.

In the face of this siege, Don turned over the two originals to Inspector Bonner, an official with the DOJ task force, who he contends contaminated the documents by removing them from protective plastic envelopes, and asking him to initial and date them, actually writing on the originals. He was appalled but did so in order to provide tangible evidence of the lack of professionalism of the task force, the actual alteration of which was responsible for original evidentiary documents. He said that she then just stuffed them into an old brown envelope.

On the following Sunday, September 20, Dexter and Coretta King called Don to give him support and the very next day the tires on his wife's car were slashed in the parking lot, where she worked.

The report goes on to criticize Don Wilson on a number of counts, namely:

1. That he revealed belatedly the existence of a fifth document (the paper with the telephone number of the Atlanta field office).
2. That he varied his story as to when and where he actually reviewed the documents (at the scene or at home that evening).

3. That he varied his reason for concealing the documents (fear of the consequences of contaminating a crime scene or the discovery of a relationship between James and the local FBI).
4. That he varied his accounts concerning the disappearance of certain of the documents (whether the two business cards had been "lost" or "stolen" from his office).
5. That he demonstrated a lack of veracity concerning the actual location of the documents (whether or not they were in his bank safe deposit box).

The report concludes that Don Wilson's statements were inconsistent and that he provided false information either to the King family, myself, district attorney Howard, or to DOJ task force and the media. The report also concludes that there can be no rational explanation for Don's "lack of candor." What is characterized as his "belated revelation" – the existence of the fifth document – is viewed as raising a serious question about the credibility of his other statements about the documents, including how he came by them.

It does not take much experience in the conduct of criminal investigative tasks, not to mention the sensitive investigative work required where a political assassination is concerned, to realize that witnesses, in positions where they may have come to possess significant information, will almost always feel the need to hold back some details or aspects of the entire story. Inevitably, they come with baggage. It may be that a witness wishes to protect someone, or feels duty bound not to reveal the whole truth. An effort to pedantically impose the standard of total truthfulness on such a witness is naïve at best and deliberately diversionary at worst. I do not for a moment believe that the DOJ task force members are naïve.

Consequently, experienced practitioners learned long ago to take such witnesses as they found them, using any information that could be elevated to the level of admissible evidence.

I accepted from the outset that there were certain events and activities in which Don Wilson had became involved, subsequent to his FBI career, in the service of his country. The fact that he could not discuss this aspect of service with me, or anyone else, was acceptable. I also came to believe that certain of the documentation may well have disappeared from his possession in a way that was beyond his control. I in no way believed that these events should prevent us from considering the materials he provided on their own merits.

As to the alleged minor inconsistencies about when he examined the documents (I believe he looked at them at the scene, but only considered them in depth at home that night), why he kept them to himself for 30 years (his reasons are certainly not mutually exclusive), or why he did not reveal the existence of the Atlanta field office telephone number document (the most sensitive, requiring the greatest caution) – his ambivalence, lack of trust, and hesitancy are not only understandable but justified in light of all of the facts, many of which are undisclosed in the report.

He was immediately attacked when he put his toe in the water of disclosure, and in addition, he was ignored and rebuffed by the chief law enforcement officer of the land, who he had seriously hoped would be at least willing to hear what he had to say. Is there any wonder that he would be less than fully forthcoming in the first instance? Considering the treatment he received, when he had decided to cooperate, is there any wonder why he would totally distrust the governmental representatives responsible for his harassment?

What is particularly appalling is that I have no doubt that the DOJ task force with all of its access to official records and information knows full well who Don Wilson is and what he has done for his country in other spheres of activity, and yet fails to even quietly apply this knowledge to the credit of the man and the relevant aspects of his story concerning the evidence he found.

Now for the report's consideration of the details as to how Don Wilson came by the evidence from James's car. The report states that the DOJ investigative team interviewed witnesses who were present at the discovery of the Mustang, its subsequent search and the search of James's rented room in Atlanta. (Wilson has also stated that he participated in an operation which effected an unauthorized search of that room.) The DOJ team also claimed to have examined all relevant reports, records, and other documents. The report concluded that no independent evidence was found to corroborate Wilson's claim that he took documents from the car or that he participated in the search operation of James's rented room. Instead, the report stated that the investigators found substantial, reliable evidence that contradicted both assertions.

No witnesses known to be at the scene allegedly remember seeing Don Wilson, and he appears in none of the photographs taken at the time.

Don Wilson has consistently said that the passenger side door was locked but ajar. He said he clandestinely opened the door. It is thus not surprising that no one would have observed him doing it. When it came open, he said that an envelope with the various documents fell at his feet. He checked to make certain that no one noticed. Then he pushed the door back with his knee, fully closed it, picked up the envelope, and quickly concealed it in his pocket because he feared that he had negligently tampered with a crime scene. He said he walked away and glanced at the documents. His initial instinct was to figure out a way to get the envelope back in the car, until he noticed the local FBI office telephone number with an extension number on one of the pieces of paper. He said that was when he made the decision to withhold the evidence.

The report contends that the Atlanta officers who arrived later on do not remember any argument between law enforcement officers. (Wilson said that the senior agent who took him along engaged in a debate with the Atlanta officers as to who was going to take charge. He has never claimed that there was a dispute about opening a front or back door as the report alleges.)

Don recalls that he drove the FBI car back from the Capitol Homes parking lot following behind the truck which was pulling the Mustang. The senior agent was riding in the truck. He drove straight into the FBI garage behind the truck. At one time, he was told that the DOJ task force heard that a senior agent did recall seeing a junior agent at the scene.

The report is unable to conclusively refute Don's description of the interior of the car as filled with trash. It implies, however, that this may not have been the case since most witnesses had no recollection of the Mustang's interior – suggesting that there may not have been anything remarkable about it.[153]

The report notes Wilson's account, finding his version of events to be unsubstantiated and "so improbable as to be unbelievable."[154] It also rejects his reasons for not coming forward earlier, rejecting his explanation that he deeply distrusted the FBI, and the DOJ itself which supervised the Bureau. Don told the DOJ task force about experiences he had early on in his career which convinced him of the racism of the Bureau.

The forensic examination of the documents

The report finally turns to a consideration of the two documents which Don Wilson turned over to the DOJ task force. The United States Secret Service (USSS) laboratory found the torn page form the 1968 Dallas telephone directory to be consistent in ageing with the page in the actual directory. In addition, the printed words on the evidence page were identical to those which appeared on page 386 of the 1963 Dallas directory. The absence of any microscopic fiber breakage indicated there was no evidence to suggest that the writing on the paper was recently produced on the old paper. The report goes on to state, however, that when their USSS examiners were provided with a similar page 386 from a 1963 telephone directory "utilizing similar pressure and angles and various backing materials,"[155] (this raises the question of how they could possibly have known how, or in what manner, the document was prepared) they concluded that this Wilson document could have been recently created by someone making the pencil entries on the torn page 386 from the 1963 Dallas directory. Hence, because the experimental page also showed no microscopic fiber breakage the scientific testing could not resolve whether the Wilson documents are authentic, the precise age of the handwritten entries or whether they actually came from James's Mustang in 1968.

The USSS indicated that the handwritten entries on the telephone directory page were too limited to determine from samples whether James, Jerry, or John Ray, or Donald Wilson or Raul (from New York) was the author but concluded that none of the above wrote the second document. No fingerprints were found.

The report finds suspicious the fact that the Dallas telephone directory page is torn just after the name Raul and what appears to be the 1963

Dallas area code, 214, since the USSS concluded that the writing on the page was made after it was torn from the book. This writing sequence would appear to refute the initial impression that Raul's full number may have existed before the page was torn out. The page was torn out before any writing was done says the USSS and the report, and the "Raul 214" may well have been inserted near the edge to create a false impression. This analysis, however, ignores the possibility that the page could have been torn twice and that the writing would then initially have been put on a fuller page. The page could certainly have been torn again, on the right side just after the "Raul 214 –" writing in order to hide the number. Hence, it is equally possible that the whole number was put on the page after it was first torn from the book and that Raul or someone wishing to protect the number tore the page again.

Alternatively, the DOJ task force did not consider the possibility that the number 214 may not at all be an area code for a telephone number but could instead be an extension or hotel or motel room number.

In fact, the other Dallas telephone number on the page – the Jack Ruby Vegas Club number – does not have an area code in front of it, but simply sets out the Dallas number "LA – 4775." In addition, the report does not connect or relate the entry on the second document following Raul's name which is set out as "x 213," or in full "Raul x 213." An empirical analysis of this similarity might make it more evident that the "214 –" was not an area code but an extension number or a hotel or motel room number as appears to be the case with the "x 213."

This possibility is completely overlooked by the DOJ task force in their effort to strongly imply that the document was a forgery, though the report admits that such a determination must be inconclusive.

One interesting, and I suspect unwelcome, conclusion of the USSS laboratory was that the writing on the two documents had been written by two different persons,[156] since this determination would be a clear indication of conspiracy; it was glossed over and never developed. Also, the laboratory concluded that the "Raul 214 –" entry was not written at the same time as Jack Ruby's telephone number, though no comment is made as to whether both entries were made by the same person.[157]

Much is made of James's failure to positively identify the Wilson documents. James never was one to leap into making such admissions.

Since Raul had access to and used the Mustang, it was quite possible that he left items and clutter in the car, on occasion, which were unknown to James. In fact, one time when James was cleaning out the car prior to driving from Mexico to California in 1967, he came across the business card of a person who was unknown to him but very possibly was known to Raul.

Don Wilson is attacked in the report for his refusal to accept federal immunity (I note that the more serious state obstruction of justice charges were not mentioned) and take a lie detector test. The grant of federal immunity would have only been effective for past acts up to the point of him meeting with them. Don feared that he could be set up.

The report concedes that the DOJ investigation is unable to explain why Don Wilson came forward with what the task force believes is an untruthful account of how he came by the documents, and why and how the possibly forged documents were produced and what they mean.

The truth is that we do not know the full significance of these documents, but on balance, I submit that the evidence indicates that they did come from James's car as Don Wilson has courageously contended and that they clearly indicate the existence of a conspiracy, as well as the involvement of Raul and the possible previous connection of one or more of the participants with Jack Ruby.

Raul

The report notes at the outset that over a period of 25 years following his conviction "James Earl Ray, those representing him and others, have specifically identified as many as 20 different persons to be Raoul."[158] James only knew him by the name which phonetically may be spelled in the French style as "Raoul" – as he did – or in the Spanish/Portuguese style as "Raul" which we came to believe was the way his name was actually spelled and which spelling I will use in this section. The report writer(s) elect to spell the name of this alleged perpetrator as "Raoul" in order to make a distinction with the name of the man who we came to believe was the actual handler – Raul.

In my nearly 25 years of looking at this case and my 10 years of representing James, I came to believe that only one person was Raul. I certainly cannot speak for the actions of "those representing him and others,"[159] and I would hope that the DOJ investigators are not suggesting that James be held responsible for the statements of some unnamed individuals. James only ever identified one person as Raul. In 1978, during the HSCA hearings, he anonymously received an immigration photograph of an individual, who he clearly recognized as the man who had controlled his movements and provided him with money from August 1967 through the date of the assassination. There was a name on the back of the photograph, but James, concerned that he was being set up, did not accept the identity although he publicly announced that he had finally seen a picture of the man he knew as Raul. This identification was publicly reported some 22 years ago.[160]

The report ultimately concludes that the character of "Raoul" was fabricated and goes on to state that many candidates have surfaced and been discarded. Early on, the report in a footnote mentions messages that were left for James at the St Francis Hotel in Los Angeles by a person named Hardin, who some people believe may have been Raul. The report states that there are no current leads as to Hardin's identity.[161]

The DOJ task force investigators allegedly interviewed Raul in person over four hours on two separate occasions. The report states that he fully cooperated with their investigation and provided a handwriting exemplar that did not match any of the writings on the Wilson documents. (I recall, however, that the report stated earlier that in fact the USSS examination concluded that it could not conduct this type of examination with respect to the principal document – the Dallas telephone directory page.)[162] DOJ task force investigators allegedly interviewed several of his relatives, numerous persons within his community, an accountant, physician, co-workers, teachers, and storeowners.

The report concludes that the New York Raul had no involvement with the assassinations of Dr King or President Kennedy and that he had no contact with anyone connected with either of those crimes. As to the New York Raul, the report specifically found that:

1. The photo array was so suggestive that identifications resulting there from are suspect.

2. The New York Raul could not speak English during the relevant assassination period.
3. He was gainfully employed full time and often active in his tightly knit community during the relevant periods of time.
4. Glenda Grabow is not reliable.
5. Neither Loyd Jowers nor James Earl Ray are/were reliable witnesses.

In a footnote, the report also criticizes other identifications by Sid Carthew (an "English political extremist"); Royce Wilburn (too young); and Warren (who remained unidentified by Steve Tompkins who now allegedly finds him to be unreliable).

We have been at a disadvantage from the outset with respect to the New York Raul, because we have not been able to have the kind of access to him that has been afforded not only to the DOJ task force, but also to the Shelby County district attorney general's investigators and the publicist of the government's case, Gerald Posner.

It is true that the photo spread initially put together by Ken Herman does leave something to be desired, but it is irrefutable that, without prompting, no fewer that nine people, in my presence, and a tenth outside of my presence, including the New York Raul's own daughter, independently and unequivocally picked him out as the person they observed in one or another setting or activity related to the assassination or in circumstances alleged by Glenda Grabow. Could all of these witnesses be unreliable?

Then there are four significant events which, in my view, clearly incriminate the New York Raul. This evidence was known to and had to be deliberately ignored by the DOJ task force investigators. It is not mentioned in the report and I suggest that this omission is the ultimate test and criterion of its credibility and that of the underlying investigation on the issue of Raul. Given the official orientation of the investigation and the report, if these events could have been discredited or explained away, there is no doubt that this would have been done.

First, there is the tape-recorded front door conversation between television producer Jack Saltman and the New York Raul's daughter during the course of which he showed her the single photograph which had been identified by others from the spread, and she pointed to and identified her father. Second, there was an earlier telephone conversation that Jack Saltman had with the New York Raul, in which, before Raul had to break off because he was involved in preparations for his daughter's wedding, he had begun to discuss his experience in Houston and his relative Amaro. Third, there is the six-minute telephone conversation between Glenda Grabow and the New York Raul.[163] Fourth, there is the testimony under oath in *King v. Jowers* et al. by the Portuguese newspaper reporter Barbara Reis who interviewed a significant member of the New York Raul's family and was told how much the member appreciated the "government's" assistance to their family.

As for the New York Raul's English – I spoke with him on the telephone in the mid-1990s and had no difficulty in understanding him or making myself understood. As to his work schedule, an investigator I dispatched to the General Motors plant in the mid-1990s reported that she got very little cooperation from the management or supervisory staff she met, but it appeared that Raul was a piece worker who had considerable schedule flexibility.[164]

Since the DOJ task force has not shared its raw investigative data with the outside world, only referring to the results and interpretations and offering conclusions, it is not possible for any meaningful critical comment to be developed. The DOJ task force contends that their unspecified raw data and information led them to conclude that the New York Raul had no involvement in the assassination of Dr King.

The report notes that James has varied some of the details concerning his somewhat random activities on the afternoon of the killing. The report cites James's alibi of being at a gas station at the time of the killing as having been discredited during the HSCA hearings by employees of the station. In fact, no one including James was certain of which station he went to in an effort to have the flat spare tire repaired. What was discredited before the HSCA was an effort by an investigator to actually falsify an alibi. James did not need to have an alibi falsified. He already had one on the record which, unfortunately, was deeply buried in the state's files. This, of course, is reflected in the statements of Ray Hendrix and William Reed, discussed earlier. No mention is made in the report of the Hendrix and Reed statements which were contained both in FBI form 302 interview accounts and MPD interview statements and deeply hidden in the prosecutor's files.

So, the report concludes that not only is the New York Raul not James's handler, but that the very existence of Raul is a creation of James Earl Ray.

On the other hand, considering the evidence contained in the report, as well as other evidence omitted and rejected by the DOJ task force, I believe that Raul did play a significant role in the assassination of Martin King and set James up over a period of ten months. I also have little doubt that his full name, address, and telephone number are known, not the least by the government which is actively involved in protecting him in consideration for this and, likely, many other services.

Conspiracy allegations emanating from the *King v. Jowers and other unknown co-conspirators* trial

In the penultimate section VII of the report, the evidence adduced at the trial of *King v. Jowers* et al. is considered. The report found that most of the witnesses and rulings offered to support the various "government-directed conspiracy claims relied exclusively on second and third hand hearsay and speculation."[165] It also contended that the assorted assassination plots were actually contradictory. In this vein, the report criticizes the introduction of hearsay evidence, reacting as though hearsay evidence is always inadmissible in a court of law and that no exceptions exist. In fact, as the DOJ task force lawyers know only too well, hearsay evidence which is covered by one of the exceptions is readily admissible and considered reliable evidence. One of the most frequently used exceptions is a statement against penal interest. That is, if someone tells me he killed someone and I testify that he made this statement, it is hearsay but admissible, because it is against the speaker's interest to make such an admission, hence, it is likely to be true. If an FBI agent acknowledges or admits that his agency or another government agency had Dr King killed, he is certainly opening himself up to potentially serious charges or sanctions. Similarly, if an inmate relates an offer to kill James Earl Ray, which he believes emanates from the government, to a lawyer of Ray and she memorializes the conversation in an affidavit sworn at the time, it is clear that the inmate may well be taking his life in his hands by providing the information and it should be admissible. These are two of the examples cited by the report in criticism of evidence that the jury was allowed to hear.

Defense counsel Garrison also put on a "John Doe" witness, who I found unbelievable: not because he alleged his own involvement in the assassination but because his description of the crime scene was factually incorrect and made it impossible to believe that he had ever been there. The testimony of several authors and the admission into evidence of an investigative newspaper article were similarly blithely criticized even though first hand evidence resulted from the investigative work.

The report states that in contrast to the hearsay accounts, only three witnesses provided first hand information relating to any of the conspiracy allegations. Words fail me. Whilst the three – Jim Smith, Eli Arkin, and Carthel Weeden – did have first-hand testimony about some aspect of the existence of a conspiracy, or its cover-up, so also did Jack Saltman (the admission of Raul's daughter), John McFerren (the Liberto statement), Dr Coby Smith (the Invaders' investigation of the violent breaking up of the March 28 march), MPD Captain Thomas Smith (Ret.) (the observed condition of the state's lead witness), Charles Hurley (the second Mustang), Professor Phillip Melanson (TACT 10 removal), Solomon Jones (man in the brush), Kaye Pittman Black, Maynard Stiles (the cutting of the bushes), Olivia Catling (the man on Huling), Hasel Huckaby (the man on Huling), Ambassador Andrew Young and Dexter King (Jowers's admissions), Judge Art Hanes Jr (the dropping of the bundle), Mrs Bobbi Balfour (Jowers's second-floor restriction), Royce Wilburn (Raul ID), Sid Carthew (Raul ID), Joe B. Hodges (dense bushes), Barbara Reis (government protection of Raul), William B. Hamblin (McCraw's admissions), James Isabel (Jowers's admissions), Lieutenant Willie B. Richmond (Ret.) (Reverend Kyles's movements), April Ferguson (Tim Kirk's admissions), Jack Kershaw (the bribe offer to James), Louis Ward (Buddy's observations), John Smith (no police), LaVada Addison (Liberto), Nathan Whitlock (Liberto), Detective Ed Redditt (Ret.) (removal), and Captain Jerry Williams (Ret.) (no security and where MLK stayed).

As discussed earlier in detail, each of these witnesses provided direct evidence about a particular aspect, fact, or event which, however small, formed a part of the cumulative whole body of evidence.

The report moves on to dismiss all of the evidence which pointed to the involvement of the federal government in the conspiracy. It rejects the testimony of William Hamblin as "idle barber shop speculation,"[166] and contends that Hamblin never explained the basis for his knowledge that one Mr Purdy was an FBI agent. In fact, Hamblin explained that Mr Purdy had been his landlord as well as that of his friend James McCraw and that they rented rooms from Purdy and knew that his primary work was as an FBI agent. Purdy's comment that the CIA was behind the assassination thus took on a significant level of seriousness for Hamblin and his boss Vernon Jones who had also known Purdy for a number of years. The report, pointedly, does not deny that Purdy was assigned to the Memphis field office.

The report states that the DOJ task force reviewed CIA records, some of which were still classified, and found nothing to substantiate the agency's involvement in a conspiracy. I cannot believe that the absence of a smoking gun in the agency's own files would surprise or convince anyone, except perhaps this task force. On reflection, perhaps these people least of all would be surprised.

Reverend Fauntroy's awareness of the sending of a SWAT team of FBI agents to Brushy Mountain Penitentiary within 24 hours of James's seemingly arranged escape in June 1977 is referred to as a "rumor." Well, the "rumor" resulted in him convincing HSCA chairman Louis Stokes to call Tennessee Governor Ray Blanton to advise him that – as Fauntroy told me in 1992 and Blanton confirmed – if he did not get over to the prison, they – the HSCA – were in danger of losing their lead witness and he – Blanton – his most famous prisoner. Blanton promptly took a helicopter to Brushy Mountain and, in fact, found that a team of between 20 and 30 FBI SWAT snipers was combing the hills surrounding the prison. One apprehended prisoner had been pistol-whipped by an agent desperate to know where Ray was hiding. Blanton knew that the snipers were not there to capture but to kill. He wondered why they were there in the first place. The jailbreak was a state matter. There was no federal jurisdiction. "Who," he asked, "invited the feds?" He ordered them out and saved James's life.

Walter Fauntroy's articulated view, that the FBI sniper team was sent to kill James Earl Ray, is trivialized by the report which apparently refused to investigate the presence of the FBI SWAT team or if it did look into the allegation, refused to comment on its findings.

US Public Defender April Ferguson testified in *King v. Jowers* et al. that in 1978, when the HSCA hearings were in progress and she was representing James Earl Ray, inmate Tim Kirk informed her that he had been offered a contract to arrange the killing of James by Art Baldwin, a local Mafia-connected topless-bar owner who had become a government informant. Kirk became suspicious of government involvement and contacted Ferguson who executed an affidavit contemporaneously with Kirk's statement, which in light of the possible involvement of the government in the offer was clearly made against his own interests.

The DOJ task force rejected the Ferguson/Kirk evidence saying that Kirk provided no "specifics or sources for his information, that ... Baldwin was working as an agent or informer for the federal government."[167] Then, in a subsequent paragraph, the report states, "We did determine that Baldwin assisted the government in federal investigations..." How far from reality is it possible to travel through distortion?

In my interview with Art Baldwin, prior to his release from the Shelby County Penal Farm and his death, he made it quite clear that he called Kirk and was involved in this federally instructed effort to kill James – around the time of the HSCA hearings. He told me that he was also told by the Memphis godfather that James was supposed to have been killed before he left Memphis and that Liberto had "screwed up." Still, the DOJ investigators state that they found no evidence to confirm the plots against James.

The report next considered the evidence introduced in *King v. Jowers* et al. concerning the involvement of the military in the assassination. In this section, the notes/reports provided to me by Steve Tompkins concerning Warren's role, the Alpha 184 team, and the Psy Ops photographers on the roof of the fire station were discussed as was Tompkins's

1993 investigative piece in the Memphis *Commercial Appeal*. Doug Valentine's reference, in his book *Operation Phoenix*, to photographs being taken from the roof was also mentioned in passing, as was Jack Terrell's testimony about J. D. Hill's statements about his role with the Alpha 184 unit. Terrell's testimony was described as a "...hearsay opinion of a deceased source."[168] Of course it was, but the report neglects to mention that it was admissible because such an admission was clearly a statement against personal interest.

Because the notes introduced at trial and much of the information about the military presence were provided to me by Steve Tompkins, the DOJ task force interviewed him. The report stated that Steve Tompkins revealed the following to the task force investigators.

1. He confirmed that he had interviewed an individual, who he named, although he had no way of substantiating the identity, and that the individual told him that he and a partner were on the roof of the fire station and did photograph everything that took place including the assassination and the assassin (taken by his partner) in the bushes.

2. He did not believe the account and, if he had testified, he would have told the jury so and he said that he advised me of this position.

3. He provided me with a cover note relating that he had not been able to verify the source's identity or story. (The note was not introduced at trial.)[169]

4. He said his skepticism was based upon his inability to corroborate the story and also upon the individual's request for money in exchange for the photographs that he claimed would substantiate his story.

5. He concluded that the individual did not have any photographs and advised me not to pay.[170]

It is true that Steve Tompkins, through a long-term reliable source I have called Warren, made contact with one of the two Psy Ops photographers and first met with the individual and heard his story at the Hyatt Hotel in Chicago. At the conclusion of that meeting, he told me that he had been followed. In our conversation after the meeting, he seemed completely convinced that the man was credible and believed him when he said that he snapped four or five photographs of Dr King as he fell whilst his partner (who I called Norton) moved his tripod camera from the parking lot to the brush area catching the shooter as he was lowering his rifle. The fact that Warren, whom Steve knew, told him that he had also seen the photographs and facilitated the initial contact with the individual, led Steve to have confidence at the time that the photographers existed. He also believed at the time that the photographs were delivered to Colonel John Downie of the 902nd MIG who was coordinating the task force which included the seconded Psy Ops photographers.

First of all, Steve never provided me with any cover note to his short report. There was no need to do so since we both knew that, at the time, other than Warren's confirmation, there was no corroborating evidence.

Secondly, though I omitted the information from my earlier book *Orders to Kill*, not wanting to disclose our efforts to acquire the photographs, both Steve and I knew and know the identity of the other photographer who lived (lives?) in Costa Rica, and contrary to the report Steve did meet with him. The officer came into the Miami area and Steve met him. On that occasion, Steve had been followed by what he believed to be an FBI team and the meeting was held under surveillance. Ironically, the tail from the airport was spotted – so he told me – by the taxi driver who drove him to the meeting site. It is true that the second Psy Ops officer sought to change the financial arrangements, asking for more money, but when he did so, Steve, I believe in anger, spooked him by pointing out the surveillance car and camera some distance away. This brought the meeting to an abrupt end.

When I discussed the trial with Steve, he made it clear that he did not want to testify and I respected his wishes and made no attempt to compel him to testify. There was no discussion about how he would testify since this possibility never surfaced. I believe that Steve eventually came to believe that we would not be able to make a deal with the Psy Ops photographers, but it is undeniable that we engaged in an extensive effort to do so and that Steve, at my request and with my funding, met with both photographers in an effort to reach an agreement.

The report stated that the DOJ task force examined records from the Department of Defense, the National Archives, and the Alabama National Guard (for the 20th SFG) and found no records that documented surveillance of Martin King in Memphis, although the 111th MIG and the Tennessee National Guard were involved in monitoring civil unrest associated with the sanitation workers' strike in March and April 1968. The official records search indicated that no other military units, including the 902nd MIG, had personnel in Memphis on April 4 1968. The report also accepts the claim "that the 902nd MIG's mission did not include domestic intelligence work."[171] In fact, and certainly available to the DOJ task force, the Ervin Senate Committee Report stated that they had received information indicating "that the 902nd was involved in the covert penetration of civilian organizations within the United States and did assign videotape teams to monitor demonstrations in Washington DC. The intelligence analysis assigned to the Counterintelligence Analysis Branch also was carried out by officers paid by the 902nd. In addition, a counterintelligence force from the 902nd provides security for the Pentagon."[172] One can only wonder how this information escaped the DOJ task force's extensive investigation.

The report states that it found some indication that one member of the 111th MIG may have been on the roof of the fire station some days before – but not on the day of – the assassination, scouting for locations to take photographs of visitors to the King party at the Lorraine.

The DOJ task force had, however, a serious problem with the testimonial evidence in *King v. Jowers* et al. of the former Memphis Fire Department chief, Carthel Weeden. Weeden clearly and unequivocally testified that he took two army photographers up to the roof of the fire station on the morning of April 4. As he left them on the roof, he said they were setting up their equipment in order to conduct their photographic surveillance of the Lorraine Motel and the immediate vicinity.

If allowed to stand, Captain Weeden's testimony independently corroborates the presence of the photographers on the fire station roof on the day of the assassination who were by every indication those former Psy Ops officers with whom Steve Tompkins and I made contact and entered into negotiations.

At one point shortly after the *King v. Jowers* et al. trial, I briefly discussed the Weeden evidence with DOJ task force attorney Barry Kowalski who, at that time, said that no one knew how long the soldiers were on the roof. Perhaps they came down after a few minutes. Weeden admitted that he did not see them leave. The report moved away from this tack, however, claiming that Weeden had admitted that "it was possible that he took the military personnel to the roof sometime before – not the day of – the assassination." Thus, the report goes on to find credible the recollection of the officer from the 111th who had said that "someone from the fire station may have shown them to the roof" some days before.

I have, subsequent to the issuance of the report, again spoken to Carthel Weeden. He has categorically denied that he ever told the DOJ task force investigators or attorneys that there was any possibility that he took the soldiers up on the roof on any day other than April 4 1968, the day of the assassination. He is certain that he took them up on that day, although he does not know where or how they located themselves for their photographic surveillance.

I submit that the corroboration of Carthel Weeden is conclusive.[173]

The report turned next to consider the Warren and Murphy allegations, some of which are contained in reports Steve Tompkins provided to me after a series of meetings with the two 20th SFG team members.

The report acknowledged that during the course of Steve Tompkin's investigation, which culminated in his 1993 Memphis *Commercial Appeal* article, he claimed that he had seen personnel records indicating that, in fact, troops from the 20th SFG were sent to Memphis. One member of that unit was a soldier I have called Warren who, Tompkins said, claimed he was conducting reconnaissance and was not there as a sniper to shoot Dr King. The report stated that Tompkins confirmed that Warren identified the New York Raul from the spread of photographs as a man he had seen in New Orleans who was involved in gunrunning.

According to the report, in his interview with the DOJ task force, Steve Tompkins stated that he was never able to corroborate Warren's and Murphy's allegations, and he no longer believes them. This is a curious contradiction since, at one point, the report states that, in fact, Steve had seen some independent corroborating records which indicated that indeed 20th SFG soldiers had been sent to Memphis.

If Steve Tompkins no longer believes in the allegations made by Warren, as the report suggests, I can only wonder what has occurred to make him change his mind. Throughout our work, he consistently said that everything Warren had ever told him was credible. He never questioned the integrity of his source.[174]

The report notes that the "Team Leader", whose name and involvement is spread all over Steve's interview notes and report to me and who we believed was dead (having gone to Costa Rica after a criminal conviction in Alabama), surfaced in 1997, contested the accusations and sued the publishers and myself. (The case was settled as a nuisance action by the publishers.) The report states that he denied any involvement and provided an account of his whereabouts on April 4 1968, and the DOJ task force found nothing to contradict his denial. The task force missed or ignored a conflict that emerged between his alibi and a statement taken from a close associate who has explicitly contradicted the alibi – rendering it useless. (In Appendix C, I include the actual interview format used by Steve Tompkins with Warren.)

I find it curious, though sad, if true as set out in the report, that Steve Tompkins has now decided that Warren was not credible and that he denied meeting with the second photographer or with Colonel John Downie, or more likely, with someone pretending to be Downie.

As the report is compelled to note, Steve did sign two affidavits at my request prior to the publication of my first book *Orders to Kill* in which he confirmed the accuracy of the account setting out the details of what we had learned about the military involvement in the assassination and presence in Memphis on April 4 1968. I also wrote to Steve Tompkins to enquire if, in fact, he had subsequently changed his opinion on these issues. As of the date of publication, Steve's e-mail answer to me simply stated that he will not discuss these matters over the telephone or by e-mail.

The DOJ task force muddies the issue of electronic surveillance. They surely learned early on, or should have become aware, that the Military Intelligence Groups only conducted eye-to-eye or non-covert surveillance. The kind of surveillance that was conducted on Dr King at the Rivermont Hotel that Jim Smith participated in would likely have been conducted by the Army Security Agency which carried out covert surveillance operations of this type.

As just discussed, the report dismisses Carthel Weeden and Doug Valentine's information that there were photographers on the roof of the fire station, and it also dismisses as hearsay Jack Terrell's trial testimony about what the deceased 20th SFG officer John Hill (J. D. Hill) told him about being involved in the aborted assassination plan. An interesting nuance is Steve Tompkins's note to me (set out earlier) about a 20th SFG officer John Hill who had Dr King in his sights, before he turned away, on the Selma to Montgomery march.

In its final considerations, the report considered *King v. Jowers* et al. trial evidence on the possible involvement of associates of Dr King in the assassination focusing on his stay at the Lorraine Motel, the removal of the TACT 10 unit and the Invaders from the Lorraine Motel, and his exposure standing on the balcony.

As to Dr King's stay at the Lorraine, the report adopts the now official view that he stayed overnight at the Lorraine on many occasions. If one simply looks at where Dr King stayed during those visits, when he went to Memphis to support the strikers the pattern is clear. On his first visit on March 17, he stayed at the Rivermont. (This is where Jim Smith and the surveillance team were set up. King's suite was extensively bugged. On his March 28 visit he was to stay at the Peabody, but when the march broke up he was taken again to the Rivermont, where he was expected to stay on his next visit.)

It was only following the FBI-promoted publicity criticizing Martin for staying in white hotels when there was this fine black-owned motel – the Lorraine – that he finally stayed there overnight on his last visit. Ralph Abernathy's testimony about their being moved to room 306 at their request as soon as it was vacated by another guest is demonstrably wrong. If the DOJ task force investigators had examined the motel registration book for April 2 and 3, they would have seen that there was no other guest in the room (306) at the time the King party arrived on April 3. This is one more example of the task force ignoring evidence under their noses which contradicts their desired conclusion.

The room change is equally sinister, though its significance is dismissed by the report. I believe former New York City Police Detective Leon Cohen's account of his conversation with Bailey. Cohen has absolutely no reason to lie, and I find it curious that the report does not indicate that the DOJ task force ever interviewed Leon Cohen in order to hear his story first hand. One of the reasons I believe Mr Cohen's account, given under oath in 1999, is that I was told the same story in 1992 by Olivia Hayes, an employee of the Lorraine on duty on April 4 1968 who was aware of the room change and quite uncomfortable about revealing it.

As to the TACT 10 removal, MPD Inspector Sam Evans told Professor Melanson and subsequently myself that the Reverend Billy Kyles asked him to move the unit away from the Lorraine. Evans did move the unit, but I was always highly skeptical that this decision was influenced by the Reverend Kyles who had no position with SCLC and was not even prominent in the strike support group. I have formed the opinion that Kyles was a convenient name for Evans to use since he was known and apparently in regular contact with the MPD.

As to the Invaders, it was Izzy Harrington who originally told me that Jesse Jackson had given the orders that they were to leave and that SCLC was no longer going to pay their bill. Hence, contrary to the report's statement, it is not that Invader Charlie Cabbage's account is uncorroborated, but that he was corroborating Izzy Harrington's recollection communicated to me around 1992.

As to Reverend Kyles's statement about his movements just before the shot – "I moved away so he could have a clear shot" – the report terms it "an artful attempt to explain the sequence of events and the fact that Dr King was shot when he moved away from the speaker's side. It hardly amounts to an inadvertent confession."[175] I do not know what underlying motivation, psychologically subconscious or otherwise, caused Reverend Kyles to make that statement, which stunned the courtroom into silence when it was played. I do know and have discussed earlier the fact, also ignored by the DOJ task force, that despite the personal mileage he has gotten from the claim, Reverend Kyles was not in the room with Dr King before he was killed and did not walk out on to the balcony with him. He knocked on the door of room 306, Martin answered, spoke to him for a few seconds, and closed the door. Kyles walked away down (north) the balcony and was never at Martin's side. In fact, he studiously avoided being at his side or even approaching him when he came on to the balcony, waiting for Ralph Abernathy to come out. The DOJ task force had only to examine MPD surveillance officer Willie B. Richmond's statement to confirm this sequence.

The report thus rejects any and all facts, accounts, information, or evidence which are contrary to the official conclusion that James Earl Ray acted alone in carrying out the assassination of America's greatest prophet. It is, of course, naïve to believe that if the government – at various levels – assassinated Dr King, any investigation of the assassination which becomes an investigation of the government by the government could produce the truth. They can never admit what has been done. In this instance the *modus operandi* is strikingly demonstrated again and again. Any evidence which is contrary to the pre-ordained result, and which cannot be discredited, is simply ignored, not even raised or discussed.

I believe that we, the King family and myself, made a mistake. When the president refused to appoint an independent "truth and reconciliation commission" and instead offered a DOJ investigation, we should have said "no thank you" and made it clear that we could not and would not cooperate with yet another "official" investigation attached to the very institutions of power, which we believed had participated in the heinous crime being investigated. We didn't take that position, and I believe we were wrong. But, in the depths of most democratic souls, there is a hope and a yearning for the ideals with which we are raised, a hope that our government will ultimately do the right thing in such a case, and a yearning also that our worst fears will not be realized – that it has all been a lie and that, at the end of the day, our democracy is a perpetrated illusion, a myth, even a disappearing fantasy when it comes up against the special interests of wealth and power who from the shadows dominate the institutions of public life and power in our Republic.

EPILOGUE

As the trial came to a close, ending the only judicial proceeding ever focused on the assassination of Martin Luther King, the dawn of the millennium was barely three weeks away. The powerful economic interests he had decided to take on in the last year of his life had demonstrated enormous resilience, and some of his worst fears had come to pass. The corporate-dominated economy and the now clearly transnational corporate state had consolidated its power over almost every aspect of public and private life in his native land, and under a formal globalization movement the transnational corporations were extending their tentacles all over the planet.

Footsoldiers like Margaret Thatcher, Ronald Reagan, the ever-dutiful Bush family, Helmut Kohl, and a list of Japanese tenders had diligently kept the faith. Working with the timeworn International Monetary Fund (IMF), the World Bank and ultimately with the new engine of globalization, the World Trade Organization, they ensured that the interests of capital were nowhere endangered by the needs of the world's three billion poor to eat, have shelter, clothing, sanitation, medical care, and education.

Martin King understood as had Ruskin and Gandhi before him that it was not the lack of money that was the problem, but the deprivation associated with a lack of money that denies access to the essentials of a decent life. In the post-Second World War period he saw the rights of people being steadily subordinated to the rights of the transnational corporations. On 1 January 1995, 27 years after his death, that inexorable movement was virtually completed.

The framework for the post-1945 economy had largely been worked out by the United States and Britain. It called for the creation of three multilateral institutions – the World Bank, the IMF, and an international trade organization. This last was not related then to the General Agreement on Tariffs and Trade (GATT), which was established as a body through which multilateral trade agreements were developed and enforced. With the demise of the Soviet Union at the beginning of the 1990s, however, there were no longer any alternatives or restrictions on the planet to the spread of corporate colonialism.

On that New Year's Day in 1995, the World Trade Organization (WTO) was quietly born during the Uruguay round of GATT. In low-income "developing countries," the World Bank and the IMF had institutionalized the doctrine that extensive borrowing was the way forward. Thus, subject economies became enslaved to repayment schedules and loan conditions which invariably required the cutback of necessary social services and population assistance programs, whilst the loan funds found their way back to Western corporations for the purchase of goods and services, often including consumables that could have been locally produced.

With the way clear for the WTO, the world's largest corporations are now represented by a global body with legislative and judicial power committed to protecting their rights against the intrusion of governments and the citizens to whom those governments are theoretically responsible. For example, any national law requiring imported goods to meet national health, safety, labour, or environmental standards may be declared an unfair trade practice by the WTO if the legislation requires stricter standards than the international standards accepted by the WTO. Conservation practices by a country restricting the export of its own forestry products, minerals, and fish products could be declared an unfair trade practice. Any member may, on behalf of one or more of its corporations, challenge any other members' standards including bans on carcinogenic substances, auto-safety requirements, labeling, and food inspection requirements.

The transnational corporations are highly represented in their national

WTO delegations and without doubt have the greatest influence. Hence, in the year 2000 we see that the focus of Martin King's concern for poor people has to be on the WTO, the world's most powerful legislative and judicial body, the new steward of transnational corporate interests. Back in 1968, he was only planning to take on those interests through their surrogates in the Congress of the United States.

What have these post-King developments meant to the people of America and the world? Just before this writing, based on DOW and NASDAQ performances and asset values – however inflated – we were hearing from every media corner, twelve times a day, that we lived in a period of unprecedented prosperity. Corporate prosperity, on the surface – including the enormous wealth of the shareholding population – appeared real. And then in 2002 the bubble burst and the fruits of greed poured forth with the DOW plummeting to unforeseen depths and NASDAQ listings losing 75 percent of their value. But even in this context, the increase in the concentration of economic power continues. In 2002, fifty of the world's largest economies were corporations, and even by 1991 the sales of the world's ten largest corporations exceeded the GNPs of the world's one hundred smallest countries. In 1992, General Motors sales revenues (roughly $133 billion) alone equalled the combined GNPs of Tanzania, Ethiopia, Nepal, Bangladesh, Zaire, Uganda, Nigeria, Kenya, and Pakistan. Five hundred and fifty million people – one tenth of all people on earth – inhabit those countries.[176]

The concentration proceeds apace with major mergers occurring almost monthly. Globalization will continue to reduce competition through corporate control over capital, markets, and technology. The effects of all of this on people is reflected in what has been often referred to as a "race to the bottom." This is because the transnational corporations are increasingly able to re-locate their facilities around the world: in effect, all countries, localities, and their workers become competitors for the corporate favors. As a result, wages and social and employment conditions sink to the level that desperation requires.

The horror stories abound and are too numerous to recount in these closing pages. It is clear, however, that a spreading global cancer has been set in motion. People are now not only increasingly disposable but needed less and less at all for the production of the world's goods. Transnational corporate capitalism is emerging in its purest form aimed only at achieving profit and power. Remember, Ruskin reminded us that what is really desired under the name of riches is essentially power over men: the power of obtaining and using for our own advantage the labour of another. The nuance in our time is the extension of that power to dispose of, or do without that labour altogether and thus destroy lives and communities.

It is instructive to see how the middle class fares in this boom period. The percentage of full-time middle-class workers who are earning salaries adequate to support a family of four has been declining steadily. The United States Labor Department has estimated that 30 percent of those who graduated between 1994 and 2005 will join the ranks of the unemployed or underemployed.[177]

The two-wage-earner household is today struggling to make ends meet. More and more middle-class people and families are falling behind. They take little comfort from the daily reports of how well we are doing. This is especially true in late 2002 when millions of middle-class share investors have had their life savings and/or pensions wiped out.

Now, what about the growing mass of the world's poor – those who Christians refer to as being blessed in spirit, but the least of those amongst us? Have we not welcomed them to America's shores for over a hundred years with the words of Emma Lazarus?

> Give me your tired, your poor,
> Your huddled masses yearning to breathe free,
> The wretched refuse of your teeming shore,
> Send these, the homeless, tempest-tost to me:
> I lift my lamp beside the golden door.[178]

Not only have we and do we refuse to acknowledge their plight, it is rare that in any public way, we recognize their existence much less their growing numbers throughout the world. Where are these two and one half billion miserable wretches of the earth whose total monetary asset worth is less than that of two hundred billionaires? Who are they? Where are they?

In 1967 to 1968, the last year of his life after he had announced for the presidency, Robert Kennedy went into the south to see for himself how the poor lived. When he saw the squalor, he cried.

I believe Kennedy's tears were real, for I sensed that at that time in his life he was emerging as a different person to the one he was four years earlier when I knew him as Westchester County citizens' chairman in his New York campaign for the United States Senate.

In 1999, President Clinton visited impoverished areas of the United States which included Indian reservations and ghetto neighborhoods. His trip was referred to as a "new markets initiative." He did not go to see how the poor were living. The poor did not exist for the purpose of his trip. Those folks lived in ghetto areas neatly named "new markets."

We have effectively made the masses of poor more invisible than ever. They have limited mobility and resources to travel so they, for the most part, stay where they are in their rural or urban areas. The media rarely visits them to report on their condition and, of course, most Americans do not go where they are. Even if they did live amongst us, there are always the problems of time and personal priorities. Although we do encounter them occasionally whilst we are on holiday in other countries, in America there is also the fact that their condition in a land of plenty makes their fellow Americans uncomfortable. It is easier to avert one's eyes than to look and become aware of the misery in our midst.

In a very real sense, the poor live in a world quite apart from those of the rest of us. Benjamin Disraeli commented on this phenomenon in nineteenth-century England:

> Two nations, between whom there is no intercourse and no sympathy; who are as ignorant of each other's habits, thoughts, and feelings as if they were dwellers in different zones, or inhabitants of different planets; who are formed by a different breeding, are fed by a different food, are ordered by different manners, and are not governed by the same laws . . . the rich and the poor.[179]

In our time a number of very wealthy individuals avert their eyes like most others but assuage their consciences by making charitable contributions to one cause or another. Better than nothing? Of course, except that the charitable instincts of some wealthy individuals have always been with us. A century before Disraeli, Samuel Johnson reminded us that "A provision for the poor is the true test of civilisation."[180] The ethics and the priorities of the state are what counts. Though such private persons, for various personal reasons, have always kept charitable giving alive, it is the nation and its caring, or lack of it, that matter and determine the quality of a society. Martin King knew just how invisible the poor were in 1968. He also knew that the American people needed to see them, to be compelled to view them in their multitudes, and where better for this exhibition of poverty to take place than in the nation's capital. At the same time, he believed that the members of Congress should meet these constituents who were unknown to them and learn, first hand, about their difficulties.

Martin King was not to be allowed to compel Americans and their government to come face to face with the least of them – the hidden wretched of their native land.

In his "Little Essays of Love and Virtue" Havelock Ellis, writing in 1922, during another period of heralded American prosperity, and perhaps sensing what lay ahead as there would be only seven years before economic disaster struck, said: "All civilisation has from time to time become a thin crust over a volcano of revolution." This was, of course, the fear in 1967 and 1968. Martin Luther King Jr was, for the transnational corporations, public enemy number one. He stood in the way of their inexorable consolidation of power. If he had played along as have many of his peers before and after, he would likely be with us today, a wealthy and honored man, a pillar of the state. But he did not choose to play that game and as we have seen the might of the steward state was brought to bear upon him, and to this day the pillars of the American Republic continue to be supported by the same foundation stones of lies and greed which he was determined to crumble to dust and replace.

Despite self-serving declarations to the contrary, unilateralism, reminiscent of Rome, is the hallmark of America's relations with the rest of the world, while at home the basic needs of 50 percent of the people are cruelly neglected. In our time such unilateralism constitutes a profound threat to humanity. It means that increasing car emissions – per capita the largest in the world – will continue with the rejection of the Kyoto convention. Its rejection of the International Criminal Court affords the United States the opportunity to decide issues of global justice by itself and in accordance with its own interests. The horrific events of September 11 have led to the passage of some of the most draconian legislation in the history of the Republic (including the rushed through, unread USA Patriots Act which renders basic civil liberties inoperative at the discretion of the State), the commission of crimes against humanity through the indiscriminate aerial slaughter of innocent civilians in Afghanistan, with similar treatment being readied for the Iraqi people.

This is not to mention the trillion dollar projections for the defense corporate establishment and the juggernaut efforts to bring all the oil and natural gas on the planet, once and for all, under the control of the largely American oil and gas transnational corporations.

The renunciation of the 1972 anti-ballistic treaty, thus allowing a new nuclear race to ensue, is effected in the context of threatening "evil" states who dare possess, or contemplate possession of, "weapons of mass destruction." An arms reduction treaty with Russia which does not dismantle warheads but only puts some in storage is misrepresented as a significant step toward diminishing the possibility of nuclear war whilst paving the way for America to press ahead with the folly of its Star Wars program and maintain its position as the world's largest repository for chemical and biological weapons.

The primary concern of Martin King in his last days was the plight of the poor. Now, 34 years later, the gap between the rich and poor has greatly widened with the US economy producing grossly unequal living standards, swelling and institutionalizing a permanent underclass with those at the bottom ill-protected in comparison with Western European standards.

With guns in abundance and readily available, citizens seem to routinely shoot each other in a culture where God is instructed to Bless America and spirituality is eclipsed by worship at shopping malls where acts of mindless consumerism are carried out by individuals who seek to fill an inner emptiness through the acquisition of things. This quest and the omnipresent all-encompassing entertainment industry distract people from serious consideration of public issues such as the loss of liberty (as evidenced by the passage of the US Patriots Act), the corruption of the public realm, and the unresolved legacy of racism.

So, since King's murder we have come to live in a nation dominated by avarice and acquisitiveness, where state violence is out of control, even outpacing its private emulators. We see a culture where people have increasingly less value and where corporate and banking institutions determine public policy and thus the interests of capital take precedence over people.

Martin King's native land has also continued to perpetrate state terrorism across the globe, while being outraged over acts of non-state terrorism, such as those committed on September 11, as a result of which relatively few people lost their lives. In comparison, America has clearly emerged as the greatest purveyor of state terrorism on the planet. If there is any doubt one only has to consider, amongst others, the incidents of American intervention in Guatemala, Iran, Nicaragua, Panama, Cuba (ongoing for 43 years), Chile, Uruguay, Vietnam, Cambodia, Laos, and, most recently, Venezuela.

America has truly emerged as a land where its masses have become as disposable as any other object which has outlived its usefulness or fulfilled its commercial function. One of the most graphic, horrible specific examples of this national condition is the program of government-sponsored medical experiments which were conducted on unsuspecting American citizens during the fifty years of the Cold War.

Thousands upon thousands of Americans, mostly poor, in hospitals, prisons and even children's homes, were used as guinea pigs for government research on the effects of radiation and plutonium, which was put into their bodies, or to which they were exposed in violation of the Nuremberg Code. It was only through the courageous efforts of the then Energy Secretary, Hazel O'Leary, in 1993 that the tip of the iceberg of this domestic governmental atrocity was revealed.[181] Prompted by revelations in the *Albuquerque Tribune*, O'Leary broke with decades of government secrecy and cover-up and arrogance on 7 December 1993.[182]

The process of colonization of whatever stripe is a dehumanizing journey. If in this context, and complementing it, we consider technological advances, the fate of the human species itself is in question. In this millennium we seem to be on the verge of realizing the ultimate goal in the scientific, materialistic course Copernicus set us on over 450 years ago.

We are now told that before the new century is 50 years old, computers will be about a million times more powerful than they are today and they will begin to resemble life forms. Add to this the fact that humans will contain more and more miniaturized machine parts and effectively merge with their machines. Such developments may then point the way to robotic homogenization and a post-biological future where self-replicating robots have physical and cognitive capabilities approaching human beings. Corporate colonizers may finally be able to do without inefficient human beings whose behavior is not always predictable and whose individual characteristics of emotions and the capacity to reason do not always allow for smooth technological functioning.

From the beginning of the industrial revolution to the present, technological advances have been equated with human progress. Whilst many benefits are undeniable, it is also true that the potential social and environmental damages are rarely brought forward for examination and discussion by the people most affected. One would have thought that television would have been the natural medium to inform the public about such significant issues. It has, for the most part, not filled this role. Instead, like the mass media overall, it is responsible for broadcasting mind-numbing commercialization and causing a dumbing down of viewers who are constantly exposed to the standardization of thought and homogenization of culture across the earth.

Hence I fear that all of the concerns of Martin King are alive and well and with us today as never before. Had he lived he would certainly have been an invaluable asset in the struggle to humanize our land. We are greatly poorer without him but as the living, can we overcome? It remains to be seen whether anything can be done to reclaim the rapidly disappearing ability of people to protect their humanity, control their lives, provide a decent life for their families and take back control over their communities if not their nation.

I am afraid that the obstacles appear to be insurmountable unless the unthinkable occurs. Should an economic disaster similar to that of 1929 engulf this nation and the world, there may emerge an opportunity to rebuild this great Republic with a vastly different set of values and priorities put in place instead of those of the old order which would be swept away not by a revolution but by a transformation. We have learned by now that a political revolution is not enough. It must be part of a broader social, economic, and cultural revolution which goes to the very essence of the type of human being developed and quality of life which is being affirmed. Such reconstruction must be derived from a thorough analysis of the old order and what went wrong from the perspectives and interests of the masses of people and not the special interests of the few.

Is such an economic disaster imminently likely? Possibly, in light of recent events. It is interesting to note that the growth of margin debt – debt incurred by stock investors – had risen on February 29 2000 to the level it was on October 1 1929 prior to the crash.[183] I recall a recent visit with my then 95-year-old former Trinity School principal, Clarence Bruner-Smith. I asked him about the depression of 70 years ago, and he said it came out of nowhere. No one anticipated it. He said that, all of a sudden, the world changed. It was driven home to him when one day, walking his usual route to school down Riverside Drive, there began appearing men shooting at pigeons with others lining the riverbank with fishing poles, all seeking food for their families.

In his 1948 work *Civilization on Trial*, Arnold Toynbee wrote:

> Civilizations, I believe, come to birth and proceed to grow by successfully responding to successive challenges. They break down and go to pieces if and when a challenge confronts them which they fail to meet.[184]

Should the unthinkable occur it would certainly be a challenge. Whether we as a people would be up to meeting it without the likes of Martin Luther King in the vanguard is another question, but I have always been amazed at the resilience of human beings of whatever race, culture, station or stripe. The New Deal met the last economic challenge with, however, the assistance of a war and by basically perpetuating the old political and economic order, giving it a kinder, more humane face, though establishing the foundation of the system and preparing the type of leaders we have today. The question remains, and I submit will loom larger even in our lifetime, as to whether a transformation of the Republic and its culture can be accomplished without the revolution Mr Jefferson believed necessary for every generation to cleanse the land and sweep away, not the assets of the public but the parisitic special interests which continue to drain the very life blood of the people's liberty.

Though still engaged in a process of personal radicalization at his death, Martin King had not yet emerged from a commitment to liberal reform of the government of his native land. He continued to believe that right and reason would ultimately prevail in the determinations of the nation's policies. He would not be encouraged by events since his death.

Martin King, now martyred and rumored some time ago to be on the road to (however expedient) beatification and sainthood by a church not his own, was finally moved, indeed inspired, by the thinking of the Christian, existentialist theologian Paul Tillich, whose seminal work *The Courage To Be* observed that human beings from birth onward have an existence and it is up to each person to struggle against the forces of determinism and try to create a life, an individual essence.[185] Individuals can only do this by making decisions, life choices, adopting, and living by values and ultimately by taking stands and making those commitments even unto death which often are painfully contrary to their environmental and genetic dictates.

Martin King's commitments to social and economic justice went beyond the contemplative intellect into the arena of an active life. The root and branch transformation of our society, which was about the shaking of all the old foundations, will require nothing less than a struggle in whatever focus it ultimately takes against the familiar, the comfortable, and the acceptable values and inclinations which constitute a very real type of determinism for each one of us. This transcendent struggle, this exalted commitment, emerged as an all-consuming passion of Martin King. He acted upon it until he drew his last breath.

This is his living legacy to us and people everywhere.

APPENDICES

Appendix A: A further analysis of the Department of Justice report

Evidence ignored, truth suppressed, justice denied

A further analysis of the Department of Justice report indicates that an extraordinary amount of evidence available to the task force was ignored, apparently because it ran contrary to the official story. This orientation approach to research renders the final document worthy of being regarded as little more than a position paper for the government's religious commitment to the lone assassin – James Earl Ray – answer to all questions.

It is instructive to see exactly what evidence has been omitted in respect of the various critical issues of the case covered by the report. Anyone interested in a fair evaluation of this case will be dismayed at the extent of the omissions. I have identified 55 examples of pieces of evidence which the task force failed to consider. For ease of review and consideration, I summarize the missing evidence in the table below.

No.	Issue	DOJ report position	Omitted evidence	Relevant pages

JOWERS

No.	Issue	DOJ report position	Omitted evidence	Relevant pages
1	Whether Jowers acknowledged involvement under oath.	No.	Yes. Jowers's 1994 deposition transcript which incorporated his TV transcript as truthful.	22, 23
2	Why Jowers did not testify in *King v. Jowers* et al.	Declared – no reason given.	Court record – Severe illness.	22
3	Who was J. C. Hardin, an individual mentioned by Jowers and who called Ray?	No information.	FBI report identifies Hardin as Liberto mother's family name.	28
4	Whether Rev. Kyles was with Dr King prior to 6:00 PM and exited room 306 with him.	Yes.	No. MPD statement of MPD intelligence officer W. B. Richmond – stating No.	31, 135
5	Whether there was anyone in room 306 when the King party arrived as R. D. Abernathy claimed.	Yes.	No. Registration records of the Lorraine Motel for April 2 and 3 1968.	133
6	Whether brush area was "muddy" and footprints could have been left.	Yes.	*King v. Jowers* et al. testimony of J. B. Hodges on thickness of bushes and brush and only muddy area being alleyway. Photographs were taken after brush was cut still showing heavy grass cover – no mud.	37
7	Whether footprints should have been left in area where Rev. Orange saw puff of smoke.	Yes.	No. Same as above.	37

No.	Issue	DOJ report position	Omitted evidence	Relevant pages
8	Whether it was possible for any MPD officer to be in bushes before officers Landers and Hodges and thus S. Jones saw a policeman in bushes after shooting.	Yes.	No. Testimony J. B. Hodges and photographs and description of area revealing two fences, 6 and 5 feet high between fire station (where MPD TACT 10 were) and bushes beyond Jim's Grill.	38
9	Whether Olivia Catling saw a man driving quickly away on Huling after shooting.	No.	Yes. Statements of Bell South Telephone repairman Hasel Huckaby that he noticed such a person there during the day.	42, 43
10	Whether there was a second white Mustang with Arkansas plates on South Main Street in position from where witness saw car leave after bundle was dropped.	Silent, but no by implication.	Yes. Statements of Mr and Mrs Charles Hurley.	FN. 43
11	Whether J. E. Ray actually left South Main Street area 10–15 minutes before shooting.	No.	Yes. Reed and Hendrix alibi statements to FBI (302s) and MPD.	FN. 43
12	Whether the brush area of the crime scene was massively cleaned up the next morning.	Silent.	Yes. Testimony of Maynard Stiles.	43

No.	Issue	DOJ report position	Omitted evidence	Relevant pages
13	Whether James chose room directly overlooking the Lorraine.	Yes.	No. Statement of landlady Bessie Brewer and James that he wanted a sleeping room – rejected a cooking room.	44
14	Whether W. Anschutz confirmed shot came from bathroom window.	Yes.	No. MPD statement – said he saw man run out of JER's room.	44
15	Whether FBI report showed rifle sighting was off – firing 3 inches left and 1 inch below target.	Yes.	No. FBI report said it was worse: 4 inches left and 3 inches below.	46
16	Whether Judge Joe Brown had good reason to say rifle was not murder weapon.	No.	Yes. Indication is that DOJ task force did not interview Judge Brown.	46
17	Whether dent in windowsill was made by rifle.	Silent.	No.	FBI report
18	Whether F. Liberto ever knew L. Jowers.	No.	Yes. Statement of MPD task force officer S. O. Blackburn.	50
19	Whether F. Liberto was involved in the assassination.	No.	Yes. Ignores cumulative effect of the number of independent witnesses.	51, 52, 53, 54, 55
20	Whether LaVada Addison believed F. Liberto's statement or not.	No.	Yes. Trial testimony and deposition – just didn't want to hear it.	55

No.	Issue	DOJ report position	Omitted evidence	Relevant pages
21	Whether F. Liberto had Mafia connections.	No.	Yes. S. O. Blackburn's statement and N. Whitlock.	55
22	Whether Jowers's lifestyle changed after killing, indicating he received money.	No.	Yes. Documents for purchase of Veterans Cab Company within one year after assassination.	56
23	Whether Alda Mae saw money in stove and changed her story.	No.	Yes. J. Saltman's interview.	56, 57
24	Whether Dr King rejected protection of black MPD unit which was usually with him in Memphis.	Yes.	No. Testimony of Jerry Williams: unit never formed, white unit inexplicably formed instead.	58
25	Whether Dr King party requested removal of TACT 10 from Lorraine to fire station.	Yes.	No. Phil Melanson and my interview with Inspector Sam Evans (Kyles request not believable).	59
26	Whether removal of Redditt was really based on a threat on his life.	Yes.	No. Messengers with information about threat were previous members of 902nd MIG – D. Valentine interview with Manual.	59
27	Whether Redditt was removed as a security risk.	No.	Yes. Redditt testimony, he was a Community Relations specialist not an intelligence agent.	60

No.	Issue	DOJ report position	Omitted evidence	Relevant pages
28	Whether removal of black firemen was based upon legitimate security reasons.	Yes.	No. Redditt testimony, and that of black firemen, Wallace and Newsum.	61
29	Whether M. McCollough ever met Jowers.	No.	Yes. Statement of McCollough to ABC producer that he knew Jowers.	63, 64
30	Whether Lt. Earl Clark's alibi provided by wife is credible.	Yes.	No. Affidavit of dry-cleaners owner's son, working on April 4 1968, and fact that no investigation done to check basic details e.g. store closing hours.	65
31	Whether MPD had walkie talkie as described by Clark's ex-wife.	Yes.	No. Question of kind of walkie talkie ignored. MPD specialist's statement no such walkie talkie (size of TV remote) existed.	70
32	Whether L. Ward was mistaken or made up story of taxi driver seeing person come over the wall.	Yes.	No. Ward always called him "Buddy" and came wrongly to believe man's name was Paul.	70
33	Whether Jowers made it all up in 1995.	Yes.	No. Milner's and Isabel's testimony that Jowers told story nearly 20 years ago.	71

No.	Issue	DOJ report position	Omitted evidence	Relevant pages

WILSON

| 34 | Whether Wilson has been consistent in his story. | Yes. | No. Public statements made by Don Wilson. | |

RAUL

35	Whether JER ever identified New York Raul before 1995.	No.	Yes. News clippings of ID in 1978.	101, 105
36	Whether Hardin who tried to see JER in Los Angeles was same Hardin mentioned by Jowers.	Silent.	Silent possible – Allan Thompson's interview and J. Saltman's interview of Jowers.	102
37	Whether G. Grabow saw NY Raul on hood of car with a rifle when JFK arrived in Houston.	No.	Roy Grabow's ID and statement confirm event.	103
38	Whether NY Raul is the Raul ID in the photo spread.	No.	Yes. Ignores J. Saltman's interview with New York Raul's daughter when she confirmed ID from photo.	107
39	Whether JER exchanged the first rifle at Raul's request.	Silent.	Yes. Consistent explanation with record showing call to store shortly after purchase.	115

No.	Issue	DOJ report position	Omitted evidence	Relevant pages
40	Whether JER moved his car from in front of Jim's Grill or stated that he did move the car.	Yes.	No. Numerous eyewitness statements in FBI 302s and MPD files indicating car was in front of Jim's Grill door from 3:45 PM – 4:00 PM and 5:45 PM – 5:50 PM.	116
41	Whether Mr Purdy who claimed that the CIA killed MLK was an FBI agent.	No evidence.	Yes. Testimony of Bill Hamblin that Purdy was his landlord for some years and he knew that Purdy was an agent.	122
42	Whether an FBI SWAT team was sent to Brushy Mountain Penitentiary when JER escaped in June 1977.	No. Governor Ray Blanton.	Yes. Statement of reporter J. J. Maloney and prison official Steve Jacks and former HSCA King Subcommittee chairman, Walter Fauntroy.	123
43	Whether Art Baldwin called Tim Kirk to put a contract on JER from a suite at Airport Hotel used by US Attorney's office and FBI.	No.	Yes. Affidavit of lawyer and paralegal interviewing Kirk, affidavit of Kirk, and statement of Baldwin confirming offer.	123
44	Whether the John D. Hill named by J. Terrell as a military member of the Alpha 184 unit was the same John Hill who said he had MLK in his sights on Selma march.	No.	Yes. Roster of 20th SFG Miss. section lists Hill.	125

No.	Issue	DOJ report position	Omitted evidence	Relevant pages
45	Whether the two-man Psy Ops photographers Reynolds and Norton photographed different areas.	Silent.	Yes. Brenner's statement to Steve Tompkins.	126
46	Whether S. Tompkins ever met with man in Bermuda – Sonesta Hotel – claiming to be J. Downie.	No.	Yes. Previous statements of Tompkins to W. F. Pepper.	126, 127
47	Whether the Army Security Agency or other federal agency had Dr King under surveillance in Memphis.	No.	Yes. Testimony of former MPD officer Jim Smith.	127, 128
48	Whether 111th MIG senior officer in Memphis at the time of assassination was in fact Maj. Jimmie Locke.	Yes.	No. Colonel Frank Bray ran operations.	128
49	Whether records of the 20 SFG revealed that that unit was in Memphis.	No.	Yes. As per army records obtained by Steve Tompkins.	129
50	Whether Carthel Weeden unequivocally placed the army photographers on the roof of the fire station on the day of the assassination.	No.	Yes. Statements under oath by C. Weeden.	129
51	Whether "Warren's" partner was a "spotter" for sniper action and not an observer.	No.	Yes. S. Tompkins' reports.	130

No.	Issue	DOJ report position	Omitted evidence	Relevant pages
52	Whether MLK ever stayed overnight at the Lorraine prior to April 3.	Yes.	No. Clippings and SCLC staff and MPD black detective security unit statements show he always stayed at Admiral Benbow, Holiday Inn, or Peabody.	133
53	Whether MLK's room was changed from a courtyard room to 306.	No.	Yes. Testimony of Leon Cohen and statement of Olivia Hayes, Lorraine staff on duty, and Lorraine register for April 2, 3, and 4.	133
54	Whether room 306 at the Lorraine Motel was occupied when the King party arrived on April 3 requiring King and Abernathy to take another room until the next day.	Yes.	No. Statements of various members of the King party, the Invaders, and R. D. Abernathy's published recollection in his book *And the Walls Came Tumbling Down*, as well as the register of the Lorraine Motel which shows room 306 vacant on April 2 and occupied by King and Abernathy on April 3 and 4.	
55	Whether the mission of the 902nd Military Intelligence Group ever allowed them to be involved in domestic intelligence activity.	No.	Yes. Report entitled Military Surveillance of Civilian Politics of the Subcommittee on Constitutional Rights, Committee on the Judiciary to United States Senate in 1978.	

Appendix B: Direct examination of Clayborne Carson, history professor at Stanford, by Dr Pepper, *King v. Jowers* et al., November 24 1999

Q. Dr Carson, good afternoon – barely afternoon. Thank you for joining us here. You've come some three thousand miles, and I know that time is precious in terms of your schedule, so I'd like to just move ahead. Would you please state your full name and address for the record?

A. Clayborne Carson, Palo Alto, California.

Q. And what is your profession?

A. I'm a professor of history at Stanford.

Q. And what do you – what is your relationship to the works and life of Martin Luther King, Junior?

A. I'm the editor of Martin Luther King's papers, and I'm director of the Martin Luther King papers project at Stanford.

Q. And how long have you been in that position?

A. Fifteen years.

Q. And have you published various works on Doctor King's work and life?

A. Yes, I have. I've published, I think, edited or authored five – I think five books on Martin Luther King.

Q. All right. And is the King papers project at Stanford University an ongoing project?

A. Yes, it is. It's a long-term project to publish all of the historically significant papers of Martin Luther King. It's been going on for fifteen years. It will probably go on as long as I go on.

Q. And in your capacity and as part of that project at Stanford, do you have the process of collecting documents and materials of all sorts of natures related to Doctor King's life, work and death even?

A. Yes, sir. The purpose of the paper is – papers project is to assemble all of the historically significant papers from archives around the world. We've contacted probably some two hundred or more archieves to make sure that we have all of the historically significant papers. Obviously, the largest collections are those at the King Center in Atlanta and at Boston University.

Q. Right. And as a part of that responsibility, did you receive from me certain documents, certain reports with respect to the assassination of Martin Luther King?

A. Yes, I did.

Q. And it should be clear to the Court and Jury that you are not in any way involved in attesting to the accuracy or the validity of this information, but you are simply reporting on what it is that you have received; is that correct?

A. That's right.

Q. So we're asking you to do that in a professional capacity and in line with your role as editor and director of the King papers project. With that background, Professor Carson, I'd like you to move, please, to the first set of responses in the documentation that I've provided to you and of the project that I addressed to a resource who was traveling and providing me with information. The Court and Jury have become aware with how that process worked so we just need to go into a question and answer mode here.

On Page 2 of – well, on Page 2 of the questions and whatever page of the response, I'd ask you to turn to Paragraph 2.1.4, and the question that was asked to be answered was: Was the operation, in re, our target, a one op, or were there other similar operations? If others, any details possible. Please, at least learn if they were domestic, foreign or both.What is the answer that you have?

A. Answer: Lots of other ops nationwide. These are the ones I was at, summer of 1967 – (June 12th through 15th, 1967) – Tampa, Florida. Two Alpha teams deployed during riots. Detroit, summer, July 23rd, riot. Washington, October 1967, riot. Chicago, just before Christmas, 1967, recon. February 1968, Los Angeles.

Q. Thank you. Question 2.1.5: When was the instant operation? The instant operation is the Memphis operation against Martin Luther King. When was the instant operation first raised with him, that is, the source. A, where and by whom?

A. Date unknown. Place, Camp Shelby, Mississippi. Briefed by Captain Name. First, a recon-op – not sure when killing King first mentioned.

Q. What – 2.1.6: What were the first details of the operation scenario put to him?

A: Was target named?

A. Yes, King. Another answer.

Q. Yes. Please continue.

A. Young added later.

Q. First answer, King. Young added later. What was site?

A. Site not set. Depended on our intel and recon. We positioned at rooftop ascent across Lorraine Motel about 1300 hours 4 April. Don't know why or how intel came in. At brief, 0430, reminded Doctor King was the leader of a movement to destroy American government and stop the war. We were shown CR, close range photos, of King and Young. Don't know – don't remember anyone worrying about killing those sacks of shit.

One but – buddy on Team 1, remember bragged about him, had him in center mass (this is a sniper term meaning cross hairs and center of chest). During that big March in Alabama, should have done it then.

(Bill, I did some checking from my files. There is a John Hill listed among the 20th special forces teams that was deployed in Selma, Alabama in 1965 for the beginning of the march to Montgomery.

I interviewed two of the team members who were there, and they said a sniper team had King in their scope until he turned left and crossed the bridge. This may be the same Hill on main team. None of the other names match.)

Another Name – (that's me) – asked about clothes. We were dressed as working stiffs working on the docks. (I believe this means their cover was day laborers on President's Island where the riverboat barge and the warehouses are located.)

Equipment was stored in suitcases, moved along, came up in cars from Camp Shelby. Only place I remember eating in Memphis was a Howard Johnson's. My spotter and I were met by a Name down near the train tracks where we were let out. I remembered this guy because he looked a lot like a buddy – (buddy of mine). This guy got us to the building where we set up. I always figured he was a spook.

From him, we got a detailed AO – (area of operations map) – not the kind you'd buy in a gas station, pictures of cars the King group were driving, and the guy got us to the building where we set up. I always figured he was a spook.

From him, we got a detailed AO – (area of operations map) – not the kind you'd buy in a gas station, pictures of the cars the King group was driving and the Memphis police tact – (tactical radio frequencies). Maybe some other stuff, I just don't remember.

Q. C: Any explanation of reason?

A. Name gave none.

Q. D: Any indication of sanction by or involvement of others, one at federal, state or local levels?

A. Everybody but my brother was there. Spooks, the company – (CIA) – Feebs – (FBI) – police, you name it. The only person I remember talking to besides CO, Name, was some guy who was the head of the city – (Memphis tact) – tactical squad. I think his first name was Sam.

Name put him on radio to describe to us what was in that hotel – (Lorraine). I do remember he saying friendlies would not be wearing ties. Took that to mean that somebody inside the King group was informant.

Did meet in person one other guy. Met him on sidewalk down couple blocks from our perch. Directed by Name. This guy identified himself with the police intelligence. Said city was about to explode, and blacks would be murdering whites in the streets.

After a few minutes, I figured was asking me to sit tight and kill any rioters if things went to hell. He seemed to know something about us and said had met with Name before this day.

Q. E: Was operation pure military, any involvement of FBI, state police, local sheriff's, poster police, civilians, anyone in targets organization?

A. Our part military. Far as I know, we were coordinating with units at NAS. This would be Millington Naval Air Station.

Q. Okay. Move over to the response to Question 3, please. Was he aware of any support from inside Doctor King's organization, SCLC, or inside the local Memphis groups working with Doctor King? Details and names if possible.

A. Scuttlebutt was 111th – (military intelligence group out of Fort McPherson) – had guy inside King's group.

Q. Moving to Number 7. Did he actually see anything at the time of the shooting? Where was he precisely?

A. I thought Team 1 had fired early. I guess I still think they may have. After that day, I only saw Captain Name twice more, and both times, he refused to talk to me about what happened. After the shot, I keyed – (radioed) – CO to ask for instructions, and after a wait – (I think this means Name told him to wait) – was told to exit building and make our way to pick-up point.

If this helps, I heard a lot of gunfire, and I think remembering – I remember thinking it was an army sniper shot. It surprised me later when I heard some wacko civilian had done it.

Name described the shooting to me, and let me tell you this. Whoever fired that shot was a professional. Even from three hundred meters, there's no way just anyone could make that shot.

Q. Eight: If the military unit did it, how does he explain the head shot, and their not waiting for the coordinated hits from the second target, A-Y-, Andrew Young?

A. When you have everybody's hands in someone's pants, it's a cluster fuck. That's what happened in Nam – what happened here.

Q. What kind of weapons were they carrying?

A. Standard forty-five caliber sidearms, M-16 sniper rifles and some K-bars – (this is a military knife). We also had some frags – (fragmentation grenades) – and two or three laws, light anti-air – anti tank weapon rockets.

Q. Ten: How did the two teams communicate with each other? When was the last contact prior to the killing?

A. By radio. The shot was fired just after the TTR – (top of the hour, I guess this means 1800) – sit rep – (situation report).

Q. Eleven: Set out details of their exiting Memphis, how – where they went.

A. Exit by foot to waiting boat.

Q. Finishes the first section. Now the second – second series of questions and answers. We'll just move through these. Number 1: Where was Young?

A. Best I remember, a bunch of them had been upstairs. My spotter got Young when they all left. He went downstairs. He had come out of his room below and looked like to me was heading for the – a car when the shot was fired. We were getting ready to do the sit rep. He was definitely out of his room.

Q. Second page, 2.15 and 2.16: What was the nature of the training – real purpose training?

A. This was a recon, slash, surveillance mission to support major army element at Millington and possible deployment of other heavy units – one of the dozens in cities with large black populations. We were walking the ground literally. We would walk city streets to identify possible sniper and ambush sites, anything that would help the guys coming into a riot to survive.

Target reduction – (Bill, he means killing Young and King) – was discussed as a option should the situation go in the toilet, and we had a riot on our hands in the AO – (area of operations). Then and only then was that option briefed.

You need to talk to him – (he's referring here to you) – about how a military mission is done. Logistics, intelligence, communications which make up seven-eighths of a mission. What I'm saying is that target reduction was brief, but we had to get to a riot before it was authorized on the net.

Do you want me to go on?

Q. Yes.

A. Here NAME digressed into an argument over radios. Said team had PRC 77s unreliable. Out of – on that roof that evening, we were watching. I had Young targeted, but only to watch.

Q. Then moving down – I asked here about the psychological warfare photo recon stuff at this point. Continue.

A. Big psy-ops (phonetic) plan to discredit King and his party using any means at hand. We weren't told much about this, but, again, SOP with fifth special forces was psy-ops included and everything. M-A-C-V-S-O-G had long time begged into this. We call this, quote, gray operations, and spreading propaganda to newspapers and radio stations. This was done a lot against black pot-heads. I wasn't involved in this, but I kept my ears open, and this was a big push. Any intel we picked up to help this effort out was passed back up the chain. Not sure about reserved element of psy-ops. Most guys in Nam I knew worked for the fourth psy-ops group at Teng Sau Nu. I know there they ran their own newspaper, radio and TV operations.

Q. Yes. 2.1.7: When was Memphis first mentioned?

A. Not sure. Original brief of twentieth recon operations including – included Memphis among cities where possible rioting was possible at Camp – Camp Landing. (Bill, this is in Florida.) Memphis was scouted 22 February by Alpha team for sniper communications and supply sites. We had a lot of stuff going in, but previous recon produced a lot more.

What we were doing is similar to Nam. Maps, terrain studies, readouts of infrared imagery from aerial recon blackbirds – (Bill, he's referring to SR 71 blackbird overflights of Memphis and other potential riot cities, this mentioned in my series) – and anything else we could find, which we shipped to S2 and Nam Trang.

Here we shipped to Camp Shelby S2. Where intel went from there, I'm not sure.

Q. 2.1.8: Who was in charge of training?

A. NAME Captain.

Q. How long was the training period?

A. Can't remember. Too long ago. Too many missions before and after.

Q. During training – 2.1.13: During training, who were you told were targets?

A. We were told these were recon missions whose purpose was to reverse the cluster fuck in Detroit where our guys didn't even have maps of city streets. Our mission was to walk the ground before the heavies – (Bill, means tanks and APCs here) – got there.

Training was entirely based on identifying communications links, supply sites, places where troops could be quickly and safely inserted where the black community was, where black churches were, where black leaders congregated – (restaurants, churches).

Q. 2.1.14: Other members of team involved, other sites.

A. Worked with Captain Name in Tampa.

Q. 2.1.15. Were all those 9–0 second operations?

A. Don't know and don't care. What I know is this. You start asking a lot of questions about the 9–0 second – he pronounced ninety-deuce – you'd better be digging a deep hole. Parentheses, Bill, he was very reluctant to discuss 9–0 second. I tried several times in this interview to broach subject. He refused to.

Q. 2.1.16: Who controlled training and actual operations?

A. Team leader and his exec. control.

Q. 3.2: Who was on the February 22nd Memphis recon mission?

A. I was on it. Will give other names if agreed they not be made public.

Q. 3.3: Did entire unit go together to Memphis on 4 April or separate? Explain.

A. No, we went in separate cars in twos.

Q. 3.4: What time leave Camp Shelby for Memphis?

A. Don't remember.

Q. 3.8: You're referring to this Name fellow – I'm sorry. 3.8: Who did spook on ground work for?

A. You're referring to this Name fellow who met us down by railroad yards. Guy smelled like a company guy. We had maps, but this guy gave us a detailed map of the AO – (area of operations) – not a regular service station map. This was like a grid map you got in the field with street and building names. Anyway, this Name, I think it was James reminded me of a friend. I got no proof though, but he was definitely a spook.

Q. 3.9: Details of conversation.

A. You got to be kidding. We just talked about the current situation, our location and radio net.

Q. And then questions 3.9 to 3.14.1: No answers?

A. (Bill, these questions, he simply could not remember.)

Q. That finishes the second section. Lastly, Professor Carson, you have a one-page report of a meeting that took place in Chicago, also at plaintiffs' counsel's request, having to do with the location of some photographers on the roof of the fire station in Memphis. Would you read that report, please.

A. Trip to meet NAME, 1 December, 1994, Chicago. Location, Hyatt Regency, downtown off Michigan Avenue. Breakfast, slash, lunchroom off of lobby. Description, about five-feet-ten inches, one-sixty to one-seventy pounds. Gray, short cropped hair, nice suit – (Brook Brothers style) – wing tipped shoes, erect, obviously ex military.

Said in Vietnam assigned first SOG – (special operation group) – base, Kan Tu, worked 525th psychological operations battalion.

Refused to discuss place of birth, date of birth or other personal info. April 3, 4 weekend, 9–0 second operation. New Colonel Name, worked with him number of assignments. Two agents in Memphis day of killing. Therefore, routine photogs and surveillance copied to Name and Name –

Q. Yes.

A. – believed distributed to other agencies. Idea to pick up anyone in photos, might be identified as communist or national security threat – such H-U-M-I-N-T-S-O-P in King's surveillance. When King came out on balcony, camera was filming. No photo moment King shot, but several of him falling. Second guy with Name watched approaching cars, heard shot and saw white man with rifle. Quickly snapped his picture several times as this guy left scene. Shooter was on the ground clearly visible. Name witnessed only his back as left scene. Said never got a visual face ID. Name and second guy rooftop of fire station, both armed with forty-five caliber automatics. Second guy carried small revolver in holster, small of back.

Pictures had been delivered to Colonel Name, but second guy with Name kept negatives. Name has no copies. Said will approach second guy for two thousand dollars, give us name and address.

DR. PEPPER: Thank you very much, Professor Carson. There is a final document, which is a chronology of important dates, that has been provided to us from January 17, 1967 to the 4th of April listing dates, times and places and subjects of meetings that took place in government agencies throughout that entire year. We're not going to go through that here, but I am going to close that and move that that be admitted as a part of the total package of evidence. Thank you for coming, and no further questions.

Appendix C: Interview with Team Leader

I ask the reader to please understand that in this instance, in case there are further court proceedings involving the Team Leader, I need to withhold specific names and facts for the court record.

As to examples of the questions and answers in the exchange between Tompkins asking my questions and Warren's answers, I offer the following examples.

Q: When was the instant operation first raised with him?

    a. Where and by whom.

A: Date: unknown. Place: Camp Shelby, Mississippi. Briefed by: TEAM LEADER (named). First a recon. Op. not sure when killing King first mentioned.

Q: What were the first details of the operation scenario put to him?

    a. Was the target named?

    b. What was site?

    c. Any explanation of reason

    d. Any indication of sanction by or involvement of others:

        1. At federal, state or local levels

        2. Names

    e. Was operation pure military. Any involvement of FBI, State Police, local Sheriff's Post, or Police – civilians? Anyone in target's organizations.

        1. names or even just positions if possible.

A: YES (to all of the above)

    a. Yes – King/A. Young added later.

    b. Site not set. Depended on our intel and recon. We positioned at rooftop across (Lorraine) motel about 1300 hours 4 April. Don't know why or how intel came in. At brief 0430 reminded Dr King was the leader of the movement to destroy the American government and stop the war. We were shown CR (close range) photos of King and Young. Don't remember anyone worrying about killing those sacks of shit. One bug (buddy) on team I remember bragged about he had him center mass (this is a sniper term, means cross-hairs in center of chest) during that big march in

Alabama, should of done it then. (Bill, I did some checking from my files. There is a JOHN HILL listed among the 20th Special Forces team that was deployed in Selma, Alabama in 1965 for the beginning of the march to Montgomery. I interviewed two of the team members who were there, and they said a sniper team had King in their scopes until he turned left and crossed the bridge. This may be the same Hill on Stone's team. None of the other names match.)

c. (that's me) asked about clothes. We were dressed as working stiffs working on the docks (I believe this means their cover was day laborers on President's Island where the riverboat/barge and warehouses are located). Equipment was stored in suitcases. Moved along. Came up in cars from Camp Shelby. Only place I remember eating in Memphis was a Howard Johnson. My spotter and I were met by a James Kilmer down near the train yards where we were let out. I remember this guy cause he looked a lot like a bug (buddy) of mine. This guy got us to the building where we set up. I always figured he was a spook. From him we got a detailed AO (area of operations) map, not the kind you'd buy in a gas station, pictures of the cars the King group were driving the Memphis police tac (tactical) radio frequencies. Maybe some other stuff, I just don't remember, and the guy got us to the building where we set up.

Q: Was he aware of any support from inside Dr King's organization SCLC or inside the local Memphis groups working with Dr K. Details and names if possible.

A: Scuttlebutt was 111th Military Intelligence Group out of Ft. McPherson had guy inside King group.

Q: Did he actually see anything at the time of the shooting? Where was he precisely?

A: I thought team 1 had fired early. I guess I still think they may have. After that day I only saw him twice more, and both times he refused to talk to me about what happened. After the shot I keyed (radioed) CO to ask for instructions and after a wait (I think this means they told him to wait) was told to exit building and make our way to pickup point. If this helps, I've heard a lot of gunfire, and I remember thinking it was an Army sniper shot. It surprised me later when I heard some wacko civilian had done it. He described the shooting to me and let me tell you a thing. Whoever fired that shot was a professional. Even from 300 just no way just anybody could make that shot.

NOTES

1. See *Texas in the Morning*, Madeleine Duncan Brown, The Conservatory Press, Baltimore 1997, p. 166.
2. The morning after the shooting, he told Bobbi that he had found a gun in the back and turned it over to the police. On that day, he allegedly told cab driver McCraw a similar story. In 1968 and 1969, he identified Jack Youngblood, a mercenary and intelligence agent, to Wayne Chastain as the mysterious stranger in the grill who had been picked up by the police. In 1972, he denied it to Wayne. He then confirmed the Youngblood story to me in 1978 when the HSCA investigation was preparing to call James. He was strikingly inconsistent about the presence of the waitresses in the grill on April 4. In 1982, he apparently instructed Akins to kill Betty. Six years later, he finally tried to obstruct my locating Betty and other waitresses.
3. Handwritten by FBI Special Agent John Simmons and witnessed by one of Pierotti's investigators, Mark Glanker.
4. Jowers believed that the Scott Street produce business LL & L was owned by Frank Liberto and his brother, but he didn't remember the brother's name.
5. This is why Curington found charges of embezzlement made by Hunt's sons Bunker and Herbert and nephew Tom Hunt in 1969 against himself and Paul Rothermel hard to take since funds were

routinely siphoned off and kickbacks from purchasers were collected and diverted, on the old man's instructions. James's former lawyer, Percy Foreman, who also represented the Hunts, was ultimately indicted for charges connected with the wiretapping of Hunt aides Curington and Rothermel as a part of the effort to prove the embezzlement charges.

6. Nathan gave me a written account of his encounter with Frank Liberto and also showed me photographs of Liberto sitting at a table in his mother's restaurant.

7. Emmett Douglass, the driver of the TACT 10 car, testified at the TV trial that he was parked about 75 to 100 feet back from the sidewalk alongside the northwest door of the fire station, and no car was in parked in front of him.

8. Though it clearly came from Washington it was broached by the Memphis agent who was controlling Baldwin in 1978. At the time, he was the government's key witness during the prosecution of Governor Ray Blanton.

9. In their view, the doubts would largely die with Ray. Eventually, after James testified before the HSCA and nothing startling came out, the idea of killing him seemed to go away. It was not raised again, and it appeared to me that perhaps all concerned had come to realize that James was not going to provide the prosecution with even the peripheral information he might have learned or pieced together later. After James had rejected these approaches, a more lethal scenario involving Art Baldwin was introduced.

10. Ward also said that at that time, there was speculation by some of the drivers that since the man seen fleeing the area wasn't carrying a gun, perhaps it was hidden in the back of Loyd Jowers's cafe as all of this activity took place behind that building.

He agreed to undergo hypnosis to see if he could recollect the names of the driver of car 58 and the dispatcher. Subsequently, under hypnosis, he said he believed that the driver's name was Paul and that after the fleeing man got into the passenger side of the MPD traffic car, the car headed north at top speed.

I later located and deposed a former yellow cab dispatcher named Prentice Purdy. Under oath in May 1995, he recalled a full-time

driver named Paul and said that he believed that he almost exclusively did airport runs. He said that he could not specifically recall
ever seeing Paul after April 4, but he did not know if or when he
had died.

11. Raul, who was much younger, came over many years after Armando.
Glenda said Armando was quite proud of the fact that he once lived
in Chicago and worked for Al Capone's organization.

12. She would then deliver the guns, packed in cardboard boxes or
crates, to Torrino's house where Raul Pereira, Torrino, and their
associates would assemble them. She would only go and pick up the
guns when particular customs agents were on duty so that she would
be waved through.

13. The surveillance team had told me that he demonstrated a high
degree of street smarts when they tried to tail him. They said he
knew exactly which moves to make to shake them off.

14. James stated the photograph was the same as the one he identified
in 1978. We had copies of press accounts of his identification at that
time. Glenda's younger brother, Royce Wilburn, later identified the
photograph of Raul as the man he first knew as "Dago" in Houston
and later learned was Raul Pereira. I took his statement under oath
and filed it along with the others under seal. Raul's face was very
distinctive. The independent identifications were convincing.

15. The material elements of the conversation are as follows:

    1. He referred to her as "Olinda," the name he always called her.
    2. He confirmed that he was still heavily involved with gunrunning.
    3. In response to her question, he acknowledged knowing a Jack
       V_____ and he asked her how many children she had and
       confirmed that his daughter was getting married.

16. Two supervisors who knew Raul when he worked at General Motors
were tracked down. I sent an investigator up to interview them. One
said Raul visited at Christmas. His employment records revealed
that he was employed between 1962 and 1992 when he retired. He
had, however, not been a salaried employee, but worked on an
hourly basis. This meant he could take time off whenever he wished
and would be laid off from time to time. It was no secret that the
General Motors Corporation and other defense contractors often

provided cover for CIA and other government assets. It soon became clear to the investigator that the word was out not to provide any information. She learned that personnel records on site only went back to 1975.

17. Former *Commercial Appeal* reporter Steve Tompkins eventually agreed to reach out to certain contacts of his in greatly varying positions in army intelligence, the Pentagon, and the Special Forces. He doubted that they would meet with me face to face. They distrusted all lawyers, and the fact that I was James Earl Ray's attorney made their assistance even more risky.

18. During the 1960s a highly secret federal interagency structure, with army intelligence at the forefront (using the task force structure), carried out officially approved tasks which ranged from official intelligence activity, "eye-to eye" surveillance, and information gathering and analysis, to blatantly illegal covert operations. I discovered a surprising degree of official cooperation between what have been publicly portrayed as exclusively competing agencies and officials. This had been confirmed in 1972, in the hearings of the Senate Judiciary Subcommittee on Constitutional Rights, the Ervin Committee.

19. In *Orders to Kill* (William F. Pepper, Carroll & Graf, New York 1995) I have set out in detail much of the information contained in this chapter, except that in the interim, additional facts have been brought to my attention which now require that I consider afresh the detail of the military structure and role leading up to and during the assassination. Some of the new information only confirms the earlier analysis but other details amend the original account. In this highly secretive and sensitive area precise truth is elusive, but non-disinformational history required that the issues be treated as dynamic examples of seeing through a glass darkly, only gradually coming face to face with the truth.

20. I was provided with a copy of the ACSI command structure and organization as it existed in 1967.

21. Jim Kellum, one of our private investigators, later reported that former members of the MPD intelligence bureau, including senior

officer Lieutenant Eli Arkin, confirmed to him that all during this time agents of the 111th were in their offices working with them. Arkin later confirmed their presence to me.

22. Warren provided a copy of the orders for the April 4 mission in Memphis. Though he confirmed they were authentic, I acknowledge there are questions about their authenticity. They confirm the following statements he made:

A team was in Memphis.

Reference was made to a 4:30 AM briefing.

The brief at 4:30 was controlling unless so ordered otherwise.

"NAS" support (Millington Naval Air Station support was on line).

Support services were provided at the "Riverside."

Local intelligence was needed; recon on the site was required (". . . prior to King, Martin L. arrival termination of mission was available on radio notice channel 012").

The orders appeared to come from the office of the Joint Chiefs of Staff and to be issued under the umbrella of the anti-black terrorist operation "Garden Plot," which was a part of the overall US Command anti-riot operation CINCSTRIKE and activated with the outbreak of any major riot. If authentic, the orders were clearly well circulated, reaching the highest levels of government. They were even sent to the White House.

The origin of the orders "LANTCOMN/CINCSPECOPS" revealed knowledge and involvement of the Atlanta Command and a special operations section of CINCSTRIKE. The critical reference is to the 4:30 AM briefing (confirmed independently by Warren) at which time sources said the deadly nature of the operation was explicitly laid out and "target acquisition photos" of the two targets and their location were shown.

23. Warren would not name this soldier or any other member of the team except his expatriate buddy Murphy, who consented and also provided information.

In earlier accounts, I attributed corroborating information gained from contacts of Steve Tompkins to an anonymous source in an effort to protect Steve who had a valuable inside source. The information was that the Alpha 184 team had been selected and coordinated by Downie of the 902nd MIG. A further check of the files revealed that the 20th SFG did indeed have a sniper team deployed to the Selma area for the beginning of the march from Selma to Montgomery. Two of the members of that Selma team confirmed that King was being targeted until he turned left, at one point, and crossed a bridge.

24. It was remarkable that J. D.'s account, coming to me twenty years after Terrell had heard it, independently confirmed the presence of a Camp Shelby based 20th SFG Alpha 184 shooting team in Memphis on April 4 1968, which had been drawn from crack reserves of the 20th with Martin King as a target. Further, J. D. had said that a team had been training for that mission for a period of several months. Warren and Murphy never knew that I had access to J. D.'s story, neither did they or Terrell know that the names of each member of the Alpha 184 team had been provided to me by another, separate source through Tompkins.

Warren identified a photograph of a CIA contract operative Jack Youngblood, whom I first met in 1978. Youngblood had long been on the periphery of the King case. They served together in Vietnam when Youngblood was assigned to a highly classified covert Special Operations Group based in Can Tho ("1st SOG"), which was financed and controlled by the CIA and involved in sabotage, assassinations, and special operations throughout Southeast Asia. Warren had last seen Youngblood in the summer or early fall of 1967 on one of his gun-running deliveries to New Orleans. He saw Youngblood with Zippy Chimento, the coordinator of Carlos Marcello's gunrunning operations in which Warren and (from what Sid Carthew and Glenda independently said), apparently, Raul were also involved. Sixteen years after I first met and interviewed Jack Youngblood, it appeared clear that though apparently not himself involved, he knew at least one of the people on the scene at the time of the killing. It occurred to me that the people he talked to about the possibility of my obtaining information from them in 1978 could very well have been these former Vietnam War buddies, Warren and Murphy, since Youngblood had said that the people he wanted me to meet believed they had been sold down the river by their government after many years of faithful service and now lived outside of the country. Warren and Murphy certainly had a grievance against the government, and left the country because they believed that they were to be killed. I was now independently obtaining their story.

25. I also forwarded a photograph to Warren to see if he could identify either of two people coming down over the wall, shortly after the killing – uniformed police were shown in the photograph running up Mulberry Street. The two figures were hatless and wearing some kind of uniform. One of them appeared to be wearing a small sidearm.

   Warren was quick to respond. The man closest to the camera, bending over as he prepared to jump down from the wall, he knew from his days in Vietnam as someone who had been assigned to that 1st SOG in Can Tho. He named him and said he believed that in Vietnam he was associated with either the CIA or the NSA, and that in 1968 he was working for the NSA. If true, he appears to have been part of the task force pulled together by and under the control of the 902nd MIG; his actual role, however, remains unclear.

26. Steve had the impression that Downie had talked to Warren and would not meet with me as long as there were active legal proceedings to avoid the risk of being subpoenaed. As with the others, Steve would carry my questions and he would reply.

27. At that time Galt was cooperating with another 902nd MIG operation. The real Eric Galt was listed in the Toronto telephone directory in 1967–68 as "Eric Galt" with no middle name or initial, and in 1967 he had begun to use the initial "S." dropping his middle name, "St. Vincent," entirely. When James in July 1967 assumed the alias Eric S. Galt, he was signing the name in the same way as the real Galt had recently adopted.

28. Though I have no knowledge of the extent of his day-to-day awareness and the details of the operation and whilst there may very well have been someone in between him and Colonel Downie, at that time the 902nd came under the direct control of the Assistant Chief of Staff for Intelligence, the ASCI Major General William P. Yarborough.

29. Jerry Ray visited James on Christmas Eve and was clearly shaken by his condition. He believed his brother was suffering pain and signed a waiver of life support which would allow James to die. His sister Carol visited on Christmas Eve morning and again on Christmas Day when she saw some improvement in his condition. She spoke with Jerry and on the same day he notified the hospital he was withdrawing the waiver, instructing the hospital to do everything it could to keep him alive. The decision was released to the media.

30. I had quietly attempted to contact the King family on two occasions in years past but they hadn't responded. It was clear to me that they were not ready at that time.

31. At the June hearing, the State argued that the previous injunction granted by the Court of Appeal was still in effect and that the judge was powerless to grant such an order. I responded that the new post-conviction relief statute, which came into effect after the Court of Appeal's ruling, rendered the injunction moot. The proposal we filed with the court in September focused on firearms identification testing of the rifle as well as the use of neutron activation procedures to compare the chemical composition of the death slug with the other bullets found in the evidence bundle dumped in Canipe's doorway.

32. If the markings on the test-fired slug, or some of them, match those on the death slug, then the experts may conclude that the death slug came from the rifle in evidence. If the markings on the test fires do not match those on the death slug but the test fires themselves have matching marks, then it may be possible for the examiners to exclude the rifle as the murder weapon. A failure of the test fires to match one to the other would render such a test inconclusive. Each panel member would independently fire the rifle and collect and mark his own test-fired slugs. This would enable each expert to conduct his own analysis and arrive at his own independent assessment of his test fires and the death slug. The examiners would then pool and compare all the test fires with the death slug.

33. During this stage, these particular individual markings on the test-fired slugs would be cosmetically marked for further more precise analysis during the second stage. In the second stage, the compara-

tive analysis of the test-fired slugs and the death slug would be conducted using an electron microscope. This has a degree of magnification far beyond that of a comparison microscope routinely used in firearms identification.

34. Based upon other statements of McCraw (particularly his account of leaving the rooming house and driving up South Main Street minutes before the shooting), I have come to dismiss the possibility of him seeing anyone emerge from the side of the rooming house which would have been some blocks behind him. I have also come to believe that the person he picked up in downtown Memphis on the evening of April 4 was not Mrs Clark.

35. Though I would later be accused of interfering with the interrogation by putting forward my views of the case, in fact, for most of the time, I discussed the evidence on the side with Glankler who informed me that he was certain that we were wrong about Raul. He said that he had seen his work records, and they were conclusive. Not having access to them at that time, I couldn't comment. When I did obtain them later, they certainly did not justify Mr Glankler's conclusions.

36. I had known Wayne for 22 years. During that time, I had observed his performance in two professions – journalism and the law. He epitomized the best in both because the hallmark of his work and his life was an unimpeachable integrity. When one is surrounded by lawyers, reporters, editors, and publishers who routinely suppress and distort the truth to serve their own purposes or the special interests they represent, a person like Wayne Chastain is not only a breath of fresh air, but also a rare role model for young media professionals and lawyers. He epitomized the highest standards of personal and professional conduct, and as a result of his example, I have, in my lifetime, had hope in the future of humanity rekindled from time to time, often when I have been in despair. It was fitting that the last action in which he was involved concerned Dr King, because Wayne Chastain's life and work reflected Martin King's ideals, hopes for mankind, and legacy. With a practice devoted almost exclusively to public interest law, focusing on the needs of the most wretched Memphians, Wayne died with few assets. Most

notable of them was an extensive human rights library. In our last meeting, in his Memphis apartment at 60 Monroe Avenue in the spring of 1999, I went over my proposed trial outline. My son Sean was with me and Wayne, impressed with the scope of the plaintiffs' case, said it appeared to be well thought out. He then took us to a set of filing cabinets and showed me where all of the relevant documents were in his file.

He wanted me to know where everything was, for, though unspoken between us, we both knew that this would likely be the last time we would meet – at least on this mortal coil.

Our departure was painful. His leaving left me feeling empty. I am certain that a part of the agony, as with James's passing, resulted from my continued frustration at being powerless to prevent the suppression of the truth and the denial of justice by the very forces which had deprived humanity of Martin Luther King's vision and leadership when he was in the prime of his life.

Not a week passes that I do not think of Wayne and sometimes see him in one or another situation of success or failure that we shared over a period of 22 years. I will miss him, but unlike Hamlet, I believe we see his like from time to time, and this keeps hope alive.

37. Don Wilson stood his ground as attacks were mounted against him. He felt let down that a member of the King family had not appeared with us at the press conference. He believed that would have given his credibility a solid boost. The family believed that it would appear that they were manipulating the situation and rather than assisting Wilson's independence it would hurt him.

38. Some time later, a *Chicago Tribune* reporter visited the area police precinct and enquired about the investigation of the tire slashing. He later told Don that the local officers advised him that they were told by two Chicago field officers that they knew all about such operations.

39. Word filtered through to me that the Department of Justice was increasingly concerned about the trial and what might come out. This came from other persons interviewed by members of the Kowalski team. Nathan Whitlock and taxi driver James Milner were

uneasy. Like Don Wilson they said that the investigators were not friendly to either the King family or myself, and side comments were made about the penalties for perjury. At one point, I wrote to the Department to complain about certain comments. Then, Glenda Grabow said that she heard them making fun of her on the telephone when they didn't think she was listening.

40. An attorney for the Memphis *Commercial Appeal* promptly made a motion requesting the judge to allow the media to be present during the jury selection process. Relying upon the rules of court, which gave him discretion, the judge denied the motion. They appealed, and the judge's ruling was eventually overturned, but it was moot since we had selected the jury by the end of the first day and would even hold one spectator in contempt and impose a fine for violating the order.

41. Professor Phillip Melanson and the Reverend Mike Clark agreed to deal with all media queries since both sides had agreed that we would follow the English practice that counsel would not give media interviews during the trial. The decision was taken to avoid the inevitable media spins and in an effort to let the evidence speak for itself. Risako Kobayashi, my assistant, would coordinate the production of evidence and the synchronization of materials and exhibits to witness testimony. Attorney Ray Kohlman, from Massachusetts, was in charge of court logistics, special research, and last-minute investigation. My sons Sean and Liam, over from England, would respectively organize for the scheduled arrival and departure of the nearly 70 witnesses and film the proceedings.

Security was handled by Cliff Dates (CDA Security), who organized security details for the members of the King family, who, in turns, were present in the courtroom throughout the trial.

42. Only he and I had previously separately interviewed Inspector Sam Evans, who was in charge of those units, and since I could not readily testify, Phil took the stand.

43. Television trial producer Jack Saltman recently confirmed to me that Spates had independently told him the same story in 1992. She had indeed seen Loyd, white as a sheet, with muddy knees, running from the bushes with the rifle. For years, she believed that he did it,

having tried back in 1969 to get the story out. She had no idea that he had taken the gun from the actual shooter.

44. Attorney Raymond Kohlman, to whom I had assigned the research task, testified that the 1967 Memphis Polk Telephone Directory showed Paul and Betty Butler living at 2639 (Apt no. P1) Central Avenue, Memphis. His employment was listed as a taxi driver for the Yellow Cab Company, and his wife was a manager of a local Gridiron restaurant. In the 1968 directory, Betty Butler was listed as the "widow of Paul." Attorney Kohlman went on to state that there appeared to be no record of a death certificate for Paul Butler. Subsequent to the trial, we would learn that "Buddy" was not Paul Butler but another driver who regularly made the airport runs in car 58.

Also, Ernestine Campbell, who a minute or two before the shooting had driven up, took a right turn on to Mulberry, and then stopped in front of the Lorraine driving away very shortly after Dr King had been shot, told me that as she started to pull away, in her right – the passenger side – mirror she saw the back of a yellow taxi cab in the Lorraine driveway. I believed that in that fleeting glimpse, she had seen taxi cab 58, Buddy's car. We urgently tried to get her to testify, and whilst at first she was willing, eventually she ran from the idea, even frustrating our efforts to serve her with a subpoena.

45. There was also written at the top of the telephone directory page (which contained the listings of the family of H. L. Hunt) the letter "R" preceding a telephone number. As discussed earlier, when I learned that the phone number belonged to the Vegas Club owned by Jack Ruby, pointing to a connection between Raul and Ruby, I went to Dallas to find and interview some of Jack Ruby's strippers as well as Madeleine Brown – Lyndon Johnson's mistress of 21 years. I saw Beverly Oliver, Chari Angel, and Madeleine Brown separately. In each instance, I placed the photographic spread in front of them and each time, without hesitation, Raul was identified as a person seen in the company of Jack Ruby in 1963, usually at the Carousel, Ruby's other Dallas club. Beverly Oliver said that on one occasion, she remembered Raul giving Ruby $20,000 in a Piggley Wiggley grocery store bag.

46. Not only did ABC not use the interview, we came to believe that it

was very possible that they had turned the tape or the information over to the government. Terrell maintained that there was no reasonable excuse for them not using his interview. In fact, there was every reason for ABC to be aware of his credibility since he had been previously a source, interviewed by them on sensitive matters on more than one occasion. When Jack learned that they had blocked out his story in its entirety, he decided that he had to testify.

47. In his pre-trial deposition, the owner of the Yellow Cab Company, whose son runs the business today, testified that he no longer had any records dating back to 1968 and also that he did not recall hearing about any such incident involving this driver.

48. So, at the time of writing, we are left only with the unwavering statement of Louie Ward who, concerned about his own safety and that of his family, kept it to himself for a quarter of a century. He said that he did call John Pierotti at one point and told him what he knew. He said that Pierotti, then Shelby County district attorney general, gave him short shrift, and Ward said he become so angry that he asked the district attorney if he was the person driving the police car that took the shooter away.

49. Jerry tape-recorded this conversation and authenticated the transcript of that recording as being accurate and the one he caused to be made. It was entered into evidence.

50. Milner testified that Jowers identified an old police buddy with whom he used to ride, Inspector John Barger, a black MPD undercover officer, Marrell McCollough, introduced by Barger, and a hunting buddy, Lieutenant Earl Clark. But he insisted that he didn't know two other men present.

51. The jury had, of course, previously heard from Bill Hamblin that his roommate James McCraw had maintained over a 15-year period that Jowers had given him the actual murder weapon on the day after the killing and told him to get rid of it, which he did by throwing it off the Memphis–Arkansas bridge into the Mississippi River. In his earlier deposition, McCraw only went so far as to admit that Jowers showed him the actual murder rifle on the morning after the shooting.

52. Dexter participated in two separate meetings with Jowers. The first session was in my presence, and the second was with Ambassador Andrew Young at the table. On both occasions, Jowers was accompanied by his attorney Lewis Garrison.

53. It is interesting that while he told Milner that he did not know the other two men at the planning sessions in his cafe and that Raul picked up the rifle the day after the killing, in the King/Young interviews, he named a fourth man (an MPD inspector) who participated, and he said that one of Frank Liberto's people picked up the murder weapon on the morning of April 5.

54. We argued that the statute only began to run after Dexter King's first meeting with Loyd Jowers when he actually heard for the first time the account of his personal involvement. The meeting was held on March 2 1998, and the action was filed on October 2 1998 within the year. No proof was offered that any of the plaintiffs had access to reliable information about the defendant's role as well as any opportunity to test his credibility. The plaintiffs, for a considerable time, diligently sought an opportunity to learn the truth from the defendant, and as soon as the meeting with Dexter was agreed, it was held without delay.

55. A doctor's letter was provided in support. It was true that Jowers had been absent after the first week, and we had considered going to his home in order to take his deposition. We ultimately decided against doing this when he informed us through his attorney that he would invoke the Fifth Amendment throughout.

    We argued that the mistrial application was not timely or warranted since we at the outset had fully disclosed our list of witnesses and the scope of their expected testimony to the defense, which had ample time to prepare. Since the defendant had made it clear that he was unwilling to testify on his own behalf either in front of the jury or by deposition, his presence or absence was irrelevant.

56. Upon request, he read the state's representations about: the existence of the second Mustang (which they falsely claimed at the time was the only Mustang); the eyewitness Charlie Stephens (who was actually too drunk to have seen anything); the dropping of the bundle in front of Canipe's (the jury had already heard Judge Hanes

testify about Canipe's statement); and the deliberative misrepresen-
tation of the dent in the windowsill, about which it was stated that
forensic evidence would conclusively establish that it would
". . . match the markings on the barrel of the rifle in evidence" (after
Attorney Lesar had introduced a FBI laboratory report stating that
this was not possible).

57. Lieutenant Arkin then confirmed that elements of the 111th Military
Intelligence Group worked out of his office for some time during
the sanitation workers' strike.

On cross-examination, he denied ever meeting or talking with
any of the Alpha 184, Special Forces team in Memphis on the day
of the assassination.

58. After Attorney Garrison completed reading his portions of the
telephone deposition, I advised the court that we had concluded that
this witness was providing misinformation and false evidence, and I
referred to page 56 of the deposition and read his response to my
question on cross-examination with respect to him arriving at his
position at the corner of the brush area near the wall. When I asked
him how long he took to get to his position from the time he
entered the parking lot area, which was adjacent to the brush area
behind the rooming house, he replied only a couple of minutes.
When I asked him if he encountered any impediment as he passed
through the area to his position, he said none except for the bushes,
through which he had to make his way. We then put up on the
screen a photograph taken within a day or so of the assassination
showing the area behind the rooming house. Very clearly visible on
the photograph was a fence which was about five feet tall and which
ran around east and west from the north side of the rooming house
all the way down to the very edge of the wall. For the witness to
have passed through this area without encountering this fence was
unimaginable. Since there were even some barbed wire strands
across the top, it would have required some effort to climb over it.

Based upon this particular fact and other statements he made,
which did not conform to facts we knew about the case including
the caliber bullet retrieved from Dr King, we concluded that this
witness was not credible.

59. Meanwhile, Marvin Glankler, out of turn, arrived at the courthouse along with a representative of the anti-drug task force, which he now headed. The judge's order required him to take the stand but with Glankler outside of the courtroom, the state's lawyer and the task force official argued in a bench conference that his testimony could destroy his cover and jeopardize the sensitive operation. It was finally agreed that Glankler would take the stand, but that the cameras would avoid showing or photographing his face. He was sworn in and began his testimony.

60. Copernicus published *Revolution of the Celestial Spheres* in 1543 but it took some time for it become a part of the collective, authoritative consciousness.

61. *Devotions upon Emergent Occasions*, John Donne, 1624

62. They were essentially caretakers for the huge American air bases at Udorn, Takli, Korat, and Ubon.

63. Suharto was brought to power with the help of the Central Intelligence Agency.

64. For example, overruns now include the Patriot Missile ($1 billion), the Crusader artillery system ($1.4 billion), a new Navy destroyer ($2 billion). The Air Force F-22 costs $200 million per plane. This makes it history's most expensive jet fighter even though the design keeps changing and the onboard computers are untested.

65. Even in his Passion Sunday sermon on 31 March 1968 at the National Cathedral in Washington, King challenged the congregation to face up to the task of making the global community a brotherhood of all people.

66. *Unto This Last and other writings*, John Ruskin, Penguin Books, London 1985, p. 226.

67. Ibid.

68. Lawrence was said by Winston Churchill to be "The greatest being alive in our time . . . like Hamlet we shall not see his like again."

69. *Autobiography of Martin Luther King*, ed. Clayborne Carson, Warner Books, New York 1998.

70. It is interesting to note that Frank, with the blessing and encouragement of Cartha Deloach and J. Edgar Hoover, published in 1972,

and that McMillan came out with his work in 1976 around the start-up time of the congressional investigation.

71. *Killing the Dream*, Gerald Posner, Random House, New York 1997, p. 342.
72. Ibid., p. 343.
73. In fairness to Posner, his reputation may have preceded him, at least in respect of some of the people, following his work on the Kennedy case – *Case Closed* – which also became the official view rationalized in print. As a result of this reputation, it is not surprising that at least some of the people with a decent knowledge of events would not want to speak with him.

     What is surprising is that some of those who should have known better – Ken Herman, Jack Saltman, and John Billings – did believe that they could show him the truth and such evidence as they knew about and convince him to treat it fairly. They have learned better, and I understand that Herman was shocked when the book came out, with what he regarded was a distortion of his comments. He is quoted by Posner as saying that I paid $14,000 for a photograph sight unseen, and $25,000 for information on the military. I did nothing of the sort, though I did pay Ken Herman $20,000 for documents that they had developed on Raul. I had a client in jail and if they had materials that would help me get him out, I was determined to secure them. That was the price paid.
74. Posner, at first, refers to the same inmate and discounts him, but then relies on other alleged inmate statements, the source of which is the FBI. This forms the basis for his allegation that Ray was a racist. Not even the HSCA concluded that James was a racist. In fact, their final report explicitly ruled out racism as a motive.
75. *The Final Assassinations Report*, US House of Representatives, Bantam, New York 1979, pp. 537–8.
76. *Killing the Dream*, p. 7.
77. *Orders to Kill*, pp. 216–17.
78. Telephone interview with Dora MacDonald on 13 March 2000. Considering what he told Wayne Chastain and New York City Police Detective Leon Cohen immediately after the shooting (that on April 3 1968, he planned to put Dr King in room 202), it makes

no sense unless Bailey was referring to the day room registrations, which, however, considering the number of times he had actually visited Memphis in the 1950s and 1960s, were far fewer. Martin King's personal secretary Dora MacDonald explicitly states that she never made a reservation for him at the Lorraine.

79. HSCA Vol 1, p. 32.
80. Ralph Abernathy's specific recollection of room 306 being occupied upon their arrival requiring them to stay in the adjoining room and be put into room 306 the next day is not referred to at all in his 1989 book *And The Walls Came Tumbling Down* (Harper Collins, New York 1991). In fact, at one point, he referred to holding ". . . a meeting in our motel suite . . ." (p. 429). Every indication at that time was also that they were in room 306.
81. Ibid., p. 438.
82. *Killing the Dream*, p. 19.
83. Ibid., pp. 24–5.
84. Ibid., p. 25.
85. Ibid.
86. *The Final Assassinations Report*, p. 556.
87. *Killing the Dream*, p. 25.
88. HSCA Vol 4, p. 231. In executive session, Redditt was told that Inspector Graydon Tines had testified that, on April 3, Detective Redditt had called him and expressed concern about one of the two black firemen in fire station no. 2. Redditt did not remember making any such call but did acknowledge that he and Richmond had written a memo to Tines stating that Newsom was giving Richmond a bit of a hard time. Neither Tines nor Redditt confirmed that Redditt had, in the language of the HSCA Report, issued a "request" or in Posner's words that ". . . it was detective Redditt who requested they be transferred." Even if it was decided to remove Newsom because he was sympathetic to the strikers and somewhat of a nuisance, how does this explain the removal of Wallace who was not active at all? In his testimony, Redditt raised the question, saying that he was simply voicing some concern about Newsom (*not requesting his removal*), so why would they transfer both black firemen? It made no sense at all.

89. Telephone interview with Reverend James Orange in October 1999.
90. *Walls Came Tumbling Down*, p. 440.
91. *An American Death: The True Story of the Assassination of Dr. Martin Luther King, Jr., and the Greatest Manhunt of our Time*, Gerold Frank, Doubleday, New York 1972 pp. 100–101.
92. *Killing the Dream*, p. 333.
93. Ibid., p. 230.
94. Ibid., p. 327.
95. Ibid., p. 236.
96. Also, I interviewed two of Jack Ruby's former employees and a third woman who used to visit one of Ruby's clubs, the Carousel, on a regular basis. All three, Beverly Oliver, Chari Angel, and Madeleine Brown, separately interviewed identified the photograph of Raul as a man who they had seen with Ruby at the club. One, Beverly Oliver, said that she even remembered Raul giving Ruby $20,000 in cash in a Piggley Wiggley grocery store bag. As noted above, they also confirmed that Ruby, on occasion, in fact, did go to Houston.

Sid Carthew's politics and mine are certainly different, but I have rarely met a person as honest and straightforward as Sid. He became outraged when he saw Hickman Ewing comparing James's story about Raul to his mother's tales about the tooth fairy. It took Sid some time to locate me, but when he did, he told about meeting Raul in the Neptune bar in Montreal in the summer of 1967. He decisively identified Raul in the photo spread. I set out his account in detail in *Orders to Kill*, and his telephone deposition was put in evidence at the civil trial. He was attacked by fringe media in England and even had a fire bomb thrown at his house as a result of coming forward. There is no doubt in my mind that politics played no role in Sid Carthew's effort to truthfully share what he knew.
97. Memphis *Commercial Appeal*, 30 November 1978.
98. *Killing the Dream*, p. 300; *King v. Jowers* et al. trial testimony of Jack Saltman on 24 November 1999.
99. Saltman testimony, ibid.
100. *King v. Jowers* et al. trial testimony of Barbara Reis on 23 November 1999.
101. "A Report of the Subcommittee on Constitutional Rights, Com-

mittee on the Judiciary, United States Senate – 'Military Surveillance of Civilian Politics, 1972'" (henceforth referred to as Military
Surveillance of Civilian Politics), p. 5.

102. Ibid., p. 21.
103. Ibid., pp. 17, 53.
104. Ibid., p. 111.
105. Ibid., p. 57.
106. *Killing the Dream*, p. 314.
107. Ibid., p. 317.
108. Ibid., p. 315.
109. *Billy R. Eidson v. William F. Pepper PhD, Caroll & Graf Publishers,
     Inc., and Warner Brothers, Inc.*, deposition of Billy R. Eidson on 31
     March 1999, p. 98.
110. Interview of General Henry H. Cobb Jr conducted by Tony Stark
     from Just TV (UK documentary film production company) in 1998.
111. *Killing the Dream*, graphic illustration between pp. 178 and 179.
112. Ibid.
113. Ibid., p. 273 and note 12, pp. 413, 414.
114. I also have photographs of the work being done in August 1968. At
     that time, as I understand it, Walter Bailey somehow was induced
     to erect a memorial to his wife on that very site, and he contracted
     for the work to go forward. This was done at a time when the actual
     cutting down of the bushes, beginning on April 5, was a potential
     impediment to the official story. Bailey had been persuaded to
     provide a clumsy cover which future writers could seize upon as an
     explanation of when the bushes were cut down. I do believe,
     however, that between April and August there continued to be
     concern about a remaining overhanging tree branch which appeared
     to partially obscure the target area from the bathroom window. I
     believe that the August work focused on this issue, as it was referred
     to in the deposition of former MPD officer Ed Atkinson, who
     overheard the problem being discussed by Earl Clark and another
     officer.
          The true facts of the brush being cut to the ground on the
     morning after the killing are now well established. Posner's and the
     state's story is untenable. All anyone had to do was to ask Maynard

Stiles or, when she was alive, Kay Black, or any number of other locally employed people or area residents.

115. Here, as is the case with other witnesses who came under pressure, Canipe's story had varied. The fact, however, that he was willing to be a defense witness and testify under oath to the events as he described them to Judge Hanes is most persuasive that that recollection was truthful. In fact, as set out in detail in Chapter 1, the Department of Justice report inadvertently confirms that the bundle was dropped some minutes before the shot.

116. Betty Spates has maintained that Herman and Saltman wanted her to change her story and say that she saw a black man give the gun to Jowers. She refused.

In attacking Spates's credibility, Posner notes visits by the Attorney General and TBI's investigators and her recantation and admission that the story that she passed the gun to her brother was false, as indeed it was.

Posner also says that Bobbi Balfour, Betty's sister, denied telling me that Jowers had told her that he had the murder weapon. I never said she did. What I did say and what Bobbi testified to at the civil trial was that Jowers told her the police had found the murder weapon out in back of the restaurant. The Spates story, which after all of the pressures put on her has been badly tainted, is I believe basically as true in 2000 as it was back in 1969 when she tried to get the truth out in order to help an innocent man. I am afraid that her credibility has been hurt as much by some of those working for me as it has by the agents of the state who wish to discredit her.

117. I first interviewed him in 1978 and have known him for 22 years. He has never altered his story.

118. *Killing the Dream*, p. 287.

119. Ibid., p. 291.

120. "United States Department of Justice Investigation of Recent Allegations Regarding the Assassination of Dr Martin Luther King, Jr., June 2000" (henceforth referred to as DOJ 2000), p. 10.

121. Ibid.

122. Ibid., p. 12.

123. Ibid., p. 22.

124. The actual exchange under oath was the following:

    Dr Pepper: "I'd just like to note, Counsel, for the record, an exception to the pleading of the Fifth by Mr Jowers on the basis of the fact that the accuracy of the transcript has been already agreed to and entered into the record, and that being the case it becomes our position."

    Attorney Garrison: "Okay. Dr Pepper, we will stipulate that the questions were asked and Mr Jowers gave these answers."

    Dr Pepper: "Okay. We accept that stipulation."

125. In April 1997, Jowers was under a great deal of pressure from his family because of his efforts to have the truth brought to the surface. Members of his family were being contacted by a range of people from media types to investigators. The family pressed him to take whatever steps he could to stop what they regarded as never-ending harassment. One evening, despondent and in his cups, Jowers called the Shelby County district attorney's investigator Mark Glankler to complain about investigators bothering his relatives. In a desperate attempt to stop the harassment, he told Glankler that the rifle in evidence was the murder weapon. Jowers has continually stated, since that late night telephone call, that he thought they might leave his family alone if he appeared to back off. Similarly, sensitive about the harassment his admissions had brought on his family, Jowers may, at one point, have disavowed his involvement to a relative although I have no information about this alleged occurrence. Despite the relative's self-serving statement, there is no indication that the disavowal was ever made. It is unfortunate that Jowers's impetuousness, often combined with his drinking, resulted in behavior which is used to undermine his credibility, but it was a fact of life with which we had to live from 1993, when we first learned about his involvement, until he died in 2000.

126. It is interesting and outrageous that the attorney general's team seems to have had access to the ABC polygraph report and material whilst Jowers and his lawyer, in violation of Tennessee law, were denied access. Who knows what the ABC News personnel really gave to the Department of Justice task force.

127. For personal reasons, Jowers has said that he turned the rifle over to a man – Raul or another – on the day after the assassination. He never had the opportunity to explicitly deny the truthfulness of William Hamblin's trial testimony that James McCraw told him that he threw it off the old Memphis–Arkansas bridge. We found Hamblin credible with absolutely no motive to lie. Over the years, Jowers, clumsily attempting to distance himself and cover any eventuality, did vary his account. For example, in anticipation that Betty Spates would tell her sister Bobbi Balfour what she observed shortly after 6:00 PM on April 4, Jowers told Bobbi the next morning that the MPD had found the rifle out behind the grill. He finally settled on the story that Raul had collected the rifle on the morning after the killing. Thus, by implication, he denied James McCraw's recollections of events including the Hamblin allegation that he admitted to disposing of the rifle. Jowers and McCraw were close compatriots and used to go along together to every court hearing.

128. Contrary to the report, Jowers also consistently maintained that he owed Liberto a big debt. Initially I thought that the "big debt" might have been a gambling loss, but, eventually I came to believe that Liberto probably did him a huge favor by getting rid of the body of the Mexican he killed after finding him in bed with Betty at the Peabody apartment. The Mexican railroad worker, who had gone home with Betty when she got off work at the diner across the street from the railroad station, became, as a result of that liaison, the father of a child whom Betty raised. On one occasion, some years ago, Betty told me that Jowers told the boy, "You know I killed your daddy, boy, don't you?"

129. The report indicates that Jowers, at an early stage, also used the name "Hardin" for Raul. This is curious, because the Hardin family name has surfaced more than once. In fact, though it is scarcely known, Frank Liberto's mother's name was Hardin, Liberto had a nephew named Hardin, and there is an indication that a man named J. C. Hardin attempted to contact and may have contacted James in Los Angeles.

130. In fact, as we know and as ignored by the DOJ task force, Reverend

Kyles knocked on Dr King's door at 5:50 PM and did call him out. Martin closed the door but then did emerge a few minutes later. The fact that Reverend Kyles actually knocked on the door of room 306 at 5:50 PM and was not in the room with Martin and Ralph, as he has always maintained, was ignored by the DOJ task force and nowhere discussed in the report.

131. Thus, it was not surprising that the only footprints found at twilight by MPD officers Landers and Hodges were in the dirt of the alley between the wings of the rooming house. At the civil trial, Hodges described the extraordinary thickness of the bushes and ground cover: contrary to the impression in the report, the area behind Jim's Grill was not "muddy." The grass cover was evident, and the only mud was in the alleyway.

132. DOJ 2000, p. 37.

133. Ibid., p. 37.

134. Ibid., p. 40.

135. Ibid., p. 42. When we checked on the age of a Paul Butler who died on August 2 1967, we found that it was incompatible with that of the man with whom Louie Ward spoke and who was allegedly killed on April 4 1968. The report says that Louie gave the driver a different name – "Buddy" – but in fact, that was consistent with Louie's original recollection. Louie only knew him by his nickname.

136. Ibid., p. 43.

137. Ibid.

138. Ibid., p. 45.

139. The report's conclusions in this issue, juxtaposed with other statements made and accepted over the years, allows us to establish the truth. This was pointed out to me by the Reverend Jim Douglas who steadfastly sat through the entire trial.

140. DOJ 2000, p. 47.

141. Much is made in the report of John McFerren's, ". . . peculiar behavior and bizarre, uncorroborated claims, . . ." (ibid., p. 53), but nothing is said about the historical courage of this civil rights leader in the most racist county – Fayette – in Tennessee as he led black people in their struggle to vote, establishing a tent city to facilitate his efforts in the early 1960s. No mention is made of the harassment

which led to him being shot, hospitalized, the subject of a products boycott, and the victim of threats and attacks from 1968 up to the present. In this context and as a successful local businessman now for 40 years, John McFerren's integrity far exceeds any of those official investigators who over the years have sought to discredit him. And discredit him they must, for if they cannot do so, then he exists as a corroborator of Loyd Jowers's allegation that Memphis produce dealer Frank Liberto was a moving force in the local assassination scenario.

142. Ibid., p. 55.
143. *Orders to Kill*, p. 238.
144. DOJ 2000, p. 56.
145. The report also ignores the fact, despite having access to the relevant records, that Philip Manual had been – perhaps still was – a member of the 902nd Military Intelligence Group. Some years ago, he admitted this to Doug Valentine, the military historian who conducted the interview. For some period of time, Manual dropped out of sight. In late 1999 or early 2000, Valentine obtained an address and phone number and wrote to him requesting an interview. There was no reply but Manual's telephone number was disconnected shortly after the letter was sent.

The report concludes that the removal of both black firemen Newsum and Wallace was the result of a concern that the surveillance cover of Redditt and Richmond would be blown. I discuss this at length elsewhere, and it simply is not substantiated by the facts. In particular, Wallace's removal could in no way be justified on this basis. Whilst Newsum was active in supporting the strikers, Wallace was not involved in any such community activity at the time. Redditt, who allegedly requested the removal, has always convincingly denied ever making such a request.

146. DOJ 2000, p. 63.
147. Ibid., p. 65.
148. The report states that she "... provided significant information contradicting Jowers. In an interview with our investigator and in testimony in *King v. Jowers* et al., she related that she got home from work after 4:00 PM on the day of the assassination. The

lieutenant arrived a short while later to take a quick nap, shower, and change clothing. Because of the schedule, he and other officers assumed following the disruptions related to the strike, he had not been home for some time. About 45 minutes after he arrived, his ex-wife heard a bulletin over his walkie talkie announcing that Dr King had been shot and immediately awakened him."

149. DOJ 2000, p. 65.

149. I was that lawyer. The MPD at the time did not, in fact, have walkie talkies, as we know them, but large radios – like a lunch box the size of two bricks – which, however, were only assigned to some officers. Though Clark could have had one of those, he definitely could not have had the kind of "walkie talkie" the ex-wife described to the Reverend Jim Douglas during his visit in February 2000. She described an instrument which in size and shape was like a current television remote control. No such "walkie talkie" was available to the MPD (or perhaps available at all) in 1968.

150. All of the others who supported Jowers are called "friends" of his with the clear implication that they told their unsubstantiated stories with a view to personal gain. Nathan Whitlock is referred to as "financially motivated" and Louie Ward is described as a man "who had worked with Jowers" (he never had worked with Jowers and did not even know him). They are lumped together with Milner (an obsessive telephone user), McCraw, Isabel, and Hamblin, each of whom had various and different pieces of information which had come to them much earlier and at different times.

151. The report even unbelievably links Betty Spates to a conspiracy to promote the Jowers's story when it was her initial account which placed him where he clearly did not want to be, and in fear of being implicated in acts that he had long kept silent about. Rather than being pleased with taxi driver McCraw's revelations, I recall that Jowers was furious that his old friend was pulling him more deeply into troubled waters.

152. Oliver Stone was interested in acquiring the rights to my story and we negotiated over a considerable period of time. Finally he set out conditions (similar to my first publisher's) which he said would make me wealthy if I would accept them.

They were: 1) that the film could depict me in any way, except using drugs; 2) they could depict my relationship with my client James Earl Ray in any way they wished; and 3) they could depict James as guilty or innocent at their discretion.

Stone's offer received the same rejection as given to Harper Collins some years earlier.

153. DOJ 2000, p. 86. As an aside, and though it has nothing to do with the evidence from the Mustang, the report alleges that Don Wilson said he participated in a "black bag" (illegal) break-in and search of James's room in the rooming house at 113 Fourteenth Street prior to the assassination. He was on duty on the night of the break-in by agents John Reynolds and Don Burgers. He was told to pick up some material that Burgers left in a public phone booth after the break-in, and take it back to the field office. He did so. That was his "participation," not the act of actually breaking in to the room. I believe this to be a misunderstanding. Wilson has said that after the Mustang was found, the room was discovered and he participated in surveillance. He also said that on one occasion, shortly after the assassination, he and a partner saw a man they thought was James, and radioed their base office for instructions which he believed would be to apprehend the man. Instead, they were told to return to their base and forget about it. The report omits any consideration or even mention of this incident.

154. Ibid., p. 85.
155. Ibid., p. 92.
156. Ibid., p. 93.
157. Ibid.
158. Ibid., p. 101.
159. Ibid.
160. Memphis *Commercial Appeal*, 30 November 1978. Later on, we realized that by providing James with a photograph of the real Raul and a demonstrably false identity, some forces were hoping to embarrass and ultimately discredit James's story. All he confirmed was that the photograph, a copy of which we were to obtain some 17 years later, appeared clearly to be the person he knew as Raul. He turned it over to his brother for safekeeping, and it

was confiscated at one time during a police search of John's apartment.

161. It is interesting that Jowers in an early statement to Jack Saltman said he had been approached by a man, who he first called Hardin. It is not clear precisely when this contact was made. It is also interesting to note that one J. C. Hardin is related to Frank Liberto, and that Liberto's mother's maiden name is Hardin. Whether or not this leads anywhere or is significant at all is uncertain, but it is strange that the DOJ task force with all of its access did not uncover this connection.

162. DOJ 2000, p. 105.

163. Even if one totally disbelieves Glenda's account of this conversation, it is simply not believable that two complete strangers would talk on the telephone for this period of time. This conversation caused Glenda to provide a voice identification of Raul as the person she knew in Houston, because she said he pronounced her name ("Olinda") in the same way he always had.

164. I don't know the extent of the work records obtained by the DOJ task force, but I was advised by the General Motors records supervisor in Southfield, Michigan that I was receiving the same batch of records that they received. An analysis of those records, however, revealed that Raul had taken substantial time off over the period of his "employment," often taking informal and sick leave. In addition, there were voluntary layoffs, temporary layoffs, and work reduction periods. The information, however, is computerized and more available for the later periods of his work history. It is simply not possible to obtain a clear picture of how often he was away from his job in the 1960s. If, however, as some of my investigators have suggested, this is an "accommodation" employment, by which the corporation (as we know is done from time to time by US corporations) has provided the cover of employment at the request of the government, the work records would be meaningless in any event.

165. DOJ 2000, p. 121.

166. Ibid., p. 122.

167. Ibid., p. 123.

168. Ibid., p. 125.

169. Ibid.
170. Ibid., p. 127.
171. Ibid., p. 126.
172. Military Surveillance of Civilian Politics, p. 25.
173. The report also suggests that photographs taken by Joseph Louw at some undetermined time after the shooting and seemingly showing no visible sign of anyone on the roof, are no indication of the situation at the time of the shooting. The famous Louw photograph of Andrew Young and others standing on the balcony, pointing, was itself taken some minutes after the shooting. The fire station photographs showing men milling around on top of the wall, with a few others coming down the wall in to Mulberry Street, would have been taken at an unspecified time even later when the photographers could have withdrawn from view if they ever were in sight. An army surveillance photographer advised one of my investigators that the surveillance would have been conducted from tripods which would have been located a considerable distance back from the edge and much closer to the center of the roof, well out of physical sight. For the photographers to set up in a rooftop position, where their clandestine surveillance could be readily observed, if not photographed, would defeat the purpose of their mission and make no sense at all.
174. Steve did raise some questions about the "orders" which were obtained from Warren, but he never indicated that they were "bogus" as claimed in the report. If he believed that, then why had we obtained them in the first place and was it really believable that this professional soldier, this "grunt," was capable of fabricating such a specialized communication?

In fact, in one note to me stressing his belief that the 20th SFG mission was primarily a "recon mission" Steve specifically quoted the language in *Orders to Kill*, as though the document was legitimate and authoritative. He said: "This was a recon mission. The orders specifically state that 'MISSION: RECON. RIOT SITE MEMPHIS PRIOR TO KING SITUATION: DEPLOYMENT MAIN FORCE MUST HAVE LOCAL INTEL." He then wrote: "this was a hit team ONLY in the case of a major riot."

175. DOJ 2000, p. 135.
176. *When Corporations Rule the World*, David C. Korton, Kumarian Press, Inc., West Hartford, CT 1996, pp. 220–22.
177. Ibid., p. 246.
178. "The New Colossus: Inscription for the Statue of Liberty, New York Harbor, 1883," Emma Lazarus.
179. *The Two Nations*, Benjamin Disraeli, London 1845, Book 2, Chapter 5.
180. *Life of Johnson*, James Boswell, July 21 1763.
181. *Plutonium Files*, Eileen Welsome, Dial Press, New York 1999.
182. Ibid., p. 424.
183. *New York Times*, April 9 2000, News of the week in Review section, p. 4.
184. *Civilization on Trial*, Arnold Toynbee, Oxford University Press, New York 1948, Chapter 4.
185. *The Courage To Be*, Paul Tillich, Yale University Press, New Haven, CT 1952.

INDEX